MOLTKE AND  WARS, 1864–1871

European History in Perspective
General Editor: Jeremy Black

Benjamin Arnold *Medieval Germany*
Ronald Asch *The Thirty Years' War*
Christopher Bartlett *Peace, War and the European Powers, 1814–1914*
Robert Bireley *The Refashioning of Catholicism, 1450–1700*
Arden Bucholz *Moltke and the German Wars, 1864–1871*
Patricia Clavin *The Great Depression, 1929–1939*
Mark Galeotti *Gorbachev and his Revolution*
Martin P. Johnson *The Dreyfus Affair*
Peter Musgrave *The Early Modern European Economy*
J. L. Price *The Dutch Republic in the Seventeenth Century*
A. W. Purdue *The Second World War*
Francisco J. Romero-Salvado *Twentieth-Century Spain*
Matthew S. Seligmann and Roderick R. McLean
Germany from Reich to Republic, 1871–1918
Brendan Simms *The Struggle for Mastery in Germany, 1779–1850*
David Sturdy *Louis XIV*
Warren Treadgold *A Concise History of Byzantium*
Peter Waldron *The End of Imperial Russia, 1855–1917*
James D. White *Lenin*
Patrick Williams *Philip II*

European History in Perspective
Series Standing Order
ISBN 0–333–71694–9 hardcover
ISBN 0–333–69336–1 paperback
(*outside North America only*)

You can receive future titles in this series as they are published by placing a standing order. Please contact your bookseller or, in case of difficulty, write to us at the address below with your name and address, the title of the series and the ISBN quoted above.

Customer Services Department, Macmillan Distribution Ltd
Houndmills, Basingstoke, Hampshire RG21 6XS, England

Moltke and the German Wars, 1864–1871

Arden Bucholz

palgrave

First published 2001 by
PALGRAVE
Houndmills, Basingstoke, Hampshire RG21 6XS and
175 Fifth Avenue, New York, N.Y. 10010
Companies and representatives throughout the world

PALGRAVE is the new global academic imprint of
St. Martin's Press LLC Scholarly and Reference Division and
Palgrave Publishers Ltd (formerly Macmillan Press Ltd).

ISBN 0–333–68757–4 hardback
ISBN 0–333–68758–2 paperback

This book is printed on paper suitable for recycling and
made from fully managed and sustained forest sources.

A catalogue record for this book is available
from the British Library.

Library of Congress Cataloging-in-Publication Data

Bucholz, Arden.
      Moltke and the German wars, 1864–1871 / Arden Bucholz.
        p. cm. – (European history in perspective)
      Includes bibliographical references and index.
        ISBN 0-333-68757-4 – ISBN 0-333-68758-2 (pbk.)
        1. Moltke, Helmuth, Graf von, 1800–1891. 2. Marshals–Germany–
Biography. 3. Germany–History, Military–19th century. 4. Schleswig-
Holstein War, 1864. 5. Austro-Prussian War, 1866. 6. Franco-Prussian War,
1870–1871. I. Title. II. Series.

DD219.M7 B83 2000
355'.0092 – dc21   00-062613
[B]

10   9   8   7   6   5   4   3   2   1
10   09 08 07 06 05 04 03 02 01

Printed in China

For my favourite 'Three L'

Frontispiece Helmuth von Moltke (1800–91) the professional soldier. His bald head is covered by his own hair in the back, a wisp of the wig he always wore showing over and behind the right ear. His costume is not the embellished, bedecked dress of the court general, but the clothes of a professional soldier, with campaign hat instead of court regalia and the upper part of the simple long coat worn by Prussian generals since Frederick the Great. He is wearing the Iron Cross, awarded for action in war under fire. He is depicted in a steadfast, realistic, straightforward gaze: no heroics, no romantics. The most competent professional war leader of the mid nineteenth century European world: confident but not enthusiastic, both fatalistic and trusting (Courtesy Ullstein Bilderdienst, Berlin).

CONTENTS

Acknowledgements   ix

Introduction   Prussia: War, Theory and Moltke   1

1   Napoleon's Legacy and the Prussian Invention   12

2   Helmuth von Moltke, 1800–57   25

3   Moltke and the Prussian System, 1857–63   50

4   The Danish War, 1864   77

5   The Austrian War, 1866   103

6   The French War, 1870–71   139

Conclusion   185

Notes   196

Bibliography   226

Index   235

LIST OF ILLUSTRATIONS

Frontispiece Helmuth von Moltke (1800–91) the professional soldier   vi

Figure 3.1 Relationship between railroads and rivers in Germany   73

Figure 4.1 The Danish peninsula   82

Figure 5.1 The Prussian Royal War Council, 1866 and 1870   107

Figure 5.2 The German states in 1866   109

Figure 6.1 North-eastern France, the German and Belgian
    border areas   165

Figure 6.2 Moltke and the mobile General Staff during the
    French War   169

ACKNOWLEDGEMENTS

To Sue Tally Bucholz, the anchor and joy of life.

To Bill McNeill who responded to an early draft outline of this project by remarking that Moltke should be the main thematic red line running through this book from start to finish: and so he is!

With thanks to my department chairs at SUNY Brockport, Bob Smith and Bob Marcus, for adjusting teaching schedules to make research and writing possible.

To Barbara Wachob, departmental secretary of steady knowledge.

To the SUNY Brockport History Department, surely one of the great history communities of the past 30 years.

To Bob Gilliam, Drake Library's incomparable Interlibrary Loan Librarian, for tracking down and bringing in masses of books and articles over the past five years.

To Lockwood Memorial Library, SUNY Buffalo, for allowing usage of their German history collections.

To my colleague Bruce Leslie for his loan of a Danish–English dictionary allowing me to read Danish work on the 1864 war.

To Philip Schwartzberg of Meridian Maps, Minneapolis, for creating the maps.

To Chris Cormack, Senior Engineer, Learning Technologies Corporation, East Rochester, New York, who kept my Macintosh systems up and running.

To Ullstein Bilderdienst, Berlin, for use of the photographs.

To Lore, Hans Christoph and Stephan Hobe for hospitality in Potsdam Germany, over a memorable Thanksgiving 1998 and generally staying in touch these many years.

To these and many others I am grateful. For the errors which remain I alone take responsibility.

Arden Bucholz
Waterport, New York,
August 2000

INTRODUCTION
PRUSSIA: WAR, THEORY AND MOLTKE

Reversing Established Orders[1]

Is it necessary to forever blame the sins of the sons on the fathers? Historians too often consider the past on the basis of what came later rather than on what came before.[2] That is one of the problems with Prussian–German history before 4 August 1914.[3] The great Fischer controversy of the 1960s hinged around it, as did the Sonderweg dispute of the 1980s and the Goldhagen disagreement of the 1990s.[4] Each of these paints nineteenth-century Germany in various ways with the brush of Nazi Germany and the Holocaust.

World War I was *the* radical break in German history, not the link between Second Reich (1871–1918) and Third Reich (1933–45). The Great War (1914–18) and Weimar Republic (1918–33), not the Second Reich, established the preconditions for the advance of National Socialism.[5] Suppose historians could describe the Prussian Army before 1914, unencumbered by the baggage which has accompanied two world wars? What would it look like? Can we imagine it so?[6]

It might look very different. The most influential Afro-American intellectual of the twentieth century – who became a radical critic of the United States in the first half of the last century – spent two years in Berlin in the 1890s. W. E. B. Du Bois developed deep attachment and profound respect for Imperial Germany. It was not, he said, a land of militarism and authoritarianism. He lauded Bismarck as an example of the power of purpose and the force of ideas: 'it shows what a man can do if he will'.[7]

Du Bois's images were not to last. After 1914 the modern mind became overwhelmed by slaughter in the last 'holy wars': the 'German cousin' died, to be replaced by the 'German Satan' of World Wars I and II.[8]

Of course it is impossible to describe Germany exactly as Du Bois experienced it. Many of the sources are destroyed. And the two greatest wars in world history left so much devastation we have still not recovered

1

from it. And it is ahistorical. The present, it is said, always derives its small and large origins from the past. Anything else would be to reverse the logic of time.

But let us try.

1864–2000: Cycles of War

A decade ago the world resembled Europe 100 years before. There was rapid technological change, an arms race of increasingly complex, costly and destructive weapons, two large, competing alliance systems, and very great specialization of labour in the bureaucracies which dealt with these matters. The basic framework of war in 1988 – its size, space and time configurations – had first confronted war planners in about 1888: armies much larger than a million men, campaign areas greater than 40 000 square miles and time pressures such that planners feared a 72-hour delay might lose the war.[9] In 1988 combined NATO–Warsaw Pact European forces were several million, campaign areas spread across ten planetary time zones and time pressures were exerted from weapons effective against targets 4000–6000 miles, but less than an hour, away. Nuclear weapons had changed international relations, dramatically raising the stakes. A basic error in 1988 appeared to have much greater consequences than in 1888.

Some of this has now changed. With the breakup of the former Soviet Union, the detargeting of missiles, the entry into NATO of Poland, Hungary and the Czech Republic, the Cold War which followed World War II for several generations is over. Explicit, overt, steady international tension caused by friction between two great alliance systems has abated. We are in a period of major power détente. Martin van Creveld has called it an era of low-intensity conflict.

However, other factors present in 1888 and 1988 are still with us. And they have been enhanced.

The rate of technology change has been raised to the next level, the level of information and smart weapons. Whereas it took one or two generations to increase firepower in the decades prior to World War I, during the past ten years the application of computers has raised the possibility of enhancing war power more rapidly.[10]

The Gulf War of 1991 displayed some of this power. Communications networks that linked satellites, aircraft, planners, commanders, tanks, bombers and ships, enabling one side to produce a completely new air-tasking order – a list of hundreds of targets for thousands of sorties – every 72 hours. A decade later, all of this has again been taken to the next level. The US Department of Defense today spends as much on satellites – tools of intelligence and communication that are crucial in getting an army through an OODA cycle quickly – as Britain spends on its whole military establishment. OODA refers to the method taught to jet fighter pilots to train them in aerial combat, 'observe, orient, decide, act'.[11]

There is still an arms race: NATO recently spent $464 billion. Russia spent more than $100 billion, China half that amount. There are still intense and ever-increasing time pressures. Control the electromagnetic dimension of the battlefield, it is now said, and you are most of the way to controlling all of it.[12] The information battle space – hundreds of miles on a side and ten trillion wavelengths deep – reminds us of the spatial dimensions war planners began to look at a century ago. Size, space and time were paramount in the strategic world of Alfred Count Schlieffen, chief of the Prussian General Staff, 1891–1905. The first modern military historian, Hans Delbrück, 1848–1929, was acutely aware of these changes and they pervaded all of his path-breaking work.[13]

Armies, Games and Complex Systems

In thinking about these matters an analogy may be useful. In the past 200 years war has passed through three stages which can be roughly equated to three widely played board games. Napoleonic warfare may be likened to the game of whist. In whist four players compete against each other. The cards are dealt out one at a time and the last card turned up becomes trump. Players follow suit and tricks are taken by the highest card. Because there is no bidding, the game just begins. Knowledge of the opponent and preparation of the players is always incomplete. Each hand is a surprise, revealing information the players did not have before. To play successfully the players adopt a series of expedients. Pure chance, and the ability to improvise after the game begins, prevails. Such was war up to about 1860. Field Marshal Moltke was even quoted as having said his strategic philosophy was nothing more than a 'system of expedients'. Nothing could be further from the truth. In reality he played whist *because* it was so different from his professional responsibilities as the first modern war planner.

By the 1860s, war was well into a fundamental transition. Industrial mass war – with its million-man armies transported by railroad and communicated to by telegraph, employing small-bore repeating rifles and steel breech-load guns – could not be played like whist. Bridge became the new game paradigm. Intricate bidding revealed long-range strategies based on carefully built up competitive strengths. These known quantities dictated long-range planning. Skilled players had the whole game in mind as the first card was played. Although expedients still played a great part, it was becoming a game which, once under way, followed the preprogrammed scheme of the opposing war plans.[14] This was the model which came into full definition and usage during the 31-year dark ages from 1914 to 1945.

In 2000 we are in a third, very different world. Postmodern war is like GO. It is a game of patterns. GO has uniform pieces whose characteristics depend entirely on their position. GO pieces do not move, they depend upon their place in the overall mosaic. Once the pattern is set, it is that which brings victory or defeat.

Except that armies are complex systems, not linear equations. War, where two armies fight, is more comparable to storms where two great weather systems clash: small variations and imperfections become magnified. War is the ultimate counteractive experience: it is a competition between two armies in which both participants will suffer some degree of death. On this stage, minor occurrences can have important outcomes.[15]

Most of the size, space, time and technology patterns of twentieth-century war have their roots in the nineteenth century. The German Wars were some of the first wars in world history to be preplanned. That is, they were thought about, written and talked about and specifically laid out on paper in complex timetables, mobilization orders, charts and plans for men, weapons, equipment and supplies. These plans were practised in war games, staff rides and manoeuvres which began at regimental level in the spring and ended at army level in early September. These forms of preplanning lasted for years.[16]

Armies as Organizations

Armies are large public monopolies, created and maintained primarily to compete against each other on future battlefields. At the uttermost bounds of this competition, one or both of the organizations will suffer some degree of death. These two factors – future orientation and death – set armies apart from all other human organizations.[17]

Armies exist primarily to deal with future contingencies, not the day-to-day problems of the everyday world. They remain focused beyond their borders at distant targets and foreign enemies. When they look in the mirror, they compare themselves – defence budgets, weaponry, readiness – not to other domestic agencies but to foreign armies. They are counteractive organizations, ready to react as a ratchet wheel to movements and actions beyond their borders. Like a ratchet, once raised, it is sometimes hard for armies to climb back down.

The thing that armies exist to do – fight wars – does not happen very often. But since the nineteenth-century Prussian invention of modern war processes, major powers always expect, anticipate and think about it. This deep future orientation – always looking ahead and watching what other armies are doing – has meant that armies have sometimes become the first modern organizations in traditional societies. Examples such as Egypt, Turkey and Japan come to mind. And, of course, Prussia.

Counteractivity was a law of human affairs before it became a law of physics. The ancient Chinese philosopher Lao Tzu described it as follows:

> There is a tendency for every existing object or arrangement to continue to be what it is. Interfere with its existence and it resists, as a stone resists crushing. If it is a living creature, it resists actively, as a wasp being crushed will sting. But the kind of resistance offered by a living creature is unique: it grows stronger as the interference grows stronger, up to the point where the creature's capacity for resistance is destroyed. Humans and human societies are thus highly responsive to challenge. When anyone, ruler or subject, tries to act on humans individually or collectively, the ultimate result is often the opposite of what he is aiming for.[18]

War as an ironic phenomenon is aptly characterized by Shakespeare. In *Romeo and Juliet* it is produced when both principals accidentally create exactly the opposite of what they intended. It is massive understatement to say that the outcome of World War I was ironic, confounding those who began the fighting. However, we can say with certainty that the outcome of World War I was totally opposite to what the planners had in mind when it began.

'Unintended consequences' is a favourite name for this situation. Under conditions of stress, which is the essence of war, unintended consequences become routine. Clausewitz called them the 'frictions of war'.

Contemporary surgeons call them 'latent errors': errors waiting to happen because of the structure and process of situations. Onerous workloads, inadequate communications and chaotic environments: the hospital emergency room and the combat battlefield are both full of such situations. Modern error experts believe that it is process, not individuals, that require examination and correction.[19] Latent errors are built into the complex processes of modern war fighting.

Military people speak of 'peacetime duty' and 'combat' as two different worlds. This is an important, nay an essential, distinction which civilians often do not understand. The difference is that in 'combat' someone else, the enemy, wants to kill you. Peacetime duty, no matter how realistic, cannot simulate this. Armies train and train and train to prepare for it. Training never includes death, except accidentally. Yet death, the fear of it and the response to it, is not only at the heart of war, it *is* the heart of war.

The fact that armies serve as instruments of death is the primary factor which differentiates them from all other human social organizations. It is also the glue which attaches one soldier to another in combat and the primary bond between army and society. The sanctity of grace – the death bond – also gives special status to other organizations such as the church, police, fire agencies and hospitals. But only armies encompass this to the terminal degree. No other modern organization has suffered nearly 60 000 casualties in 12 hours as did the British Seventeenth Army on the first day of the battle of the Somme in 1916. No other organization has absorbed such numbers of deaths as occurred to Germany during World War I. Had the German war dead been buried at home as they died, it would have entailed almost 1300 funerals per day for each of the 1560 days of World War I.[20]

For most human beings, such intimate relationship with death is entirely extraordinary. Yet at certain times and places it is customary, normal and usual for armies in combat. That is why combat is so different from peacetime duty. Armies must look ahead and prepare for the worst-case scenarios which do not happen very often. For that is sometimes normal war.

The German Wars

Several of the grand masters of German military affairs have written spellbindingly on these wars: Gordon Craig on the Austro-Prussian War and Michael Howard on the Franco-Prussian War.[21] There is no need to retell their stories, except to use the methods, sources and insights which have turned up since their work. Organizational, knowledge and learning theory are the methods. Theodor Fontane (1819–98) is the source. Helmuth von Moltke (1800–91) is the individual in need of new insight. Let us briefly describe each of these and suggest how they blend together to form the central mosaic.

Knowledge and learning theory

A powerful perspective from which to understand modern armies comes from those who focus on the organizational impact of knowledge. The definition that applies to armies is the systematic use of organized knowledge applied to the practical skills of war making.[22] This results in the division and subdivision of labour so that tasks become coterminous with established areas of scientific and engineering knowledge. Modern organizations break down their tasks, and organize themselves, partially or wholly, on the basis of knowledge.

The systematic use of organized knowledge applied to the practical skills of war has many implications. The more complete the application, the longer the task cycles become, and the more procedures become inflexible and harder to change. Personnel become more specialized since organized knowledge can only be applied by those who possess it. The organization itself becomes more complex in order to focus the knowledge of separate specialists on single pieces of work. As individuals become more specialized, and as the task is further divided, more information is needed. Finally, power passes to those who have the knowledge necessary for important decisions. Knowledge is that component, the possession of which gives one section of a bureaucracy a 'knowledge advantage' over other sections and departments. In 1864 Moltke had this on 2 May, midway through the war. In 1866 he got it on 2 June, 32 days before the battle which decided the war. By April 1870 – months before the war began – Moltke and the General Staff had it all.[23]

Important illustrations of this are transportation and communication. Nineteenth-century railroad and telegraph companies were the first modern business organizations. It was they which provided the first fast, regular and dependable services essential for high-volume production and nationwide distribution. They were the first to require managers to coordinate, control and evaluate the activities of far-flung separate operating units. To carry high volume safely and efficiently, up-to-date information was constantly needed.[24] To coordinate size, space and time on such a vast scale a new kind of organization was created, the knowledge organization. The Prussian General Staff was such an agency: the first organization in the world to put both rail transportation and electric communication together to fight a complete war.[25]

A second example of the impact of knowledge on modern organizations is information theory. Structures of organizations and parts thereof vary according to the uncertainties they confront, according to what sources of information they depend on and how that information is best got to the decision-making units. It is argued that organizations develop functionally towards those locations where information about the future is located.[26] That is one reason why the General Staff over time became so important in Prussian war mechanisms as a whole.

In high-technology organizations, skill is measured by the capacity to routinize activities that come to a given work role.[27] Uncertainty within the organization – units, soldiers or commanders who do not follow orders and procedures – undermine productivity. Military continuing education, pioneered by Prussia, aimed to educate soldiers from corporal to general so that, in similar situations, they responded in roughly similar fashion.

In sum, the structure of organizations is partially determined by their growth towards sources of news about the uncertain future. These uncertainties are distinctive in different parts of the organization, depending on tasks and environments. To deal with uncertainty continuing education taught routines. In the bowels of what appeared to be a very ancient, traditional organization, the Prussian Army, its control mechanism, the General Staff, became powerful because it often had the earliest vision of the future and application routines with which to master this future.

A final insight into the Prussian Army is provided by learning theory. Organizations that purposely build structures and processes to enhance and maximize organizational learning are called 'learning organizations'. The nineteenth-century Prussian Army was such an organization. The learning goal of armies, the productivity goal if you will, is to improve its ability to win quickly and decisively at low cost. This goal was repeatedly stressed by Moltke, who considered George Washington's victory at Yorktown a stunning achievement: a war-winning battle achieved with low casualties.[28]

To enhance learning, the Prussian Army introduced competition and conflict into its educational process by inventing the war game.

Competition and conflict are an essential condition for learning. Conflict caused, for example, by error, contrary evidence or opposing views, acts as a motor driving the learning process.[29] War games institutionalized this motivational sine qua non in early nineteenth-century Prussia. From the 1820s to the 1860s Moltke participated in dozens of war games every year, from intimate sand table and map games to outdoor manoeuvres in which divisions and corps played against each other across many square miles of terrain.

Good quality organizational learning involves error detection and correction. Called 'single loop learning', it permits the organization to carry on its present policies and achieve its present objectives. 'Double loop learning' occurs when errors are detected and corrected in ways that modify the organizations' norms, policies and objectives. The General Staff, using history and war games, routinely engaged in double loop learning.[30]

The organizational culture of the Prussian Army was unique. Within that culture, Prussia invented the four main core competencies of twentieth-century war: organizational, representational, educational and analytical. Each of these contained a host of knowledge-based specialities: the General Staff, the chief of staff system, the '*Auftrag*' or 'mission-type' command philosophy [a command and control principle which allows subordinate commanders great freedom of action in executing their orders], continuing education, cartography, and above all, the war plan and its testing vehicle, the war game.

One purpose of this book is to describe and analyse the German Wars within organizational, knowledge and learning theory. To describe the impact of increasing demands for knowledge on the practical task of war fighting. As size, space and time considerations burgeoned, as technologies changed, the bonding of war with knowledge was one way through.

Theodor Fontane

Theodor Fontane was the most important German writer between Goethe and Thomas Mann.[31] Fontane had three lives. First he trained as a pharmacist, became a reserve soldier, worked in London, participated in the 1848 revolution in Berlin, was a government official and journalist for the conservative *Kreuz-Zeitung* and wrote the classic *Travels in the Mark Brandenburg*.

Then he became a war correspondent. From 1864 to 1875 he wrote six volumes of war histories, 4000 pages, more than the string of literary masterpieces which were to make him famous in the 1890s. Fontane wrote about war as a newspaperman, as a wandering journalist who visited both sides, travelling back and forth. He was once arrested by French partisans behind German lines of occupation and nearly shot as a spy, and only rescued from a French prison by the combined efforts of Bismarck and the American ambassador.[32] Fontane, the newspaper correspondent, wrote history from the bottom up, using and describing small details of time and place. His war histories are illustrated by hundreds of woodcuts.

Finally Fontane became world famous as a novelist. He published eight novels, several of which are considered among the classics of German literature. Only *Schach von Wuthenow*, the tragedy of 1883, combines his military, social and psychological experiences. Why was *Schach* a best-seller in the 1880s? Because it described the ethos of the German Wars of 1864–70, which the Prussians of that day, a generation later, felt they were losing.

Helmuth von Moltke, 1800–91

Finally there is Helmuth von Moltke. He is the unifying theme that ties the story together. More than any other individual he developed Prussian war planning processes to the end of its first stage, then validated this development by proving it could win wars. Three wars in six years.[33] He is one of the first of a new breed: the modern, self-made, technically educated, professional officer.

Suppose Moltke's achievement was essentially neutral, like all technology? Suppose Prussia was one of the creators of modern high-technology industrial processes and organizations? Do the actions of later generations, especially in World War II, permanently dishonour this? In reversing established orders we are not asking readers to condone, explain away or exculpate twentieth-century horrors. Only to more carefully weigh judgement on its backwash. To avoid painting all Prussian–German history with the brush of the first half of the twentieth century.

This book is written to advance the hypothesis that Moltke is a much more remarkable individual than anyone has noticed up to now. A rare combination of artist and soldier, it was Moltke in his sixth decade of life, when many of his generation were dead or had retired, who developed and validated deep future-oriented war-planning processes.

This striking invention, which dominated all twentieth-century war – the Gulf War of 1991 was its most interesting recent example – was not 'militaristic', but, like all technology, essentially neutral.[34] It carried with it no necessary political baggage and did not doom Prussia and Germany to the path and track it followed thereafter. After 1871, Moltke the 'Superman' of modern war processes, became what he had been before, the mild-mannered 'Clark Kent' who went about his life in a normal unaggrandizing way, tending to his modest estate, reading, playing whist, and leading the General Staff into increasingly intellectual venues.

'The Prussian army was as much a marvel of organization for the world of 1870 as Henry Ford's assembly line was for the world of 1920.'[35] In the destruction and grieving of industrial mass total war which dominated the twentieth century, we have lost the Prussian Army before 1914. It has become a mythological demon, one of the putative seedbeds of the only two global catastrophes in world history. Its legendary core, the General Staff, was outlawed in 1919. Its traditional heartland, Prussia, was downsized in 1945 and largely eliminated in 1989. Have we lost the ability to recapture it?

This work is not intended as a definitive statement. Quite the opposite. It is written to open up discussion, to suggest possibilities for further research and to lay out a framework to study modern armies using a slightly different approach than normally employed.

1

NAPOLEON'S LEGACY AND THE PRUSSIAN INVENTION

Napoleonic Transformations

Modern war begins with Napoleon's Italian campaign of 1796, reinforced by his wars against Austria, Prussia, England and Russia in the next decade. Three aspects of Napoleonic war tell us it begins modernity. First there is terminology: the names used to describe it. For example 'avant-garde' was originally a French Revolutionary term meaning something that invades unknown territory, exposes itself to the dangers of sudden, shocking encounters, conquers as yet unoccupied land.[1] With this phrase we are no longer in the safe world of eighteenth-century limited warfare, where armies under siege went home, soldiers did not fight in bad weather or at night, wars did not threaten the existence of states, and campaigns went on for years with only a few battles.

Napoleonic war brings a new time consciousness. Napoleon was the first commander to issue time-specific orders. Later with standardization of time and electricity, time becomes altered, reduced, conquered. Industrial mass war brings mobility and acceleration. Some have suggested that the idea of speed built into military strategy at this time helped define modern Western power.[2] The new time consciousness enters philosophy with Henri Bergson's fluid reality: attention came to be focused on the historical process rather than on the eternally valid, unchanging order of things. Interest was transferred from 'being' to 'becoming'.[3] Time became a positive and useful element, the stage for action of military élan vital.[4] There was a Yin/Yang quality to it: an unending, boundaryless continuum.

With Napoleon comes an increasing reliance on future expectations. Whereas previously small professional armies were often sent home between wars and spent hardly any time at all getting ready for war, modern armies spend nearly all their time preparing, not fighting. They are constantly looking ahead. The more a particular time is experienced as new, modern, different, the more demands are made on the future; the more expectations increase. In periods of rapid change, such as the French Revolution, there is an acceleration of this process.[5]

Names, time consciousness and future expectations tell us we are in a different military world from the old regime. What created this new world?

Some changes had already begun before 1789 and were only accelerated by the wars which followed. But mainly war changed because of changes in ideas, politics and society which in turn transformed armies, tactics and strategy. And war changed as a result of material and technical factors, specifically weaponry, organization, road building and cartography.

The result of executing one king, exiling many of his nobles, and anointing a middle-class officer as emperor transformed not only society but the military. Careers were now open to talent. An even bigger change was to harness the new national state to the army. This opened recruitment to huge numbers of men who before this would not have considered joining an army. The new nation state, created by the participation of 'citizens', was threatened by the old royal states, populated by 'subjects'. Agricultural elite armies began to confront democratic mass armies.

Examples of these changes are easy to come by. By the spring of 1794 the French Republic had the largest army ever raised by a European power: 800 000 men. It was a national army, representing the people in arms, commanded by officers promoted on the basis of ability, not nobility. Its soldiers fought because they believed they had a political stake in military outcomes. Their enemies sought to extinguish the young French Revolution, an unheard of goal for eighteenth-century limited war, and French armies countered with the goal of exporting the revolution beyond French borders. In 1796 one of its commanders was Napoleon Bonaparte. He received command of an army which, in two campaigns, drove the Austrians out of northern Italy. His army was out of control: it lived by requisition, was self-supporting and created its own government. Later Napoleon took it to Egypt, where he destroyed the existing army and state and then moved back to Paris to become first consul.[6] An army that moves from the Mediterranean to the North Sea and fights between Paris and Moscow, remaking political boundaries along the way, is very different from one that operates between the Rhine and the Danube to besiege cities.[7]

Meanwhile other things had been happening. Artillery changes, associated with Jean de Gribeauval and the brothers du Teil, improved the technical qualities of artillery, reduced its weight and allowed Napoleon to employ massed guns for tactical breakthroughs.[8] As the Chevalier du Teil said, multiply the artillery at the point of attack to decide the victory.[9] Artillery concentrations began to win battles.

Innovations in organization had led, before 1789, to the creation of divisions and corps. This separation had begun in the 1780s. Armies then contained two kinds of tactical units: cavalry and infantry. This new situation created units composed of separate, self-contained, interchangeable parts. They moved separately, but were capable of quickly reuniting to act together. The army regulations of 1791 institutionalized this change.[10] Self-contained units of 20 000–40 000 men became Napoleon's main element of manoeuvre. Blending volunteers and conscripts, veterans and recruits, old companies and new brigades, they were folded into a new construct, the corps. It had its own artillery and cavalry. With the disappearance of aristocratic officers, soldiers had less distance from and more attachment to their officers, who treated them not as subjects but as citizens.[11] Men from the same region ate, lived and fought together. Regulations were simplified, reducing dependence on exact drill and cutting down training time. French armies had a penchant for attack and more cohesion in defeat than the old armies which tended to scatter in confusion.

Maps began their modern transformation in the eighteenth century, providing for the first time a correct two-dimensional representation based on mathematical triangulation. Prior to that geographers estimated distance by the duration of travel. They lacked sophisticated instruments and used each others' maps as primary sources. As late as 1807 the Caucasus Mountains in southern Russia were estimated to have an elevation of 50 miles![12]

The French Academy changed this, using the new techniques of triangulation: that is, geodetically accurate maps based upon trigonometric numbers, careful topographic recording and modern printing techniques. In the middle of the eighteenth century France began a detailed topographic survey of their country at a scale of 1.25 miles to the inch.[13] These maps were so rare they were considered top military secrets.[14]

France wrote the first modern cartographic textbook and right from the start the needs of the army were considered.[15] It was estimated that

180 sheets would cover the whole of France, and that this could be done working with two engineers per sheet. By 1789 army map survey procedures were established. Each spring, commanders gave field teams instructions. Fieldwork – trigonometric measuring and plane table drawing – went forward during spring and summer, with winter for analysing, copying and preparing the actual maps. The French Revolution did not bring about any profound or enduring changes in cartography. France, which had the early lead, now lost its momentum.[16] But in 1809 Napoleon possessed one of the first examples of this new breed, a rare hand-drawn set of 1 : 100 000 maps of Europe west of Russia.

Stein's highways in the County of Mark were examples of road improvement in Germany. Beginning in the 1780s, Stein laid the foundations of a modern system of roads in part of the Ruhr coalfields. Prussia also completed the Finow, Plauen, Templin, Fehrbellin, Bromberg and Klodnitz canals. The German Customs Union of 1834 gave more impetus to improved roads and turnpikes and the first glimmerings of railroads. But the Germanies of this day were 39 sovereignties and many went their own way. As Goethe described the antique lifestyle of Duke Karl August of Saxe-Weimar: more was consumed in a day at the top than could be produced in a day at the bottom.[17]

What did all of these innovations mean for military activities?[18] There are diverse views. One is that tactical forms were essentially unchanged. Infantry volleys and bayonet attacks still decided things, with cavalry an auxiliary weapon and artillery most effective for defence, although the final Napoleonic campaigns gave the guns a greater offensive role. Brigades, divisions and corps were the characteristic form. Supply did not change much. In this view the defence remained stronger in combat between similar weapons systems.

However, the main features of Napoleonic warfare were its political goals, rapid tempo, future orientation and, above all, its battles: many more were fought using larger armies, traversing much greater spaces and with far more decisive results.[19]

Deep Future-oriented War Processes

Agricultural elite Prussia fought democratic mass France in 1806–7 and was swiftly and completely overwhelmed, losing not only its army and its identity, but nearly its state as well. A single philosopher of war, Carl von Clausewitz, described Napoleon's essentially unlimited goals. Napoleon set out to destroy and recreate not only the armies but the states of his opponents. Here is the philosophical underlayment of total war. New technology – weapons, transportation and communication – increasingly opened up unlimited possibilities. Defeated by this new kind of army, Prussia set out to create one of its own. The major Prussian response, the invention of modern war processes, may be analysed in three categories: they describe changes at the top, middle and bottom of the army. At the top deep future-oriented war-planning processes: organizational, educational, representational and analytical. In the middle the professional NCO corps. At the bottom, the reserve force system. Additionally, there were four pieces of mechanical technology intimately involved in this military revolution: the telegraph and railroad, the breech-loading rifle and rifled steel artillery.

The General Staff system

At the top, Prussian processes comprised a new way of thinking about war. It began in 1795 with Christian von Massenbach, Prussian officer and military writer. Looking out at the early outlines of Napoleonic warfare, Massenbach sensed a new era. He sought to apply rational, Enlightenment ideals to war. Before this the future was considered either a mirror of the past or the whim of the gods: the domain of fortune tellers and soothsayers. War was a one-off situation, a single accidental surprise, confronted on unique occasions without much fore- or afterthought.

Massenbach discerned that it might be something else: a risk to be managed. He asked over what time frame would Prussia be exposed to danger? He proposed scenarios, a series of linked observations about the future state of the world. Officers should carry out mock battle exercises, factoring in contemporary intelligence and playing them out within the specific geographic context of past wars. Finally he described mathematical benchmarks to calculate outcomes systematically.[20]

Massenbach sensed the acceleration of time that had occurred in the first six or seven years of the French Revolution. Perhaps he speculated that this represented a kind of substitute for the older messianic notion of a Day of Judgement as spelled out in biblical revelations. His ideas were the military equivalent of the famous conflict between the ancients and the moderns which had been fought earlier in the seventeenth and eighteenth centuries. Until then it was thought that human life's epitome had been fifth-century BC Athens. Since fifth-century Athens, human life had had its ups and downs, but it had never surpassed that golden era. Several generations before Massenbach, Enlightenment rationalists finally concluded that the quality of life in contemporary France *had* superseded fifth-century BC Athens. Furthermore, that the future might continue to improve over the present, if education were utilized to prepare for it. From this point on, people gradually began to look mainly ahead not back. Gradual secularization meant that biblical expectations of a good life after death were slowly replaced by expectations for the good life now. In these slow but steady changes in perspective lie one of the foundations of modern war processes.

Whether he understood that the rate of change was accelerating is not clear. But Massenbach's terminology contained certain temporal assumptions. The idea of acceleration was gradually transformed from a passive sense of what was happening to an active process for generating a new reality. A concept became a metaphor, then a programme for action.[21]

Massenbach's ideas lay dormant for ten years. They received a jump start after Prussia's defeat in 1807 and had become institutionalized by the time Moltke joined the Prussian Army in 1822.

The organization which did this was called the General Staff. It comprised four functions: organizational, representational, educational and analytical.[22]

Organizational describes the General Staff system: an agency for thinking about, planning for, and ultimately directing future war. Comprised of four dozen officers, half were in Berlin – referred to as the Great General Staff or 'GGS' – and half were assigned to active corps and divisions – known as the Troop General Staffs or 'TGS'. After being handpicked from each War College class, these officers served an apprenticeship of several years, usually in the Berlin map and historical sections, and then began working in one of the sections. Summers they went into the field to do the trigonometric measuring and plane table drawing of the topography. In the spring and autumn they participated in war games: staff rides, sand table or map exercises and outdoor manoeuvres.

What did the Berlin General Staff, the GGS, do and how was its product used and tested? Its main function was to study and research potential enemies and future fields of action. This had three major components: intelligence, scenarios and plans.

Gathering intelligence on potential enemies was continuous. In fact for decades the GGS was organized geographically: the Russian section, the French section, the Austrian section. Each one assumed a foreign language and culture competence. A second component was to construct scenarios based upon current intelligence estimates: to create hypothetical dangers and 'what if' situations. The third component was to draw up war plans: specific operational solutions for each hypothetical danger. War planning was centralized in Berlin because the main job of the chief was to advise the war minister on what wars the state might have to fight. However, until Moltke became chief in 1857, this responsibility was not fully carried out; possibly because there were so few near-war situations between 1822, when Moltke joined the Prussian Army, and 1850, when it carried out its first mobilization since the Napoleonic Wars. For the same reason, such plans as were drafted were rarely communicated to the army as a whole. It was an academic exercise and the GGS was a small, inconspicuous think tank, buried within the War Ministry, without practical purpose.

To draw up scenarios, these soldiers had access to the best maps in the nineteenth-century world. The second function of the GGS was representational and it was embodied in the Land Survey Section. Created in 1816, this section laid down detailed procedures – trigonometric, topographic and cartographic – for creating an image of the land. From 1816 until 1921 Prussian–German cartography was in the hands of the military, and this unit led the world in cartographic reproduction. All beginning GGS officers worked in the Land Survey Section: four out of six chiefs, 1820–1914, served several years there. Moltke's first three probationary years were spent in the Land Survey Section.[23]

Most General Staff officers were trained in the first modern school for higher military education in the world, and the third function of the GGS was educational. The War Academy was founded in 1810, simultaneously with Berlin University. They were set across from each other on Unter den Linden. Although the GGS did not direct the War Academy until much later, they were, nevertheless, closely tied together. Officers from the GGS comprised much of its teaching faculty and from each graduating class the best officers were directly recruited. Moltke's three-year War Academy stint, 1823–26, immediately preceded his assignment to General Staff work.[24]

General Staff education depended heavily on history: on recapturing the past in order to derive lessons for the future. The military history section of the GGS did this work. From the 1820s through to the 1940s it researched, lectured and published vast quantities of military history.[25] There was a monthly journal, the *Militär-Wochenblatt*, and published series of war histories.[26] General Staff officers were expected to be conversant with military history: it was the experiential background to future wars.[27]

The fourth function was analytical. This encompassed drafting war plans and testing them out in war games. War gaming was a virtually continuous set of exercises to test out how the plans might work in particular situations, against mock enemies. These exercises were based on historical battles, as described in General Staff histories. They emphasized specific geographic contexts, as portrayed on General Staff maps. They included up-to-date intelligence from the GGS 'language sections'. Games took place indoors at map or sand table, and outdoors on GGS rides, and on regimental, divisional, corps and royal manoeuvres. In every case war games were competitive: two sides were selected and they played against each other.[28]

War gaming became the central building block of deep future-oriented war processes. As such it served four purposes:

1. It was a training ground for practical decision making. Using verbal and written responses to simulated war conditions, often in the actual geographic setting of historical battles, officers drafted orders to meet them.

2. It was a means of testing and evaluating plans in a simulated situation, of trying out, of competitively testing, many possibilities.

3. It was a data bank and research method from which new insights were generated and novel military ideas evaluated against historical and contemporary reference points.

4. It was a testing vehicle for personnel. Officers were pitted against each other under the watchful eye of their superiors. Careers were made, put on hold and accelerated at war games.

One can question the artificiality of such a situation, but given the scarcity of war experience following 1815, war games served as essential metaphors, as analytical tools for thinking about possibilities.[29] It is worth emphasizing that war games were not necessarily predictive, they were exercises in understanding what future problems might be.[30]

What was the relationship between the parts of this process? Officers began with knowledge of the land, trigonometric measuring and plane table drawing, studied the history of notable battles conducted on that land, then war gamed indoors around the map or sand table, using the maps and the history to replay the battle, taking it apart to understand what had happened. They also learned how to solve tactical, operational and strategic problems and how to record them in operations order format. Then they went outdoors. To GGS rides – essentially war games between two sides chosen by its chief – then to brigade, divisional and corps war games. Finally some units got to participate in the royal manoeuvres held in early September, usually two corps playing against each other under the eyes of the king and his closest aides and advisors. This was a highly competitive game, with lots of observers. The GGS planned, coordinated and judged royal manoeuvres. As soon as the outdoor season ended, on 1 November, they examined and compared after-action reports from all the major outdoor games.

Reform at the top level of the Prussian Army – organizational, representational, educational and analytical – constituted the most visible, famous and emulated aspect of the Prussian invention. However, innovation at the middle of the army was equally significant.

The Non-Commissioned Officer corps

French revolutionary edicts of the 1790s – laying out the framework for the new national government's educational philosophy and a school system which was oriented towards practical and occupational needs – were not lost on Prussian reformers. Out of the ashes of Prussian defeat in 1807 came Fichte's call for rebirth by national education. Some of this was institutionalized between 1809 and 1810 through the aegis of Wilhelm von Humboldt: public elementary schools for everyone, secondary schools for a few and universities at the top. Each embodied Johann Heinrich Pestalozzi's philosophy that education was not the authoritarian imposition of knowledge from the top down but the cultivation of the innate capacity of each individual.[31] This principle was later embedded in the '*Auftrag*' technique, the Prussian method of writing military orders.[32] For the Prussian Army all of this had momentous consequences: the beginnings of the first modern NCO system.[33]

The earliest Prussian soldiers who can be described as modern 'noncommissioned officers' are mentioned in 1824. The commanding general of the guard corps, Count Karl von Mecklenburg-Strelitz, asked the war minister for more mid-level regimental leaders. The fastest way to get them was to create a school for NCOs within the guard corps and that is what he did.[34] He expanded a part of the infantry teaching battalion to train young graduates of the Potsdam Military Orphan House and the Annaburg Boys Military Institute for duty with the standing army.

The school was to recruit 300 students between the ages of 17 and 20, who stood at least 5 ft 2 in. tall, and passed tests in science, morality and physical strength. For three years they studied reading, writing, mathematics, German, geography, history, astronomy, physical training, military discipline and marching. When training was completed and they had served three years in their regiment, the best of them would become NCOs. They would wear the officer's sword with silver sword-knot and be addressed as adults, with the formal *Sie* instead of with the *Du*, universally used with children and soldiers. They had earned respect. But the going was slow. From 400 in the first class, 1825–29, only 177 graduated to active duty and only 15 attained NCO status. But a few of these became generals.

Following this lead, during the first half of the nineteenth century a whole educational structure was created for Prussian NCOs. It comprised three levels: specialized schools to train NCOs to better accomplish their normal duties – for example the Military Shooting School at Spandau, the Riding School at Schwedt and Central Gymnastic School in Berlin; schools preparing NCOs to advance to higher rank within the NCO Corps – such as those at Potsdam, Jülich, Biberach, Weissenfels, Ettlingen and Marienburg; and schools for promotion to officer rank – the War Schools at Anclam, Potsdam, Erfurt, Neisse, Engers, Hanover and Cassel.

The Prussian NCO system had five unique characteristics.

Educational standards were high. Students in the 18-month Advanced Gunnery School in Berlin studied artillery, gunnery, chemistry, fortifications, mathematics, German and plane table, artillery and fortification drawing.[35]

Specialization of knowledge was substantial: it may have been greater in the army than in civilian life at this time. Military riding schools taught horse care and breeding, as well as jumping, dressage and war fighting. The Royal Central Gymnastic School trained NCOs in free exercises, gymnastics, fighting, quick running, long distance running, jumping, running an obstacle course and gymnastic pedagogy. Engineer schools curricula included mining, sapping, walls and tunnels, carpentry, wheelwrighting, blacksmithing, locksmithing, dikes and dams, rope making and sailing. Supply schools taught such skills as baking, butchery and cooping.[36]

Continuing education was the norm. Each spring every line infantry regiment sent four NCOs, every *Landwehr* battalion two NCOs to school. They learned and practised mobilization and supply, foraging, gun repair, equipage for horses and wagons, entrenching, and the feeding and grooming of horses. Teachers were part of a *Lehrfach*, a specialized branch of knowledge, described using the same vocabulary as university-based disciplines.

The NCO corps was one of the first organizations in Prussian society to offer achievement-based advancement to those who had no other access to social mobility. NCO education was open-access and promotion was based very substantially on knowledge as demonstrated by successful school completion. In the artillery, chief gunners were not chosen primarily on the basis of laboratory work but by examination.[37] In the NCO corps careers were open to talent. After three months' service every eligible young man could take the officer qualification exam.

Finally, NCO pay and emoluments may have offered a better quality life, both on active duty and in retirement, than comparable civilian positions open to these men. It was not only the salary, it was the fringe benefits that counted here. For example, chief gunners received 33 marks per month, but, in addition, they got a billeting allowance, food money, a clothing allowance and medical care.[38] At a time when there were no pension systems in existence in the German states, they could retire on half-pay after 12 years' service.

For modern war fighting all of this is essential. High standards and specialization of knowledge, continuous and open access education, and living standards better than average created highly disciplined, well-motivated and loyal troops. Not only did no active or reserve units turn against the government during the revolutions of 1848, but their technically proficient and dutifully inspired work ethic provided the essential glue for Prussian company-level success in the German Wars.

The reserve force system

At the bottom of Prussian Army reforms was the reserve force system.[39] When Napoleon defeated and imposed peace on Prussia in 1807, he restricted its army to 42 000 men. To get around this, Prussia sent home part of each company and brought in new recruits, training in this way more than 30 000 men over a five-year period, then sending them back to civilian life. When recalled in 1813 the men served in the same unit they had trained in, and were commanded by the same NCOs and officers they had known before. 'Citizen soldiers' thus effectively doubled the size of the army without diluting its quality.[40]

After 1815 Prussia continued this system, although fundamentally reshaping it. Instead of a long-service professional army, only some officers, NCOs and soldiers remained as career professionals. Each year the army conscripted 40 000 men for three-year terms. Upon discharge conscripts became part of the reserves for two years. After that they joined the *Landwehr* for seven years and then served eight years in the *Landsturm*. Called up in the summer for manoeuvres, reservists rejoined the units in which they had previously served. Each regiment was drawn from a single geographic area. Bonds of military experience and civilian culture – language, food customs, geography, school and work – fused them together.[41] These reserve forces hugely increased the size of the army. By 1845, Prussia could mobilize nearly 500 000 men.

Hardware technology

With armies, it is often said, there are three main things: to move, shoot and communicate. Transportation, weapons and communications underwent a revolution in the first 60 years of the nineteenth century.[42] Telegraphy proceeded slowly. It was expensive and competed with the stagecoach, river traffic and post riders. Railroads pushed telegraphy: they needed each other. By the 1850s the basic German telegraphic structure was built to go along with the 3000 miles of railroad track laid down.[43]

Railroads speeded up and made certain and continuous the traditional transportation process familiar to everyone: walk, ride a horse or take a boat. Top speed was perhaps 12–15 miles an hour on a fast horse for a short distance. Railroads enhanced this familiar pattern with speed, certainty, continuity and mass. Now larger numbers of people and goods could be carried much faster and much longer: three to five times as fast and as long as the engines were fed with fuel.

Telegraphy allowed instantaneous communication. This was a mental as well as a physical revolution. It was not the person who was being propelled, it was their ideas, shot across space at the speed of electricity. At 100 times the speed of trains.

These inventions permeated armies slowly. There was limited use of electric telegraphy in the Crimean War. Napoleon III used railroads in the 1859 Italian War.[44] Very extensive use was made of both in the American Civil War. General George McClellan, Union commander-in-chief in 1861–62, was a former railroad chief engineer.[45] As early as the Kanawha Valley campaign, June 1861, McClellan used the telegraph to change the battle plan three times in 72 hours.[46] Later at Shiloh in April 1862 both sides brought up forces by rail. Moltke followed these developments closely.

As for weapons, two in particular played a great part in the German Wars: rifled artillery and the breech-loading rifle. Rifled cast steel cannons were available in 1843, breech loaded by 1859. The advantage of these was range, firing speed and accuracy. They had roughly twice the range of smooth bores. Their firing speed was roughly five times that of muzzle-loaders and their shots were approximately four times as accurate.[47] Thus devastating fire superiority was possible. The Prussian breech-loading rifle was invented by Nicholas von Dreyse in 1835. Simply and strongly constructed, its weaknesses were a fragile firing pin, a stiff bolt action and a poor gas seal which dissipated the rifle's blast and velocity at long range.[48]

Friedrich Engels described the advantages of the breech-loaded Dreyse rifle over muzzle-loaders in a series of articles of the mid-1850s. The time of loading was reduced, the body position was changed from standing still to sitting, lying down or moving. Shooters, he said, could load while advancing, firing volley upon volley and still arrive at the enemy position with guns loaded. The eye position was changed: breech-loaders did not have to take their eye off the enemy. Ammunition was better quality and cleaning the rifle was easier since the barrel opened at both ends.

In sum the Dreyse could be loaded and fired – lying down – four to five times faster than any other infantry weapon of its day, with 65 per cent accuracy at 300 feet and 43 per cent at 700 feet. Rapid fire from the hip, prone or from behind a wall – firing, ejecting and firing again – was annihilative against close-order companies painstakingly loading down the muzzle from a standing position, with their eyes on their weapons. In Denmark Prussian casualties were consistently 10–25 per cent less than the Danes.[49] In the early battles against Austria they were so effective that later in the same war some Austrian regiments refused to fight against them again.[50]

When modern organizations first began to arise in the nineteenth century, the only model was the military.[51] Inspired and provoked by the French Revolutionary armies of Napoleon, the army that Helmuth von Moltke joined in 1822 had begun a momentous transformation, the invention of modern war processes at top, middle and bottom.

2

HELMUTH VON MOLTKE, 1800–57

In October 1800, when he was born, his kingdom had gone to sleep on the laurels of Frederick the Great.[1] By April 1891, when he died, the kingdom of Prussia had been resurrected, it dominated the first new Germanic great power since the fifteenth century. And the means to that end – a new form of war process – had been created which would become the model and paradigm for twentieth-century armies around the world. Helmuth von Moltke's life mirrored, represented and created one of the enduring and surprising inventions of the nineteenth-century world.

On the surface Moltke personified the conservative values of a large German–Danish family. Beneath this there was nothing typical or traditional about him or his family. His father was a Prussian lieutenant who – having given up his profession for the woman he loved – the daughter of a wealthy Hamburg banker who would not have a Prussian officer for son-in-law – failed at farming and ended up paying the bills for his eight children by joining another army, the Danish. Helmuth, third born of six sons and two daughters, lived his childhood during the years of Prussia's defeat, humiliation and French occupation. By 1814 these catastrophes and others had broken up his family. His mother sought refuge in a convent, his father in the officers' club. The children were farmed out. At age seven or eight Moltke was sent for board and education to live with a Lutheran minister – who gave him Homer and the Bible to read in quiet solitude – until he could enter the Danish Cadet Academy in Copenhagen, where he received free tuition from age 11.[2]

Denmark: Education and Profession, 1811–22

The first half of the nineteenth century was a golden age for the life of the mind in Denmark. It was the age of Hans Christian Andersen and Kierkegaard, of Oersted, the inventor of electromagnetism, and Grundtvig, originator of adult education. Copenhagen during the Napoleonic Wars was a sparkling refuge. Bearing the political marks of a small and declining kingdom – it had been a great power in the eighteenth century – Danish intellectual life was powered by the cultural explosions of the French Revolution.[3] If only a small city of 130 000, Copenhagen was a highly literate capital which aspired to world class. In 1807, after Napoleon had ordered Denmark to adhere to the Treaty of Tilsit and the continental system, Britain sent a fleet into Copenhagen harbour, bombarded the city and took the Danish fleet captive. Angry Denmark allied with Napoleon.[4] Moltke was a well-known family name in Denmark. Numerous related branches lived throughout the country. Moltke-Huitfeldt, for example, was one of the wealthier, with country estates such as Glorup, where Hans Christian Andersen often lived and wrote and at whose count's silver wedding anniversary 1600 estate peasants danced and dined until dawn.[5]

For more than a decade Moltke lived in Copenhagen, where he and two brothers came under the aegis of the family of retired General Friedrich von Hagermann-Lindencrone.[6] Louise, his wife, was the best woman poet Denmark produced. Their city home and large country house were the centre of a group of writers and intellectuals at Copenhagen University, the nucleus of Danish intellectual life. This group included Adam Oehlenschlaeger, professor of aesthetics, the first great Danish romantic poet and author of the Danish national anthem; Sibbern, follower of Schelling; jurist Anders Sandoe Oerstedt and his brother Johann Christen the famous natural science researcher; Jacob Peter Mynster, preacher, later Bishop of Seeland and Heinrich Steffens, the philosopher. All of these men gathered in Louise's country house and activated the family life which Moltke shared. These writers were drawn to the whole panorama of European literature and ideas: they read and put together Shakespeare, Sophocles, Goethe and Schiller: uniting classical antiquity, the Renaissance and oriental and northern fairy tales. Lessing was valued as much as Tieck, pagan Germans respected equally with Christians.[7]

Moltke absorbed their passion for the life of the mind. They reinforced his classes in the Danish Cadet Academy which were pitched at solid *Gymnasium* level and included logic, ethics and anthropology as well as lots of mathematics, foreign languages and such pure military courses as field rendering, fortifications and the mathematics of artillery. Moltke read Oehlenschlaeger's plays and the history of the

Danish–Nordic sagas at the same time as Shakespeare, Goethe and Schiller.[8] Although some writers credit Moltke with seven languages: German, Danish, English, French, Italian, Spanish and Turkish, it is far from clear how strong all of these were. He had a gift for languages, that is clear. Some of them he studied formally, especially German, Danish and French. Some he learned by translation work and through marriage, most notably English. Some he perfected by using them in their native culture, such as Danish, Turkish and Italian. Some he used professionally and at court, such as German, French and English. Through it all, in conversation he apparently preferred to use German, if his interlocutor understood it sufficiently.[9]

Moltke was raised outside of his family from age seven on. Close to a large, well-appointed but, most importantly, leading intellectual family of one of the largest and most interesting cities in Europe. What did he learn? To become a modern forward-looking, achievement-oriented person? That specialization of knowledge was going to drive the world of the future much more than the world of the past? That armies are future-oriented organizations created for competition one against another?

No. None of those fundamentals which would later drive his career to world renown. Rather a certain approach to life. A central means to understand and reconcile the world outside himself: the life of the mind and its ability to dominate everything else. And a corresponding belief, that attitude is destiny. What he learned as he grew from 11 to young adulthood was far different from the enthusiastic *Schwärmerei*, false emotion and harsh orders of practical military life.[10] The young Moltke became aware that at the top of European societies, intellectuals were highly valued because through the life of the mind, one could address practical reality. Moltke's uniqueness was that theory and practice were so closely intertwined that his wildest ideas were always grounded in the specifics of practical reality. Somewhat like Clausewitz who wrote most of his ground-breaking 600 pages during the years Moltke grew from 11 to 31, the real and the imagined, theory and practice, ideas and life were never far apart. Intellectuals in armies are often considered a contradiction in terms. Moltke was not.

The other lesson Moltke imbibed was the artistic process and the importance of art in life. Poetry is essentially one of the most open playgrounds of the mind. Especially when practised by a woman. To think about the physical world in imaginative terms was normal, valuable and

fun. Art and life are often divorced from one another. Real world prac-
titioners sometimes pooh-pooh the arts, downplay and denigrate them.
In this family, in these circles, art was joined to power.

Between cadet academy and army was the royal Danish court. In
return for free tuition at the former, Moltke served a year as page in the
latter. About this he said little. We can say that he certainly watched the
leading actors, jostling with each other for those plums of influence, promotion and acceptance that could only come from the centre of power.
However, the Danish court of this era was different. Royal personages
were neither divinities nor democrats. They were closer to ordinary people. And, in their eyes, the artist was assumed to have almost magical
qualities.[11]

As he entered the profession he would follow for the next 70 years,
Moltke was moulded by the large intellectual traditions of European culture. He was the antithesis of the narrow Prussian officer sometimes
characterized as a man of 'brainless virility and punctilious brutality'.[12]
He was an artist, an intellectual *and* a realist.

His three years' active duty in the Danish Army, 1819–21, stepped
him back into the eighteenth century. The Danish king's alliance with
Napoleon caused Denmark grief in the postwar treaties – the loss of
Norway, Helgoland and the fleet and a huge reduction in state funds.
Denmark, which had scarcely been a great power before 1815, was
clearly a secondary one thereafter, left only with good marital relationships to other European royal families. Its army, stepchild to the navy,
was an antique. Tiny in size, recruited from a population mainly exempt
from service, with salaries so low regimental and company commanders
had to engage in private business to live. Positions above the regimental level were often held by princes of the reigning house. Pensions were
so small older officers stayed on for ever.

Its single modern aspect was its officer recruitment system. This was
achievement based. Moltke passed stiff written examinations for page
and for officer at the top of his age cohort. He took tests in German,
Danish and French, mathematics and science and was examined in gymnastics, riding and dancing. In this agricultural elite army, officers were
considered part of the upper establishment. They were gentlemen. That
meant education, foreign languages and social graces. By family origin,
and even more by upbringing in Copenhagen and at the Danish court,
Moltke fit these requirements well.

Assigned to Rendsburg and the Oldenburg Infantry Regiment commanded by Wilhelm, Duke of Holstein, Moltke was appointed to its best

company, the *Jäger*.[13] Although he settled down in his father's profession and organization, the Danish Army was ultimately unsatisfactory.[14] It is hard to say exactly why this was so.[15] Perhaps pay was so bad that those who stayed had to have their own money. Moltke had none. Although his mother helped him out from time to time, he needed to look after himself. Undoubtedly he could feel the huge gap between the university world of ideas he had experienced in Copenhagen and the realities of a small-town peacetime garrison life in an antique organization. They were out of sync.

The Prussian Army, 1822–35

In 1821 Moltke visited Berlin where his uncle, aunt and brother lived. For a soldier, Prussia loomed much larger than Denmark: it carried the war reputation of Frederick the Great; it had been on the winning side in the wars of liberation against Napoleon. Furthermore, in Prussia the military was an integral part of the state. And if the peacetime Prussian Army was run in a tightfisted way, it bore no resemblance to the Danish Army. As a born Mecklenburger, he wrote to the Prussian king about a transfer, and, when he got a favourable reply from the Military Cabinet, began to process out of the Danish Army. He lost four years' seniority and was required to take a series of formal examinations.

These examinations were the result of the Prussian law of 1808 which had decreed that henceforth an officer's rank in peacetime would only be warranted by knowledge and education.[16] He was examined for several days by the Central Military Examination Commission in Berlin. He took tests in German and French, mathematics, field fortifications, geography, statistics and world and German history. The admissions process concluded with an hour-long verbal examination before a board of officers. He was rated 'very good', commissioned and sent to Frankfurt where it turned out that his boss, General von der Marwitz, was married to a Countess Moltke. He wrote a novel, *The Two Friends* and took a six-week leave to visit his mother. In fact she was supporting him financially since his father could not. He perfected English to add to his Danish and French, reading Walter Scott, Lord Byron, Shakespeare and later Dickens.[17]

From the start Moltke stood out. A little more than a year later, in 1823, he passed the exam for the War Academy. His essay on the Scandinavian peninsula – geography, climate and culture as related to its history and current military strengths – was judged so unusual a copy was deposited in the General Staff archive.[18] The War Academy during these years was in some turmoil. Its fundamental and continuing conflicts – between education for character or knowledge, and between general or professional education – were at their early peak. One-third of Moltke's studies were mathematics and science, one-third literature, history, languages and geography, one-third professional courses, such as topographical drawing, tactics and General Staff duties. Moltke studied under a gifted faculty many of whom also taught at the University of Berlin. His favourite teacher, Canitz, recognized full well what Napoleonic warfare meant. Since then, he said, the existence of the state hangs on the first shot of every campaign.[19]

Two subjects he got deeply into at the War Academy were drawing and music. Drawing, or, as it was called, trigonometric plane table sketching, became a passion. Moltke became a doodler, on the one hand, and a gifted and rapid sketcher, on the other. He discovered he loved music. Decades later, his own home had what amounted to a private musician in residence.[20] During these Berlin years he heard in concert the music of Bach, Haydn, Mozart, Beethoven, Schubert and Mendelssohn.[21] His musical tastes became well defined: he liked clarity, depth and grace. Clarity is to transfigure, to free from darkness and obscurity, to illuminate. Depth is to go to the innermost part of something: it suggests profoundness and intensity. Grace is an aesthetic quality illustrated by suppleness and ease, spontaneity, harmony and natural elegance.[22] Many of these adjectives were later applied to Moltke's writings, drawings and war plans.

Moltke and the Learning Organization

Almost as soon as he finished the War Academy and returned to his regiment he became a teacher in the division school. In 1828 he published a book. Examinations for entrance to the officer corps, a war college for advanced study, divisional schools for regimental officers, the publishing of books on military subjects, a General Staff: what does all of this tell us about the Prussian Army in the 1820s? Without realizing it, Moltke had joined a learning organization.

This novel invention was based upon a dual synthesis: the Enlightenment notion that the appropriate bridge between present and future was education and the related concept of specialization of knowledge.

The Prussian General Staff and Army became pioneers in discipline-based, institutionalized knowledge. How did this work? As a learning organization, the Prussian Army had five characteristics. Knowledge production within the GGS was essentially ongoing and continuous. It included the first modern mathematically based topographic map sets, series of historical essays, lectures and books, intelligence reports on foreign armies, proposed war plans to fight these armies successfully, and regular, sequential war games, map exercises and manoeuvres to test out these plans. Knowledge produced under this aegis was uniformly biased in favour of future operational considerations. It was didactic. It had practical ends in mind.[23]

The Prussian Army recognized the importance of continuing education.[24] Officers and NCOs were always in school – upgrading skills, learning how to use new technologies, reviewing new methods, preparing for promotion. Preparation was destiny and continuing education was one way through.

The central trunk of Prussian military education, the war game, took advantage of one of the modern psychological fundamentals of learning: that conflict – caused by error, contrary evidence or competition – is an essential motivation driving the process. Conflict was built into General Staff processes; for example, it was the essence of counteractive war gaming.

Double loop learning replaced single loop learning. Single loop learning involves the detection and correction of error. When errors are detected and corrected in ways that modify the organization, it is double loop learning. Double loop learning changes organizational culture, its basic assumptions and shared beliefs.[25] The greatest double loop learning experience for armies is often defeat in war. That is what happened in 1807 when the Prussian Army and kingdom came very close to extinction. It happened for Moltke during the battle of Nezib in 1839 and in the mobilizations of 1850 and 1859.

Specialization of knowledge produces organization-specific competencies and unique routines, those specific processes that became the trademark of the Prussian Army.[26] Deep future-oriented war-planning processes became its central core competency. By 1860 no other army in the world had this capability.

Knowledge production, continuing education, competition and conflict, double loop learning and organization-specific core competencies. Moltke assimilated these novel approaches to the military. Let us follow a few specific examples.

Moltke as Land Artist

One of the major knowledge products of Prussian war planning was cartography. In June 1826 Moltke graduated from the War Academy at the top of his class and returned to his regiment. By the autumn he had been appointed teacher at the division school in Frankfurt an der Oder, first in French, then in field drawing and sketching, finally as part of the school directorate. It was during this time that Moltke discovered he was a gifted artist. So good that he published a book, *The Military Drawing of the Land,* widely used as a basis of instruction, and won provisional appointment to the GGS topographical section where he spent the next three years.[27] One of his colleagues of those years, von Kameke, wrote later that the reason Moltke was not taken immediately into other sections of the GGS was that he did not have enough money, and could not get enough to supply himself with the required horses for General Staff rides. So he spent a few years in the topographical bureau, where horses were not required.[28]

Mapping, like Moltke's experience in Copenhagen, was both an artistic and a technical endeavour. Prussian officers sketched out their battlefields on paper, tactical assessments were visual, briefings were cartographic. Prussian officers were land artists. It was an artistic way to attain and learn practical knowledge. The use of maps was not just to guide movement: they believed that to look at a map was to see patterns that existed in space but were not apparent to the normal observer standing on the landscape. The ability to draw well was a means to express an idea, to analyse and compare, to think and communicate visually.[29]

General Staff officers were expected to be skilled at trigonometric measurement of distance, planimetric measurement of area and topographical sketching, taking the spherical surface of the land to the plane surface of the paper. The system in use was Müffling's Prussian polygonal projection. Every degree of terrain was mapped with 60 plane table sheets. At scales of 1 : 20 000, every four square miles, with its three to five trigonometric points, was transferred to a single sheet.

Chief of the GGS Karl Freiherr von Müffling's big project to map the entire kingdom of Prussia moved steadily forward during the 1820s. Moltke spent three years doing this work. He completed two maps per year, working in the land in summer and autumn and completing the maps during the winter in Berlin. To do this he lived with local families and, following the Prussian quartering laws in effect throughout the nineteenth century, became beloved by the children of the von Kleist family in Grüttenberg and the von Kospoths in Schoen-Briese.[30] The von Treskows near Posen took him to Karlsbad with them.[31] He became virtually a member of the family for these old Silesian nobility who took until noon for the *grande toilette* and did not always say what they thought. They lived in beautiful castles set in wonderful parks with French-style gardens and paintings by the old masters on the walls. Moltke sketched the counts and countesses, wrote poetry and met all the neighbours. In these experiences, Moltke discovered that, like the Hagermann-Lindencrone family in Copenhagen, for the country nobility of old Prussia, art was an essential part of life.

Moltke produced seven or eight complete map sheets during these three years. Some of these were so good they became part of the modern German Ordnance Survey series.[32] In the process he became a keen observer of the land and its inhabitants, and began to display the talents which later made him a celebrated visual and literary artist.

Moltke as Historian and War Gamer, 1832–35

In March 1832, after a four-year apprenticeship, Moltke won regular appointment to the 60-man GGS. He immediately began to participate in its ongoing work; the production, distribution and use of knowledge.

At the time its major focus was the end of the Seven Years War, 1759–63, especially the battles of Minden, Kunersdorf, Landshut, Liegnitz and Torgau. Beginning with a reconnaissance ride to familiarize themselves with the specific terrain, they pored over topographical maps, and examined orders, plans and war diaries from the General Staff library, until images of these campaigns took form. Using the knowledge thus accumulated they lectured to each other within the General Staff and wrote essays on specific topics such as topography, weapons and strategy. Single campaigns were written up, one after the other, and the work critiqued in a general meeting. Then each part was given to a single officer to edit and the manuscript was completed, published and distributed.[33]

If history was the raw materials, war gaming was its testing ground. War games originated with two Prussian officers, the Reisswitzes, between 1810 and 1824. Originally a game played with plaster terrain and porcelain models at a scale of 26 inches to the mile, it evolved into metal symbols – blue for Prussia and red for the enemy – moved about on a relief map at 8 inches to the mile. Two commanders played against each other, moving one at a time the same distance as actual troops could in a day. A set of rules, an umpire – the conductor – who mediated between the opposing sides, and dice standing for the element of chance in war. If blue, with 200 men, attacked red, with 100, four sides of the die were coloured blue, two sides coloured red. When the dice were thrown, if blue turned up, they had won. Casualties were then apportioned.[34]

When GGS Chief Müffling first saw the game in 1824 he immediately described it in the *Militär-Wochenblatt*.[35] 'It's not a game at all', he said, 'it's a veritable war school!'[36] It was not only legitimized, it became fashionable when King Frederick William III, his son Prince William and officers of the Berlin garrison played. Regiments were furnished with war game kits. Competitions were held. Fifteen years later, as corps chief of staff, Moltke's team won the annual all-army war game competition.

War gaming was practised at three or four distinct levels. One was indoors around the map or sand table. The other three were all done outdoors. There was the biannual General Staff ride. Every year in spring and autumn, the chief of the General Staff chose two dozen officers, divided them into red (enemy) and blue (Prussia) and, using the exact terrain of a well-known historical battle they had been researching, lecturing and sand table gaming, went out into the natural world to work through the problem. A third level was played by regiments and divisions during summer training. A fourth level was the royal outdoor manoeuvres, held in early September during which divisions and corps manoeuvred against each other. Under the eyes of the king, they played out a scenario drawn up, conducted and judged by the General Staff.

General Staff officers spent many months each year war gaming. It was the keystone experience of Prussian war planning because it integrated the other three elements: organizational provided the personnel, the setting and the motivation, representational the maps, charts and visual literacy and educational the uniform body of training, procedures and history. The war game exercised these elements in a profoundly theoretical yet eminently practical manner. It was a way of thinking about war in its essential two-sidedness.[37]

Yet in spite of all Moltke's immersion in education, he was, above all, the professional officer looking for promotion. His New Year's wish to his mother in 1831 was, 'May this year bring you peace and me a war!'[38]

In March 1832 Moltke was jumped ahead of 11 of his General Staff colleagues and advanced to first lieutenant.[39] He had been in the

Prussian Army ten years and at this point was spending a lot of time in travel, research and writing. During a travel and study leave, he visited Austria, Italy and several German states. He visited fortified positions in Linz, the Tyrol, Verona and Peschiera, looked at war machines such as the mortars of the Baden reserves and Württemberg artillery. Moltke did a lot of writing about the Russian Army. A preliminary study on coastal defence and landings in Pomerania for the 1833 manoeuvres, and a memorandum on the military relations between England and Russia. In autumn 1834 he studied Denmark, its military and naval establishments, taking a three-month 'study leave' to Copenhagen and Schleswig-Holstein to do it. He visited his favourite sister Auguste, who had married Henry Burt, an Anglo-Danish estate owner with West Indian and English property. A widower with two daughters from his previous marriage, Burt's youngest, Marie, was eight years old. They got along especially well.[40]

When he got back to Berlin he wrote up his conclusions on Denmark in a report which the king read. The big difference between land war and sea war, he said, was greater dependence on material. At sea there was much less improvisation and a lessening of morale factors. Individual fighters in a sea battle were not so dependent on themselves as the land fighter. Sea battles have no communications and supply lines. Ships fight their battles with what they have on board. When the enemy is met, it is all over in half a day. There is a small loss of men, a great loss of materials. Instead of emphasizing attacks by ships of the line, he talked about land–sea coordination in any war with Denmark.[41]

By 1834, the General Staff volumes on the wars of Frederick the Great were nearing completion. Moltke worked on the campaigns of 1760 and 1761, especially the Bunzelwitz campaign. Bunzelwitz was a fortified camp near Schweinitz, just west of the Oder River. Between August and November 1761, Frederick the Great's 55 000 men confronted 70 000 Austrians and 50 000 Russians. Surrounded by marshes and swamp land, a series of battery positions, redoubts and fortified villages was constructed and, with 450 cannon, Bunzelwitz was developed into a strong defensive position. Although the Austrians finally mounted an ineffective attack, the Russians backed off. Frederick had captured the attention of his enemies' main field armies for most of the campaigning season with no losses himself.[42]

In 1835 Moltke sat on the officer examination commission for 143 cadets and ensigns and during the summer months served as company commander in the Kaiser Alexander Guard Grenadier Regiment, Berlin, one of the oldest, most elite and highest profile regiments in the Prussian Army. It was the last time he actually served in a line position in his life. The autumn General Staff ride in Silesia was a contest between the V and VI Corps, who fought it out in the terrain of Frederick's brilliant victory at Liegnitz in 1760. After that he was a guest of the Prince of Holstein-Glücksburg and accompanied him to combined Prussian–Russian exercises near Kalish.[43]

But Moltke wanted to travel beyond these confines. He put in for the Prussian embassy in Paris. When this failed, he left for a six-month travel leave to Vienna, Constantinople, Athens and Naples, on half pay.

What of Moltke's own strategic ideas during this period? Eberhard Kessel says that what comes up from all of his writings to 1835 is: artillery preparation before an attack, the necessity to secure defensive positions in a retreat, the freedom which movement gives, the value of a flank attack. Classic themes which recur in the history of war.[44]

The Ottoman Empire, 1835–39

In 1835 Moltke went to Turkey. He stayed four years and experienced his first and only combat defeat.

Initially he and his colleague Lieutenant von Bergh of the 1st Guard Infantry went on a several months' travel leave south. Bergh had good connections all along the way: he knew who to see and always provided for them well. When they got to Constantinople the Prussian ambassador Count Koenigsmarck took them into his house and with him on diplomatic rounds. They were presented to Chosref Pasha, Ottoman commander-in-chief and war minister, and gave him the present the Prussian king had sent, a war game kit such as used in the General Staff in Berlin.[45]

The next day Moltke gave a demonstration of it. Chosref immediately asked him to stay and instruct his officers. His friends were due to leave for Izmir and the Greek islands the next day. Moltke stayed, mainly as he wrote, for financial reasons. Captains in the Prussian Army received half of the annual stipend Moltke was paid during four years in Turkey. Most often strapped for funds, he had tried a number of ways to supplement his income. In the two years just prior to leaving Berlin, he had translated Gibbon's three-volume *Decline and Fall of the Roman Empire* into German. It helped his English, but when he had it mostly done, his publisher reneged and he never got a penny.

Turkey and the Ottoman government were in flux.[46] Ten years before Sultan Mahmud II had destroyed the heart of the old Ottoman military establishment, the Janissaries, and began to create a modern army along the lines of those in Europe. These forces lost to the Greeks at the naval battle of Navarino in 1827 and again to Russia in 1829. Meanwhile Mehmet Ali, who had come to power in the former Ottoman province of Egypt after Napoleon had defeated the Ottoman Army there in 1798, was trying to modernize his army with French military assistance. In 1831 he had defeated an Ottoman army and began to move in the direction of the Ottoman capital. In desperation Mahmud II called upon Russia for help: he concluded the military alliance of Unkiar Skelessi and Russian troops landed in the Bosporus. The badly frightened European Great Powers called a conference to arrange the Peace of Kutahia of 1833. Under these dire circumstances and with neither knowledge nor enthusiasm, Chosref Pasha was ordered to create a modern army.

In 1835 Moltke found an antiquated army in full seventeenth- and eighteenth-century regalia with a thin veneer of modernity.[47] Speaking and writing in French, Moltke began turning out memoranda and position papers for Chosref. One dealt with the creation of a reserve military force. Others described recruitment and military education. General conscription, he wrote, one foundation of a modern army, was only possible with laws supporting and protecting individual worth. Officers had to begin their military careers by starting at the bottom. Education was the sine qua non for a modern army.

He made a reconnaissance of the fortresses of the empire, travelling north-east to the Danube River fortifications at Varna, and north-west to the mountain passes in the Balkan Mountains. He travelled with Chosref as the Ottoman commander reviewed the firing of the huge fortress guns along the Dardanelles. Stone cannon balls of enormous size were fired from one side of the bank. With an enormous roar the balls lifted off but came nowhere near the small boat which was their target. He advised Chosref on building new streets and roads, a new water system, forts and fortifications and artillery. He put forth a plan for a new military school and advised over what to do to prevent epidemics.[48]

They accepted his advice, but did little with it. The Ottomans wanted to look good on the surface, Moltke concluded, but cared little for real change. Everything turned on personal favour. The road to Belgrade was not finished because it would have removed a pleasant prospect the sultan liked to see when he travelled outside the capital city.[49]

In August 1837 three more Prussian officers arrived, captains Karl Freiherr von Vincke-Olbendorf and Friedrich Leopold Fischer from the General Staff and Heinrich von Mühlbach from the engineers. In 1838 came the campaign against the Kurds and Egyptians. By this time, Chosref had become virtual head of the governmental bureaucracy and he sent the Prussian officers up to the front lines, Moltke and Mühlbach to Malatia and Karput and Fischer to Konya. They left Constantinople on 2 March 1838, took ship across the Black Sea, and then had a long cross-country ride. By 17 March they arrived at the headquarters of Hafiz Pasha, field commander-in-chief.[50]

The army that Moltke saw spread across this landscape was in terrible shape. Insufficiently trained, weak in numbers, divided into small groups spread over a wide area, with disorganized artillery and supply. Sanitary conditions were a disaster.

Moltke noted it was a political mistake for Muslims to fight Muslims. This could never become a popular war. He noted the unfavourable geographic relationships; the Egyptian Army could threaten the capital city at any time with the same army they had assembled along the Syrian border.[51]

They undertook a reconnaissance of the border area between the Tigris and Euphrates rivers, and got to know the various units, their strengths, weaknesses and circumstances. Travelling by horse and wagon through the lands Herodotus had described, Moltke found the organization and training of the artillery especially poor. Gunsights were mostly broken. Measurements were only for very short distances. The chief of artillery gave Moltke a pair of shoes as a gift: he was a former shoemaker.[52]

During winter 1838–39 the troops stayed out in bivouac in Malatia and in spite of Ramadan, the fast, they drilled in bad weather. Sanitary conditions got worse, units lost 30–50 per cent of their strength through illness and desertion.[53]

Moltke was constantly suggesting operational plans to the Ottoman commander. One was a concentration near Urfa with a forward position at Biradschik on the Euphrates River. For Moltke, Biradschik was tantalizing: Egyptian commander Ibraham Pasha must attack it if the Turkish Army assembled there. He concluded that, in contrast to modern European armies for whom the offensive alone gave the advantage, the Turks were mass not individual fighters. With their passivity they were more effective in defence. Under these circumstances, the strength of defending Biradschik was evident.[54]

Hafiz Pasha took some of Moltke's advice. In April the forces moved south-west. Snow lay in the mountains, while on the plateaux and plains there were 29 days of unbroken rain. Moltke estimated the march itself through the rugged terrain cost 6000 men. By the middle of May the main army was assembled in Biradschik: over 30 000 men with 110 guns. Light infantry was on the frontier; a forward position, enlarged and built up, was set at Nezib, a mile east. Nezib was on a hilltop, over-looking approach march routes, but surrounded by a series of low, rolling hills. Biradschik stood in a sack formed by the Euphrates River, with its castle and market backed up to the river. Mühlbach wanted to build some bridges across, Moltke rejected this: troops fight the best when they have no way out.[55]

On 28 May the Egyptian Army crossed the frontier. By 4 June it stretched from Nisib to Aleppo, eighty miles with 40 000 men and 160 guns, an open provocation for an attack. Moltke suggested a pre-attack reconnaissance of the enemy march route.[56] The pasha refused. Two days later the Egyptians gave a cannonade and made a reconnaissance in force against Biradschik. The next day they retreated: they had found the Ottoman position too strong for a frontal attack. Hafiz Pasha was triumphant![57]

Moltke was not. He watched as an Egyptian flanking and encirclement movement began against Nezib. They crossed a small river and passed behind a series of low hills to take the Ottoman position from behind. At first Moltke suggested that this was the time for an offensive: an attack against the Egyptian positioning march, extended for several miles across the Ottoman front. When this was refused, he asked Hafiz to mass the artillery to protect his flanks, and requested that he, Moltke, be put in command of it. But the Ottoman commander refused to act. His religious advisors warned him the omens were not propitious![58]

The battle of Nezib, 24 June 1839, lasted two hours, from 9 to 11.[59] The Ottoman Army did not really fight, it fired here and there, lost its forward positions and ran away. Even so, the Egyptian Army was unable to destroy the Ottomans and its remnants marched back to Malatia. Before news of the defeat had reached the capital city, Sultan Mahmud II had died.[60] It took Moltke a long time to get back to the capital. And ever after for Moltke 24 June was a difficult day.

He finally left Istanbul on 9 October and slowly made his way north through Budapest and Vienna. He reached Berlin two days after Christmas 1839. He was surprised to be acclaimed a celebrity, inducted into the order of the Pour le mérite, asked to lecture and publish. His four

years in Turkey made an impact on official Berlin. Famous geographer
Karl Ritter and cartographer Heinrich Kiepert came to his lectures.
Within a short time, in addition to a dozen articles, he published three
volumes: a book of maps, his famous *Letters from Turkey* and a history of
the Russo-Turkish campaign of 1828–29.[61] The second of these was illustrated with a dozen charming pen and ink sketches.[62] It became a best-
seller 30 years before Heinrich Schliemann's discoveries of Assyrian
remains at Hissarlik – a few dozen miles to the north-west of Nezib – made
that part of the world exotic and rare to the German reading public.[63]

Back in Berlin and writing on the Russian–Turkish campaign of
1828–29, the transportation possibilities of steamships and railroads
immediately caught his eye. Moltke found the top leadership of the
Prussian government very pro-railroad. In his absence the government
had passed the landmark Prussian Railroad Law of 1838 and King
Frederick Wilhelm's bequest of a million thaler to jump-start building of
a rail line linking the western and eastern Prussian provinces, meant
that when Moltke talked about railroads he found ready and knowledgeable listeners.[64] He understood that military necessity paralleled
commercial need. Reading Friedrich List's *National System of Economics*
he became aware of the national political importance of railroads in an
emerging era of world trade and wrote a series of articles, memos and
reports in support of a Berlin–Hamburg rail line, finally joining the
board of directors of the new corporation.[65] Meanwhile the main framework of the German railroads was being laid down. Of two main lines
begun during the 1840s, one linked Vienna–Brno–Dresden–Hanover–
Cologne–Antwerp and the other Vienna–Breslau–Frankfurt–Berlin–
Hamburg. Railroads were beginning to be used in small ways by the
army. A year before he returned, the Prussian Army had moved 8000
troops the short 23-mile trip from Berlin to Potsdam.[66] Eight thousand
troops were 20 per cent of active duty strength.

Moltke: Marriage and Troop General Staff Duty, 1840–45

Within the age cohort which included hundreds of field grade officers,
Moltke had now achieved uniqueness. None of his colleagues had any
practical military experience. None had served as responsible advisor to
an army commander,[67] or been decorated with the order star and honour sword by the Ottoman sultan and the Pour le mérite by the Prussian

king. Such fame for an officer within the general literate public went back two generations – to the wars of liberation. But this was peacetime and more significant for now he had caught the attention of the royal family. And what they found surprised them: a very bright officer, graceful and adept at court, with the additional cachet of the artist. In a society of deference, rife with patron–client relationships, this was gold. His next three appointments put him into close, daily contact with three of them: the king's nephew and most military relative, Prince Friedrich Charles, the king's younger brother, Prince Henry and the king's nephew, Prince Friedrich. Moltke got along well with the royals. This was certainly one key to his career success. Elegantly turned out, perfectly tempered, he fitted in everywhere.[68]

In 1842 Moltke married the stepdaughter of his favourite sister Auguste. Raised on her father's Danish estates, she was 17, he 42 in April of 1842 and the marriage lasted until Marie's death 26 years later.[69] By all accounts it was a great success, a conclusion attested to by their correspondence. He wrote to her almost every day when they were apart and these letters became a published best-seller in the 1890s. As reviewers noted, this delicious legacy beautifully demonstrated to the German public that the nobility had personality, deeply held philosophy and depth of spirit – characteristics which might equally well be applied to their marriage as a whole.[70]

As they had no children, Marie von Moltke became one of the first 'service wives'. In the early 1840s they lived in Berlin and went riding every morning in the Tiergarten or Grünwald. Berliners could see the Moltkes coming back from a long ride just as they were getting up![71] When Moltke travelled with the royal family as he often did, she took extended trips to her family in Denmark. For those official occasions when they both had to show up for formal royal and army functions, Marie memorized the Prussian flags and uniforms, and knew the location and history of each regiment so she could recognize and chat with its officers. She read the *Militär-Wochenblatt*, which contained news of appointments, transfers, retirements, and articles of military interest.[72] She was not a frivolous woman and not a part of the high nobility, fluffy and social. She was a professional officer's wife.

In April 1840 he had been appointed to the General Staff of IV Corps. Because it was headed by Prince Friedrich Charles, the king's favourite nephew, this had the same character as a court appointment. Nevertheless Moltke's activities modelled those of the GGS in Berlin: he planned troop manoeuvres and exercises, especially the great year-end exercises. He took officers of the troop General Staff on reconnaissance rides. Moltke went with his colleagues into the Harz Mountains, through Braunschweig, and into Holstein from Mecklenburg. Finally he wrote strategic essays, dealing with the 1842 reductions in the Danish Army, and the Elbe River region from Riesa to Rogatz, south of Magdeburg, comparing its very different employment in the 1806 and the 1813 campaigns.

Moltke finished his book on the Russo-Turkish War of 1829, and, during his wait for the required review by the GGS censor, lamented to his brother how hard it was to find a publisher for military history. The number of potential readers is so small, he said, and the need of maps so great, that the cost of publication is enormous, and authors received almost nothing.[73] Meanwhile, Moltke and the prince got along well and he became Moltke's patron.[74]

In 1845 he was transferred to another prince, personally closer to the throne: King Frederick William IV's second youngest brother, Prince Henry of Prussia. He lived in Rome, following his artistic temperament and inclinations. When he got to Rome, Moltke found his prince in bed, dressed in a Scottish half frock. Prince Friedrich Charles had found Moltke cool and measured, Prince Henry found him lively and engaging.[75]

His duties were light. He went to the prince daily for an hour or two, informed him of the latest news. Moltke spent his time getting to know Rome and its region. He went to all the ancient sites, visited the museums and opera, sketched and drew everything. He read the writers who had written on Rome: Niebuhr, Ranke, Gibbon. Finally, he assembled a book containing map images of a single square mile, combining historical descriptions with cartographic depictions.[76] This book, *A Guidebook to Rome*, was published in 1852, financed by King Frederick Wilhelm IV at the urging of Alexander von Humboldt.[77] Humboldt, a titled court chamberlain, who often lived in Rome, was the most prestigious authority on science in the Germanies at this time. His book *Kosmos* was read all over the world. Moltke was beginning to attract important patrons.[78]

The following summer his prince died. Moltke hastened north and reported directly to the king at Sanssouci. He was told to bring the body of the prince back on the Prussian steam warship, the *Amazon*. But he became so ill he had to leave the ship at Gibraltar, cross overland and meet it again in Cuxhaven.

General Staff Section Chief and Corps Chief of Staff, 1846–55

During the next nine years, from 1846 to 1855, Moltke became intimately familiar with the problems of war mobilization at the army corps level. Appointed General Staff officer to VIII Corps in Koblenz, he joined this unit in December 1846. His boss, the elderly commanding general August von Thile, found Moltke colourless. He voiced no opinion on Moltke's character, remarked on his reserve and taciturnity, and emphasized his indifference to religion. He seldom takes part in public worship services, wrote the old man.[79]

For two months in the summer of 1848 Moltke was section head in the General Staff in Berlin. Reyher, its chief, wanted to get to know Moltke: the latter was of the age and rank for corps chief of staff. What was Moltke made of? He liked what he saw and, as soon as a corps job opened up, Moltke got it.

But meanwhile there was a war going on in Denmark and Moltke watched it closely. Between March and August a small German force – the X Federal Corps – mainly a Prussian division plus Hanoverians and few other units – fought against the kingdom of Denmark. For a time it appears Moltke was being considered as its chief of staff and he put himself forward, writing a number of articles later published in the *Militär-Wochenblatt*. What did he say? Two main points stand out. One is that divided German political leadership led to disorganized and ambiguous strategic goals and objectives. Secondly, that Danish control of the sea was a major factor. The German states had no navy, meanwhile, the Danish navy blockaded German harbours and interfered with German land operations.[80]

In August 1848, just as he finished the Danish research, Moltke was appointed chief of staff to IV Corps in Magdeburg.[81] A corps General Staff chief had a lot to do. He was the commander's manager. Moltke and two aides had charge of marches, quarters, movement, supplies, manoeuvres and exercises, intelligence, training, fortresses, maps and finally, executing the corps war plan.[82] His first boss was a son-in-law of Wilhelm von Humboldt, an elderly and loquacious man whose audiences lasted for hours. But he was often ill and went to bed, leaving Moltke in charge. In 1852 he was replaced by Anton Prince Radziwill, a high noble great seigneur of the old school. These situations demanded a firm hand on the corps wheel. It was Moltke's hand.[83]

Writing to his brother Adolph in September 1849 he said that Schleswig looks pretty well up for grabs.[84] A storm in a glass of water, but a bad situation if the glass of water is your home. Moltke, aged 49, was thinking of retiring 'if we don't have a war'.[85] He got a failed mobilization instead.

The mobilization of 1850

From 6 November 1850 to 31 January 1851, the kingdom of Prussia carried out its first war mobilization in 35 years. It was a disaster from start to finish. There had been rising tensions between Austria and Prussia in the aftermath of the revolutions of 1848 and the drive on the part of some Germans for a liberal, national Germanic state to be crafted from the disparate 39 existing sovereignties. Hoping to head off trouble, and keep Austrian power strong in central Europe, in late October 1850 Tsar Nicholas met with Austrian Emperor Franz Joseph and Prince Wilhelm, the brother of the King of Prussia, at Warsaw to mediate this tension. Each side presented their case, and on every point, the tsar decided in favour of Austria. Meanwhile in Berlin the king was receiving conflicting advice: mobilize and support diplomacy with a show of force, or do not bother because the army was not ready for a demonstration and certainly not for a war. He came to no firm conclusion.

That is, until Prussia was threatened. On 1 November, an Austro-Bavarian corps entered Hesse, occupied Hanau and approached Prussian territory. Seventy-two hours later the king ordered general mobilization.[86] Half the Prussian Army was mobilized but was in no position to fight a war. The Austro-Bavarians advanced and brushed against the rearguard of a Prussian unit at Bronzell, south of Fulda in north-east Bavaria. Confronted by artillery, cavalry and *Jäger*, and after firing a few shots, the Prussians retreated and were finally ordered to evacuate the area completely, giving up without a fight.[87] Otto Freiherr von Manteuffel, Prussia's minister-president and the king's chief advisor, fearing the worst and finally convincing the king, showed up himself at Olmütz at the very end of the month to give way to the Austrians on all points.

The first Prussian general war mobilization in almost four decades had failed. It revealed six major problems.

No top leader of the Prussian state was committed to fighting a war. The king and his key advisors wavered this way and that but ultimately shied away from it. The king cherished the notion that the Austrian emperor was the 'natural' ruler of the German states with the Prussian king, his loyal retainer, at his side.[88] This attitude had immense implications.

There was very little up-to-date, current planning for the mobilization of over 400 000 soldiers. To feed and clothe the army, they used the war plan of 1844, but things had changed in the intervening six years. Implementing rules, regulations and procedures specifying the details of how the mobilization would be carried out had not been written and circulated. For example, consider supplies: war-mobilized corps supply trains needed 3000 soldiers, 114 NCOs and 20 officers. On 6 November, the day mobilization was ordered, each corps had two officers and one NCO assigned to do this work. As reserves arrived, it was discovered few knew anything about dealing with horses, wagons or how to set and run a supply column. As a result many of the reserves and *Landwehr* troops, which accounted for half the army, were without weapons, equipment or quartering locations to protect them from the late autumn rains. General Count Groeben, the commander, said that these troops were truly indescribable: he could not see himself leading them into battle.[89]

Another problem had to do with railroads. There were no railroad officials or military officers experienced in war mobilization. Trains were in the hands of the Prussian Trade Ministry which fitted military transport into the normal peacetime train schedules. This meant long delays, especially on single track lines, slow movement from station to station, and surprises, such as providing food to newly arrived, but unexpected, troops detraining at a new point of the compass.[90]

There was little or no warning that war mobilization was about to begin. Many units of the standing army were at half strength or less and their subordinate units were out of garrison training or on special duty.[91] I, II and III Corps had only two infantry regiments immediately available, VII Corps only one, VIII Corps only two battalions in its home district, IV Corps no line regiments and no cavalry. Corps had let their reserves go off active duty in the autumn and new recruits were not yet fully trained. Cavalry remounts were unavailable. Half of the officer positions were unfilled and there was no time to fill them.

There was little or no coordination at the top levels of the army. And such as there was, was slow and contradictory. On 6 November mobilization was ordered. On the 12th the orders went out. On the 22nd they were changed. Several days later, General Groeben received a telegram from the king ordering him to avoid battle.[92] The War Ministry, and below it, the command and staff headquarters, were in chaos. Although by December the Prussian Army was more or less arrayed in four war-mobilized corps, it was in no position to fight a war.

Finally, there were enormous management problems during the 60-day mobilization. Take, for example, paying the bills. Each corps command had over 1000 bills per month to pay, this meant 8000 letters and copies. Secretaries worked seven-day weeks, dawn to dusk, including Saturday and Sunday, to get this done as the command moved from Dessau to Merseberg, a distance of 65 miles.[93]

Moltke's IV Corps was mobilized in about three weeks. He was so overwhelmed that his wife Marie served as secretary in order to get the mobilization orders out in time.[94] He himself tried to make contact with other chiefs of staff: with his old War Academy colleagues Glizczinski of the Guards, Schwartz of II Corps and Falckenstein at III Corps.[95] Except for Falckenstein, they were glad to hear from him. But his overall conclusions were blistering. For 35 years our administration has allowed the reserves to have weapons but not to mobilize. For 40 million thalers we learned that if we do this we need to prepare for it. At the end of these expensive two months, we had 400 000 troops and could have seized Baden, Hesse and even Holstein. Instead, we have nothing to show for it.[96] For Moltke it was double loop learning: it was the process which had to be changed.

His specific conclusions were clear. All troops should be at home garrisons before mobilization. This required a special alert period prior to war declaration. Corps chiefs of staff had to meet with the chief of the GGS regularly to coordinate things. Supply officials in the War Ministry and General Staff officers had to coordinate during peacetime. Clear relationships had to be established between the standing army, the reserves and the *Landwehr* long before thinking about any war mobilization.[97]

Moltke called the mobilization a comedy.[98] Thirty thousand Austrian and Bavarian troops, he wrote, skilfully deployed during our mobilization, could have totally destroyed the Prussian III, IV and Guard Corps of over 100 000.

Aide-de-camp to Frederick, Prince of Prussia, 1855–57

By 1855 Moltke had served 33 years in the Prussian Army. Pension regulations allowed and enabled retirement. Moltke had thought about it before. Just at this point Prussian King Frederick Wilhelm IV began to give signs that his younger brother, Prince Wilhelm, might soon take over. This occasioned a wholesale shift in duties within the royal family. The military cabinet and Oberstkammer Count Dohna believed they had to prepare the next crown prince, Friedrich, age 20, for his upcoming duties by finding him a military adjutant. The king's oldest adjutant General von Schoeler immediately brought up Moltke as the best choice. He knew Moltke personally, he said, Moltke's qualification reports from Reyher, his career in the General Staff and experience in Rome spoke for him. But Dohna wanted more opinions.[99] He asked around. General von Thile, his old commander, weighed in: Moltke, he said, had a winning openness of character and great understanding of our public institutions and relationships: how the prince and government worked together. He gets along easily in society. Endowed with lots of talent and a faultless personal integrity, surely he would be a good mentor for the prince.[100] In May 1855 Moltke was given a practical test: he accompanied the prince to east and west Prussia. He passed: they got along easily. The next day Field Marshal Count Dohna interviewed Moltke, asking him all kinds of questions about his politics. He was satisfied with the answers.

On 1 September 1855 he was appointed.[101] This was a complicated appointment. The prince did not believe he needed a military advisor. He was not against the man but against the office. Moltke rode into the country with his prince as quiet as a mouse. An adjutant asked him to talk more with the prince. Moltke replied, 'he could ask me questions'. In spite of which, after a time, Moltke and the prince began to get on well.[102]

Moltke's court relationships were already close. They got closer. One Sunday he showed up at Sanssouci. Apologizing to the colonel assigned as duty officer that morning, he said he understood that the king did not usually give audiences on Sunday, but it was his only available time and he needed to see the king. Friedrich Wilhelm IV received him in Frederick the Great's sleeping room, where the great king had died and the clock had stopped at exactly the hour of his death. Moltke reported on his recent trip with the crown prince. They talked for nearly half an hour. At the conclusion, the king shook his hand. An awkward and unusual move because Moltke, in correct audience fashion, had a gloved left hand and his helmet in his right. The king told him to go and talk with the queen who would be so pleased to see him. He did so. Queen Elizabeth was most friendly. He had just about completed his visit when he bumped into General Ludwig von Tümpling, an old acquaintance – they had both served on the VIII Corps staff in Koblenz – who invited him to stay for lunch.[103]

First personal adjutant to the crown prince meant a big change in life style. Moltke knew the etiquette of court: now he applied it, meeting the ruling princes of Europe: Queen Victoria, Tsar Nicholas, Emperor Napoleon III, Kaiser Franz Joseph. He became a man of the world, getting to know London, Paris and St Petersburg. He lived at Balmoral, banqueted in the Granowitaja Palace and had dinner in the Galerie de la Diane.[104] Travelling with the crown prince was upscale and very busy. Moltke travelled across Europe: to London for the prince's marriage to Princess Victoria, to Moscow for the coronation of Tsar Alexander II, to Paris for the opening of the Paris Exposition. His wife did not accompany him but went to be with her Danish relatives. Their apartments on 9 Schoenebergerstrasse and 44 Linkstrasse were often empty for weeks.

His prince took service with 1st Guard Regiment, Potsdam. Meanwhile he also attended ministerial meetings: war, interior, finance and trade. The prince wanted to learn what there was to learn. Moltke went along. In the autumn of 1856 the prince became commander of the 9th infantry regiment in Breslau. Moltke had to move south-east. He rode in the Silesian Mountains, toured the battlefields of Frederick the Great. By 1857 Moltke knew the province well.[105]

He was introduced to a wide variety of men at the top of Prussian government and society. For example Theodore von Bernhardi: broadly educated on the Baltic estates of his mother's second husband, politically interested, knowledgeable in military history, a student of Clausewitz, a citizen of the world.

All of these ceremonies, dinners, parades and court hunts opened up a world he had not known before. His letters fill up with European images: castles and countryside, Balmoral and Windsor, St James's and Buckingham palaces, Kenilworth and Warwick, the Crystal Palace, Sydenham and the factories of Manchester, Oxford and the British Museum, the British nobility, democracy.

From Russia came descriptions of authoritarian and communal village life. Upon returning he talked with Bernhardi about Russia freeing the serfs at a dinner of the prince.

From France he described court life in the Tuileries. The Empress Eugénie, beautiful and elegant, made an overwhelming impression.[106] But Empress Eugénie was also impressed. She could not decide if he was a dreamer, laconic and taciturn, or someone tense and anxious, full of startling comments which went right to the point. Napoleon appeared to be something else. Moltke wondered what he had created and also what he had destroyed.

How did Moltke and the prince get along? Was the prince charmed and influenced by Moltke? Eberhard Kessel writes that it was in some ways an odd combination, an ultra-conservative prince and a fairly liberal and open Moltke. But on the personal level they got along well.[107] This appointment was an essential rite of passage. During Moltke's adjutantship with his son, the father grew to know and respect Moltke. In this indirect way, Moltke was brought into close personal relationship with his future warlord.[108]

As it turned out, Moltke and King Wilhelm were the same kind of people: economical and simplicity loving, moderate and unpretentious. Both used the unwritten part of letters to make notes and disliked replacing old clothes with new. Thrust into the limelight almost against their wills, both men knew themselves well and held steadfastly to their own identity. Four years older than Moltke, the latter's unique genius slowly dawned on Wilhelm over time. Later he was wont to watch Moltke in social gatherings as a mother watches her daughter at a ball, proud – and lucky – that he had 'discovered' Moltke and anxious to figure him out.[109]

Two events in October 1857 changed everything. The current General Staff chief, Reyher, became gravely ill and on 7 October died. The next day Prince Wilhelm became regent for his ailing brother.

Although the General Staff chief's position at that time was technically equal to division commander, the last two chiefs had been full generals of infantry, with the same rank as the war minister.[110] Moltke, one of the youngest major-generals, had no brigade command experience. Karl von Reitzenstein, a well-known General Staff officer, had already been division commander and military commissioner to the Bundestag in Frankfurt. Moltke thought he would be chosen.

However, it was no accident that the Prince of Prussia in one of his first acts as regent on 29 October 1857, removed Moltke from his position as adjutant to Crown Prince Frederick and appointed him chief of the General Staff.

3

MOLTKE AND THE PRUSSIAN SYSTEM, 1857–63

Helmuth and Marie: Professional Officer, Service Wife

Moltke was 57 when he and Marie moved into the stately mansion on the sunny side of 66 Behrenstrasse in the midst of 'official' Berlin.[1] One whole floor was devoted to their living and official quarters. The offices of the General Staff were located on the first and ground floors; upstairs, the 'lady of the house' and the busy general had to be ready to entertain every Tuesday. There were other social requirements. Aside from official court balls and festivities – for example the Ordensfest on 18 January, the Grosse Defiliercour a week later, and several court balls held up to Fastnachtdienstag – every 22 March Moltke hosted the king's birthday dinner for the entire General Staff in Berlin.[2] This was an affair: probably 40 officers in the 1850s, 60 in the early 1860s, jumping to over 100 thereafter. To organize this they had a house staff of perhaps half a dozen, plus orderlies and adjutants.[3]

They had lived in Berlin before and knew the routines. Marie undoubtedly liked staying put after moving, in typical officer's wife fashion, from Berlin to Koblenz to Magdeburg and back. By all accounts they were devoted best friends.[4] If Marie's horse was lame, Moltke did not ride. Parsimonious by nature, he took his lunch with him when he went on a day trip, coming home weak with hunger. Moltke played whist every evening.

They spent a considerable amount of time in separate lives. Some measure of Moltke's success in the military was due to the fact that he got on well with the royals. He was always elegantly turned out and perfectly tempered, fitted in everywhere, and quiet but always with an intelligent comment when asked. He charmed the royal relatives, from Prince

Henry and Prince Wilhelm the king's brothers, to Prince Friedrich, the king's son. And Moltke spent a lot of time with these men. He travelled incessantly: to Moscow, London, Paris, Rome, Vienna, and the palaces of the Prussian Hohenzollerns. At various times he was away for months. What of Marie? For one thing she had no children. For another her languages, although good, were probably not court level.[5] Most important, she was little more than the English wife of a royal officer, without the more independent status that an ancient Prussian lineage or her own money might have provided.[6] Although she had some good connections – she moved in with her mother's cousin, Countess Lottchen Brockdorff, in Rome in 1846 while her husband accompanied the body of Prince Henry back to Berlin for burial – in general court and royal entourage duty did not include wives, unless they had their own status on the court rank list. It was a man's world and even reigning wives lived somewhat apart. How did Marie adapt to this lifestyle?

She was a 'service wife' who did what she could to advance her husband's professional career. It was she who memorized all of the colours, flags and uniforms of the Prussian Army, so she could recognize individual regiments. It was she who joined the queen's sewing circles during the wars, to sew clothes for the wounded. It was she who was embarrassed by the cheers of the soldiers as she and her husband made their way by open carriage after the Danish War in August 1864. Embarrassed? She thought it a shame that the soldiers in this way became aware that Moltke was married: a soldier should not really marry, family duties might interfere with full devotion to the fatherland.[7] Finally, when her husband travelled with the court or entourages, Marie stayed home or went to Denmark.[8]

The General Staff Organization

The GGS Moltke now headed was loosely organized around the three functions described in Chapter 1: representational, educational and analytical. Most officers served a stint in the Land Survey Section, taught in the War Academy and researched in the Historical Section. Many gathered intelligence by serving as military attachés in foreign capitals. They participated in drawing up war plans and testing them out in war games. General Staff officers got out of the shop often. They usually travelled several months of the year.[9] Nearly half of Moltke's General Staff budget went for travel: horses, trains, food and lodging.

There was constant circulation between the GGS in Berlin, and the corps and divisional General Staffs outside it. Called to Berlin for war games, reconnaissance rides or special duty twice a year brought two dozen officers.[10] Called to Berlin for temporary assignment came another dozen.

As he was appointed, Moltke wrote to his brother that the position of chief of the General Staff was technically equal to one of the 18 divisional generals but, as his appointment was only provisional, he did not get even as much pay as them.[11] Yet he directed 94 men in Berlin and loosely oversaw the troop General Staffs of nine corps. The budget was 36 000 thalers.[12] Moltke's reporting chain went up through bureaucratic channels. It was two years before he won the right to report directly to War Minister Adolf von Bonin.[13]

The GGS was a small, relatively obscure bureaucracy, subordinate in everything to the War Ministry, virtually unknown or ignored by the traditional power positions of the regular army, the commanding generals of the corps, those tiny fiefdoms on which the final power of the state rested. In 1857 the GGS lacked the prestige of successful accomplishment. It was only a modern idea, untested and unvalidated in the real world.

Immediately upon taking office Moltke got a royal order that General Staff officers were to be promoted more rapidly than others in the army at large. He needed this in order to recruit good men from the tactical arms. He created a central section, a chancellery or office manager to help schedule, arrange and organize the increasingly complex work patterns. He tried to break off the Land Survey Section and the Historical Section, so that each would become an independent publishing office. The war minister rejected this.[14]

Moltke tried to collect good men from all his past assignments to do the most important work. And a few stayed with him from the 1850s through to the 1870s. These officers learned and carried forward the General Staff core competencies. Friedrich von Hesse, chief of the third or French section, also worked in the trigonometric section. Werner Ollech did history, mobilization and war plans preparations. Hans Stiehle, his adjutant, came from the Magdeburg General Staff. Vieth, Petersen and Doering had all spent time with troop General Staffs. Gunther Vieth, an artillery officer good on technical details of fortresses and coastal defence, stayed until 1871. Johann Petersen authored a whole series of operational studies marked up in the margins in Moltke's handwriting. Herman Doering, recruited from the corps staff of Prince Friedrich Charles, succeeded Ollech in mobilization. Hans Count

Wartensleben, from the Halberstad Kurassiers and IV Corps, worked with Ollech in the second section specializing in railroad transport. He led the 1858 General Staff ride in Silesia with dependable and never flagging energy.[15] The brothers Bronsart von Schellendorff, first the older Paul, later his brother Walter, worked under Moltke for years, as did Julius von Verdy du Vernois, Brandenstein, Strempel and more. After 1866 this group acquired the collective handle 'Moltke's demigods'.

Although none of these men attained high rank, two of them wrote enduring books on their experiences, Verdy du Vernois his memoirs and Paul Bronsart von Schellendorff the classic *Duties of the General Staff*, which went through five editions from the 1880s until 1905.[16]

Moltke maintained and cultivated good relations with able General Staff officers throughout the army, regardless of their position. A good example is Albrecht von Blumenthal. Ten years younger than Moltke but, like him, an 'orphan' raised in cadet academies, Blumenthal joined the General Staff Land Survey Section as probationary field cartographer about the time Moltke was corps chief of staff in 1848. Married to an English wife, his rise in the next decade and a half – aided by royal patronage – was meteoric. Brought into the GGS full time at about the time Moltke became its chief, he rapidly assimilated the Moltke system and became a first-rate chief of staff. In 1864 he worked for Wrangel, in 1866 and 1870 for the crown prince. In each of these positions Moltke and he communicated daily.

What was Moltke's relationship with these 'demigods'? Beyond the military organization and the special training and knowledge they shared, what was their basis of trust? Here is one example which may stand for all the rest. In the week following the battle of Königgrätz, Moltke repeatedly urged Blumenthal, the First Army's chief of staff, to move south and catch the Austrians before they got clean away. They exchanged letters and repeatedly traded aides-de-camp. Some of these exchanges were heated. Blumenthal resisted Moltke's urgings: he said the First Army was not ready, it had been ordered to change direction too many times, they could not do it any faster. On 27 July, when it was all over, and peace negotiations had begun, Blumenthal wrote to his wife in English – he had sent her home to England when the war broke out – laying out the whole scenario. The letter fell into Austrian hands, it was widely published in the south German newspapers and a copy sent to Berlin. The king laughed. Moltke refused to read it: it was a private letter addressed to Blumenthal's wife, he said, and not intended for anyone else.[17]

Moltke as Strategist: the Concept of Risk

Right from the start, Moltke was very different from Reyher, his immediate predecessor. One big difference was Moltke's strategic vision and
concept of risk in war.[18]

If the future was a mirror of the past, the study of historical battles was
one way through. And the Prussian Army did lots of this. Since weapons,
transportation and communication methods changed slowly, the study
of past battles brought one close to the possibilities of future war, especially if this study was conducted in the exact topographical context in
which it had been fought before. If the future was the domain of God,
then prayers and worship became important. In Prussia the church and
the state were fused together. Nowhere was this clearer than in the army.
Willingness to die for God and fatherland was a significant strength
undergirding Prussian morale from private soldier to general officer.
Remember that General von Thile's only negative comment on Moltke's
performance in Magdeburg was the latter's lack of attendance at church!

Napoleon planned each day's actions at midnight, hours before it
began. He had the main lines of the campaign clearly in his head several days, perhaps weeks, before that. But he could also ride out during
the battle with new orders. Most often he had visual contact. He was a
workaholic who got little sleep: he lived to fight wars. A recent historian
calls Napoleon 'the scrambler' who, in spite of constant attention to
military questions, repeatedly pulled victory out of defeat, often at the
last moment after opening every campaign with a strategic blunder.[19]
Because of greatly increased size and space dimensions, such intimate
methods of operational control – and such chaotic and stressful personal
behaviour – were beyond Moltke's means and alien to his lifestyle.

Moltke was no theoretician. He was a pragmatist interested in achiev-
ing the best practical results at the least cost. Although Jomini wrote 20
books during this time and Clausewitz's work slowly came to promi-
nence, Moltke wrote no strategic recipe and no lengthy philosophical
texts. What Moltke added to war was unrelated to the rules, formulas
and tables of Jomini. But it was close to Clausewitz's central point about
destroying the enemy's will to fight. Moltke's processes were a practical
method of how to do this using the technological and organizational
tools of the mid-nineteenth century.

Above all, Moltke interjected the concept of risk. The ability to define
and manage risk based upon size, space, time and technology came
slowly to Moltke.[20] What were the components of his system as this was

embodied in Moltke's processes? There were four elements: the time horizon, scenarios, risk measurements and benchmarks.[21]

The time horizon posed the question: over what time period will the army be exposed? This had both internal and external ramifications. Internally, it created a time consciousness that was not there before. War plans would only work within a specific time frame. Orders to execute had very precise time statements. Careful time measurement was built into war games where the conductor gave each side only a limited time to act. During the first half of the nineteenth century, pocket watches gradually came into general usage. Time-sensitive orders of Napoleon, to be executed within 24 hours, now gave way to smaller, more specific segments. The Prussian military day was roughly divided into four-hour blocks: first light, before noon, afternoon, before dark. The night was also used: marches often began between 2 and 4 a.m. The synchronization of time across space, a hoped for luxury for Napoleon, became an expected necessity for the Moltke system.

The time horizon was also critical for the external environment beyond Prussian borders. Each of the three German Wars had a time frame at the expiration of which the favourable external environment – defined as allied, neutral or inactively waiting states – might have turned unfavourable. In the Danish War this was the neutrality of Britain. In the Austrian War it was the inactivity of France and the Italian alliance. In the French War it was the inactivity of Austria and the neutrality of Britain. In all three, good relations with Russia were carefully maintained.

Scenarios simulated what events could unfold and how each might affect the others. War games and strategic memos described a series of linked observations about the state of the world at some predetermined future time. A series of 'what ifs' were constructed, then critiqued. Beyond suggesting what the problems might be, another goal was to speed up response time. For example, suppose the army was able to adjust its operations to suit conditions in the space of a single day, instead of three or four days, what other possibilities did that open up? War gaming was essentially an exercise in looking at these other possibilities. Railroad transportation allowed scenarios to be constructed for the first time with some degree of mathematical precision. Moltke was always being asked to conjure up scenarios for one situation or another. His artistic imagination did this easily and fluidly.

Risk measurement estimated exact exposure. How many forces would be exposed over what period of time? In tactical situations this could become very technical: Dreyse rifle fire at three to five times the speed of its opponents occasionally allowed a platoon or company to fight a regiment or even a brigade successfully. At Lundy in the Danish War the exposure time was 20 minutes. In 1866 this meant the risk of allowing two Prussian armies to fight an Austrian force larger than both of them until a third Prussian army arrived on the Austrian flank at Königgrätz. The exposure time was three or four hours. In August 1870 at Wissembourg, a squadron opposed two French divisions for several hours.

Benchmarks are the points of comparison against which performance is measured. Historical comparisons, such as Lieutenant von Naumann's famous book on why soldiers retreat, were used extensively in war games.[22] The comparative perspective melds in with the time horizon. Moltke asked: How to measure performance in war? He realized that measuring benchmarks during war depended upon good communication with friendly forces and good intelligence on the enemy. He also recognized that command and control developed and evolved during a war, as his armies responded to changing combat conditions. This notion was introduced midway through 1864, and was employed increasingly in 1866 and 1870. Evolution and development in command and control during a war became a Moltke trademark. He called it 'operations'.

In using rudimentary risk management did Moltke identify the critical path, that is, the 10 per cent which accounted for 90 per cent of the outcome? It is not clear. In the Danish War superior numbers and supplies, rifled artillery, and rapid-fire rifles resulted in greater firepower at the tactical level and the winter campaign largely neutralized the Danish fleet. In 1866 the critical path was nine Prussian railroads, allowing Prussia to concentrate two armies on one side, stopping and holding the enemy, while bringing a third army around the flank. In 1870, the French Army accounted by itself for part of this critical path: much of it never arrived at the battlefields, and, when it did, it had inadequate food, weapons, ammunition, supplies, plans and leadership. In other words it was unprepared to fight a war. These failures allowed German forces to make mistakes and still win the war. No matter how good the intelligence beforehand, until men begin to die and respond to death in an actual war, peacetime armies are opaque organizations. There is no clear indication that Moltke knew beforehand that his armies would be confronted by this high degree of opponent incompetence. But he nevertheless focused on the few essential aspects which gave his army advantages against specific battlefield opponents.

Moltke's approach to war gradually began to incorporate the concept of risk-adjusted value: the upside possibilities minus the cost of insuring the downside. The result of this was a surplus: of time, space, weapons and force levels, creating a series of back-ups, outlets or sequential possibilities. If one was closed off, others opened. He called this a 'system of expedients'. Some writers have emphasized the word 'expedients', implying that Moltke had no strategic system. In reality Moltke emphasized 'system'. A system with built-in back-ups, fall-back positions, surpluses, extras. Moltke tried to stockpile a series of means or recourses, so that if one did not work, another would. How was this done?

War Fighting Management Procedures

Most important were the planning tools: Prussian war planning was a modern knowledge process: his opponents did not have it. For another, Moltke generally assumed his opponents would carry out an aggressive attack strategy that they finally did not do. Although Denmark from the start went on the defensive, of the two Great Power opponents, Austria chose not to attack and France was unable to. By acting on attack assumptions, Moltke built in extra time and space within which Prussian forces could operate. Thirdly, in briefing the king and his military cabinet, Moltke tended to speed up the time frames, providing a greater sense of urgency than in fact existed. In sum, he always argued worst-case scenarios. But his opponents seldom fulfilled these scenarios. They did not arrive when they were expected or with the force anticipated. The extra time and smaller force gave Prussia breathing room, time for things to go wrong, for commanders to make mistakes. In issuing orders, he followed the same rule, allowing extra time and space for his commanders. Moltke's plans contained built-in back-ups of one kind or another.

Some have argued that Moltke had no overarching strategic philosophy, and that once the war began, as he himself once said, there was not much the commander-in-chief could do.[23] Moltke said this for many reasons: because of the imperfect communications of his day; because Prussian *Auftrag* command philosophy gave lots of initiative to commanders; to give credit to the army and corps commanders, some of whom strained for it, many of whom deserved it; to deflect credit from himself, a relatively quiet, self-contained, 'Alpha Type B' personality, for whom the limelight was uncomfortable and unnecessary. We hasten to add, however, that Moltke turned into an 'Alpha Type A' personality once a war began and stayed there – the effective operating war commander-in-chief, buffered by the king's continued trust and support – until the fighting stopped.[24]

Auftrag or mission-type orders expressed the overall goal of the commander, but allowed subordinates to carry out this goal as best they saw fit. Limitations on the means to this end were only imposed if needed to coordinate with parallel commands. Mission orders assumed uniform education and training: that different officers, faced with similar tactical–operational situations, would reach roughly similar conclusions as to actions and orders. For example, Prussian officers were trained to 'march to the sound of the guns': to support each other in combat. All knew the army was programmed to 'march separately, fight together'.[25]

The arrangement of *Auftrag* orders was also unique. Written orders were issued from army to corps to division to brigade levels. Below that verbal orders were used. When possible coordination was achieved by having a staff officer from each subordinate command receive the order at the regular operations briefing of the higher command. Structurally, mission orders had five parts: enemy and friendly force situation; general statement of the mission and the commander's intent; objectives and any specific instructions.[26] Information was grouped in such a way that the eye would catch details at the very same place in every order, thereby lessening the chance that commanders might overlook essential items.

Simplicity, lucidity and brevity were the watchwords of orders. Subordinates were provided only what they needed to know, leaving execution details to them. An order from Prussian Royal Headquarters in the third week of August 1870, instructing the Third Army to change its axis of advance from west towards Paris to north towards Sedan, took up only six lines! A week earlier orders from the same headquarters, directing movements of the Army of the Meuse and Third Army, together about 200 000 men, took up less than one page.[27] Again, order writing was learned at the War College and practised regularly in war games, staff rides and manoeuvres.

Orders were drafted and passed along using only a few staff officers, whose goal was speed in composition, transcription and transmission. At army level in 1870 six officers were assigned to this task, and they normally had only five or six hours to receive, respond, draft and deliver orders to subordinate units. Thus in early August 1870 orders setting the First and Second armies in pursuit of Marshal Bazaine's retreating Army of Lorraine arrived at their respective headquarters between midnight and 2.30 a.m. And every division in these two armies was ready to move out at 6 a.m. Such speed in execution was the rule, not the exception.[28]

Furthermore there was follow-up. From the 1866 war on, Moltke adopted the principle of dispatching knowledgeable staff officers, thoroughly familiar with his intentions, to lower headquarters. Their purpose was to gather situational intelligence, and also to interpret, amplify and spell out mission orders.

Mission-type orders worked in tandem with two other unique Prussian General Staff principles. One was the principle of consultation. General Staff officers had the formal right, responsibility and duty to advise their commanders. Commanders were virtually required to listen to their chiefs of staff. General Staff officers' comments – spoken in private – which went against the conclusions of their commanders, could be written down as a matter of record. A second principle was the concept of joint responsibility. Commanders and their first General Staff officers, known throughout the army as '1-As', shared command decisions. Either one could sign off on orders, each spoke for the other. Again, although heated discussion may have gone on in private, both agreed to support the final decision in public. These two principles sometimes meant that function overrode rank.[29] But it was clearly based on confidence that a General Staff officer's judgement, educated and tested repeatedly in war games, could be trusted.

Even antique generals knew this system: Field Marshal Wrangel's orders on 1 February 1864, as he went to bed on Prussian territory south of the Danewark, were that 'On February 10th I want to sleep in Denmark.'[30]

In reality, it was a system. The rest of the sentence which begins with the definition of strategy as 'a system of expedients' goes on to say that strategy is more than a science, it is the carrying over of knowledge into practical life, the development of original themes and main ideas appropriate to each situation. Strategy is the art of acting under the pressure of difficult circumstances.[31]

And it was the Prussian war planning system which was set up to carry out this revolution. A system that was established to avoid one-off situations, confrontations which happened only once, on a single occasion. One might almost say that the Prussian Army almost never confronted these. They had war gamed and studied the history in the topography. They approached each individual, separate situation within a contextual framework of historical experience and terrain knowledge. War gaming through scenarios put dozens of situations into the minds of officers. They play-acted them, making mistakes. Mistakes are deep learning devices. A frame of reference was created into which real life might in various ways fit. In contemporary parlance, they had repeatedly imagined the situation, their response to it and its successful outcome. In a real time situation they had only to get back to that space, to return to that part of the brain filled with these images that all went in one direction.

Only a portion of the potential of Moltke's process was used in the actual wars. Traditional or stubborn commanders did as they wanted. Timid, wilful or stressed commanders made mistakes. Amid the chaos of the battlefield some lost concentration. Fear overcame training.

And Moltke had clear overall plans of how to fight each of these three wars. These plans had been in the works for several years. They had been tested out in war games, the contingencies, the various levels and kinds of expedients had been worked through, criticized and assessed. And Moltke tried, in all cases, to carry out these plans in each war.

The Moltke system institutionalized modern war processes. Why is this achievement underrated?

Because he seldom appeared to be the master that he, in fact, was. As Delbrück said, great persons have the right to step out self-confidently, as empowered, and masters of circumstance. Moltke did not do this. A modest quiet person, he was known in the German media as 'the Silent One'.[32] It was his mind and strategic ideas which were revolutionary, not his public persona or mode of presentation. In person, as a conversationalist, Moltke was often taciturn. As a speaker he was curt, quiet, reserved. He was not a debater. But as a writer he was unusually eloquent: spirited, expressive and classical.[33]

Moltke read continuously and voraciously. He appeared to forget nothing he had once looked at. In the mid-1850s, on a visit to his brother Adolph, administrator of the Rantzau estate in Denmark, he was picked up at the railroad station by his brother's two nephews, driven by their tutor Schaubach. In conversation it turned out that Schaubach was from Meiningen. Are you related to Adolf Schaubach who wrote the book about the German Alps, Moltke asked. Yes, he was my uncle. Yes, he died six years ago. Tell me about his life, he must have been an excellent man, Moltke continued. It turned out that Moltke had read everything Schaubach had written, and remembered every word.[34]

Up to 1857 the Moltke system existed but its parts were scattered about. None of these processes were done consistently, on a large scale, beyond Berlin. As there had not been any practical application of its product, the GGS was considered a sort of historical and theoretical office. The old school dominated. Tactical battle was it. Until a war was declared, corps commanders did not bother much with war plans. Time was not a critical factor.[35] They remembered past experiences, put all their eggs into the basket of tactical battle and trusted to God and fate. The GGS was considered mainly an educational and theoretical organization. The practical side of war was left to the War Ministry. How did Moltke change this? How did he explain his ideas to the army outside the GGS?

Moltke as Army Educator

In terms of operational warfare, Moltke believed in field combat not fortress war; tactical defence, operational and strategic offence. He understood that the whole relationship of infantry, cavalry and artillery had changed. Cavalry, the refuge of elite families and dashing forces, was no longer able to force a decision in war. Its main job was reconnaissance and protection against enemy cavalry.

The thesis that infantry could no longer frontally attack infantry was supposedly disproven in the war of 1859 where French bayonet charges had overwhelmed the Austrians with their new rifles. Moltke would have none of it.

That artillery should prepare the ground for an infantry attack was untried and untested. That Napoleon had used it only meant that a military genius could do whatever he liked. Artillerymen were considered technical misfits, military geeks who substituted algebra and trigonometry for dash, bravery and élan.[36]

Until it was proven in war, few top officers understood these new tactical and operational relationships. Moltke's immediate colleagues got these ideas as a first wave. Troop General Staffs got them as a second wave, buffered and in some cases rejected by their traditionalist leadership, the corps commanders. The army as a whole received it third hand. The king was unclear, although his military entourage understood fully that Moltke was a unique thinker, way ahead of his time. Only they were not sure his ideas would work. Moltke had to sell them by the experience of successful war.

How were Moltke's ideas broadcast and institutionalized? One thing the General Staff did was to examine contemporary wars carefully. In 1854–56 over a million British, French, Turkish and Russian troops fought in the Crimean peninsula. The Prussian General Staff sent a team of observers.[37] The British fought for the first time entirely with rifles. The Russians, armed with muskets, marched on foot. Since no railroads connected their supply depots in Moscow and St Petersburg to the Crimean ports which supplied their opponents, Russian supplies never arrived. Siege and offshore artillery bombardments became important.[38] The lesson of the Crimean War was: connect armies in combat with supply storehouses by rail, otherwise they will go hungry and lose. Although this war caught his attention – the war began with Turkey and Russia squaring off near ground which he knew well having reconnoitred it in 1836 – it was the Italian War of 1859 which really caught his eye.

In 1859 took place the first large-scale wartime railroad movement of troops in history.[39] French Emperor Napoleon III transported 130 000 troops from France to Italy. Once there, French troops armed with technologically inferior rifles but better training and artillery overwhelmed and inundated Austrian troops armed with better rifles they did not know how to use. Columns of French infantry, bayonets fixed, crashed into Austrian regiments who threw away their weapons and fought hand to hand. Austrian training had been too complicated to work under combat conditions using a language of command not understood by many soldiers.[40] France suffered 24 000 casualties in just a month of fighting, but won the war.[41] Austria concluded that future wars were to be won not by new technology, but by traditional battle tactics, the bayonet charge of close-order troops.

Moltke drew no such conclusions, but how did he communicate his views to the army? Up to 1857 the General Staff had not been much concerned with military practice.[42] No surprise: since 1815 Prussia had fought a single war and mobilized once. Both had failed. After the abortive mobilization of 1850, nine more peacetime years. A peacetime army divorced from practical reality: a General Staff concerned with researching, writing and publishing, but not with war fighting.

The situation of the *Militär-Wochenblatt* may serve as an example. It was founded in 1816, in the aftermath of the Napoleonic Wars, at the suggestion of Prussian occupation troops in France who thought they should write down and circulate recent war experiences. They wanted to discuss and formulate the many 'lessons learned' in these wars and celebrate the achievements of the fatherland.[43] Ernst Mittler, a book dealer in Berlin, got wind of this, contacted his relative Captain Thomas Decker in the newly constituted General Staff. Ruhle von Lilienstern, a senior colonel, liked the idea. He had published his memoirs of the campaigns of 1806–11, and founded his own monthly journal; he convinced the king to support this new project. When the *Militär-Wochenblatt* began, its goals were to publish official announcements and orders from the king, official quarters and movement postings of army units, appointments, promotions and retirements, critical reviews of military books, short military essays and biographies and death notices. By the time Moltke joined the General Staff, in the late 1820s, the *Militär-Wochenblatt* was more literary and historical and less of a house organ. Series of articles became published books, issues were entirely devoted to single themes. By the 1850s it was entirely under the Military History Section aegis. Although it remained an official army house organ, filled with bureaucratic minutiae – personnel changes, medals, decorations, awards and deaths – it retained its scholarly aspects with book reviews, intelligence on foreign armies and eyewitness descriptions such as from the war in Denmark in 1848.[44]

When Moltke became chief, the *Militär-Wochenblatt* was edited by Major Ollech, director of the Military History Section.[45] In 1860 came the hundredth anniversary histories of the battles of Kunersdorff and Torgau. In 1861, with the crowning of King Wilhelm in Königsberg, came a series of articles on the coronation of 1701. There were 70 book reviews a year.[46] Press runs by this time were almost 3000 copies every two weeks, plus a dozen special supplements a year. Thirty book stores carried it for purchase. Many of the most influential officers in the army wrote for it. It was well known for dealing with the past: history, memoirs and retirements. But it was not oriented towards current war fighting.

Moltke changed it into a vehicle for serious communication to the army about operations in future war. In a special issue of 1864 he wrote his famous essay 'Remarks on the Influence of Improved Rifles on the Attack', suggesting that straight-ahead close-order frontal attacks were a mistake. Another essay, 'Presentation of the Italian Campaign of 1859', criticized the Austrian Army's conclusions that a bayonet attack remained the ultimate tactical movement.[47] A third, 'Instructions for Large Unit Commanders', became the foundation of German large-unit operations for the next 70 years.[48]

So one way Moltke changed the army was by filling its main house organ with his own ideas. But this was mainly about the past. What about future realities?

War Planning

Moltke began to lay down specific operational plans for future war. Noted French military commentator General Guillaume Bonnal saw a striking continuity in Moltke's ideas for a war against France from the day he took office right through to 1870.[49] In November 1857 his first piece of work as chief of the General Staff responded to a request from War Minister Count Waldersee regarding a possible war with France.[50] If France attacked Germany, he replied, it will have the character of a sudden adventure. French peacetime strength between Paris and the north border garrisons is 150 000 men. Strasbourg is in railroad connection with Metz, Paris and Lyon and is twice as close to Stuttgart as Munich and Nuremberg. France would probably attack along the line Strasbourg–Ulm, with Metz and the upper Rhine as a secondary route. France would find it easier to avoid the north, with neutral Belgium and the Netherlands, and go south, splitting off south Germany, seizing the Rhine bridge at Strasbourg and surrounding the VII and IX Federal Corps there.[51]

How to defend against this, he asked? Two early mobilized corps should secure the German bank of the Rhine allowing the mass of Prussian forces, plus the X Federal Corps, to unite between Cologne and Mainz and, with 200 000 men, take Jülich and Saarlouis and attack across the right or left banks of the Mosel River. Meanwhile one Prussian corps plus the IX Federal Corps would remain in Bamberg as reserve against Austrian adventures.[52] Prussia could mobilize in six weeks, he told the war minister.

In March 1858 Moltke published regulations for leading and carrying out corps General Staff rides, modelled on those he used in Berlin.[53] Reyher's General Staff rides had been chiefly concerned with small technical details: march orders, troop divisions, issuing orders, compass work. Moltke assumed tactical competence and went on to focus on operations and strategy.

He began to rethink transportation.[54] His first move as chief was to address the chaos which had been revealed in the mobilizations of the early 1850s. In March the General Staff issued its first draft statement on the use of Prussian railroads for large-scale troop movements. The May General Staff ride emphasized the problem of time and depth of columns: the coming together of so many troops has only one goal: battle.[55]

In September royal manoeuvres tested these ideas out in large scale: V Corps against VI Corps in Silesia. Moltke was the judge and in his party was Friedrich, Prince of Prussia.[56] When it was over he ran a preliminary test of the military travel plan. Sixteen thousand troops, 650 horses and over 70 supply wagons moved from their manoeuvre grounds back to garrisons in Leipzig by rail. The exercise revealed that the capacity of railroads for military transportation was much greater than suspected, that much more prior planning was needed, including far more coordination between the four agencies involved, the GGS, and the War, Commerce and Interior ministries. Moltke perceived that railroads were highly interactive systems. Scheduling had to be precise and timetables met. One late-running train created problems miles away and hours later. He began to imagine the possibilities. Scatter army corps across the land by rail, then concentrate them at a single point in time and space. He suspected that extension and decentralization might alter command relationships. He asked War and Commerce for more railroads, especially double-track lines in the western half of the kingdom backing up to the French border regions. Moltke wanted each corps assigned a double-rail line so traffic could go simultaneously in both directions.[57]

In September, upon returning from manoeuvres, Moltke discovered that the current war plan for France was a holdover from 1855. It had not been altered or upgraded. He changed the process.

Henceforth, the official war plan was valid from 1 April of each year. On 1 November, as soon as the traditional campaign season and all the outdoor war games and manoeuvres had been completed, war plan revision began. Lessons learned from divisional, corps and royal manoeuvres – each one critiqued verbally and in writing – were examined. Updated intelligence on major opponents was added. And come 1 April – the war plans for France, Austria and Russia having been modified and revised – they were published and sent out to the corps.[58] The war planning cycle now had two phases, the execution phase from 1 April to 1 November, and the revision phase from November till March.[59]

The Mobilization of 1859

In spite of this work, two years after Moltke's appointment as chief came the first war mobilization since 1850. It was a disaster.

In late spring France and Austria mobilized against each other and began to feed troops into northern Italy. The Italians had asked for French help in freeing Venetia, held by Austria since 1815, one step in Italian national unification.[60] With France engaged in Italy, German states eyed the possibilities directly west. Austria took the lead in the Federal parliament of the German Confederation by proposing military preparatory measures. In May Hanover proposed an observation corps move to the Rhine River.[61]

The political situation was dicey. The Prussian king and his advisors were hesitant and uncertain. They wondered what Holland and Belgium would do, toyed with a limited war against Alsace and Lorraine or an attack straight west to the Saar River.[62] They feared France would send 120 000 troops south, and keep 236 000 in the country. Gingerly, hesitantly, Prussia moved towards action.

Moltke had begun to introduce timed stages into Prussian mobilization. At the end of April, as the Italian war broke out, the prince regent ordered the first of these, a state of 'war readiness', for line troops. Line troops accounted for less than half of the army as a whole. War readiness meant cancelling leaves, bringing troops back from manoeuvres and schools, preparing equipment, looking over the mobilization plans. In other words, making sure units were ready to go to war.

A month later the second stage of mobilization was put into effect for some troops. An advance guard took up a position near Trier, close to the Belgian and French borders. Fifteen days later III Corps was mobilized. Now 30 per cent of the regular army was in the field. But no one seemed to be in charge. The king had appointed no overall commander-in-chief, he seemed to be moving in the direction of armed neutrality, but nothing was clear. By this time a major battle, Magenta, had been fought south of Milan and another one, Solferino on the north Italian plateau, was coming up. But the Prussian Army was not ready for combat and Prussian operational goals remained undefined.

Into this breach Moltke stepped.[63] On 14 June he called the chiefs of staff of the corps and divisions to Berlin. They went over mobilization plans and discussed various options for a war against France along the border provinces of Alsace-Lorraine in the south and in the north-western provinces along the Belgian border. General Staff officers were dispatched to Austrian headquarters, to France to observe the French mobilization and demobilization and to the battlefields of Solferino and Magenta.

But it was too late. The main battle of the war, Solferino, was fought ten days later. On 8 July came the armistice and a few days later peace negotiations began. By then two-thirds of the Prussian Army was mobilized and under way, but it was in no position to do anything.[64] What had happened? When the order to mobilize was given only half the corps were ready to do so![65] Railroad transportation was ready: war materials – ammunition, food, wagons and supplies – had been collected and stockpiled from all over Germany along three railroad lines.[66] But civilian traffic took precedence: troops crawled to the Rhine. Many units were not fully equipped or armed. Poor preparation at regimental and brigade levels resulted in a makeshift operation. Moltke was stunned. He debriefed his observers: half a dozen officers who were eyewitnesses at Austrian and French headquarters, and looked carefully at the after-action reports from the battlefields.[67] He wrote memos and essays, gave lectures and convened GSS conferences. This exhaustive discourse went on for months. What did Moltke learn from all of this?

As for the management of armies, Moltke recognized that plans and preparation were critical, improvisations once the war began increasingly difficult. A single commander had to direct all forces and he had to depend on a host of staff officers, from whom information, good judgement and specific recommendations were expected. Especially under combat conditions, information tended to level the playing field between commander and '1-A's'.[68]

As for French and Austrian operations and tactics, his major conclusions were very close to those of later historians. The Austrian high command was at fault. Austrian foot soldiers had not been trained to move, shoot and cooperate as companies and regiments.[69] The Austrians, with better weapons and numerical superiority at decisive points, lost because of poor training and leadership. French infantry weapons were ineffective at certain ranges, so they had to charge with bayonets. The Austrians failed to use their superior weapons which should have been effective at the killing zone ranges the French weapons were not.[70] Moltke drew the correct conclusion: effective firepower from the new rifles depended on continuous individual and unit training and aggressive command leadership from top to bottom.

Operations and tactics were closely related. New weapons meant that a flank attack in sight of the enemy – such as he had witnessed at Nezib against the Ottoman Army – was no longer feasible. In Italy neither side used the advantages they had at the start, both moved slowly and did not exert control over the battlefield once the fighting had begun. The battle, poorly fought by the Austrians on the first day, might have been recovered on the second but the Austrians did not attempt it. Moltke began to think in terms of daily combat sequences during the course of a campaign. He understood what Grant said to Sherman at the end of the first day of the battle of Shiloh: 'we'll lick'em tomorrow'.[71]

Moltke considered Napoleon's campaign of 1809 in Bavaria, where he had divided his forces off the battlefield, but concentrated them at the battlefield. Railroads, he surmised, might allow this on a much larger scale.[72]

In the General Staff these intellectual perceptions were put to immediate practical use. Two weeks after the fighting in Italy had ended, Moltke convened a conference of Prussian military and civil railroad officials. He proposed that Prussian railroads be organized for war. A Central Railroad Commission would sit in Berlin. Each major rail line would have a line commission, with subordinate commissions at each loading station. Within the GGS, the second bureau became the mobilization section and within it a separate office was established for railroads. Mobilization orders were henceforth sent by telegraph, instead of by post or messenger. This reduced notification time from 120 to 24 hours, an improvement of 500 per cent.[73] To war mobilize the field army, periodization and phases were introduced. For example, 21 days was set for the mobilization of transportation. Priorities were established so that military traffic took precedence over civilian. Corps would henceforth be transported in their war order of battle. The unit train rule was created: one war strength unit – infantry battalion, cavalry squadron or artillery battery – would be moved on a single dedicated train. Troops furthest away and ready first would move first. Field exercises were held to test out these procedures. The V Corps put on a practice alert in Frankfurt which reduced their mobilization time by 50 per cent. This became the benchmark.[74]

The rest of the year they worked these ideas out in General Staff rides, manoeuvres and war games.[75] In October the General Staff ride went through the Mosel and Ahr region, working through the possibilities of a simultaneous French attack from Metz against the Mosel and across Belgium. For perimeter defence, a Prussian Mosel Army was created from VII and VIII Corps, with the rest of the army put on transports. A battle was fought in the area of Euskirchen, with the advancing IV Corps interlocking with the Mosel Army. They estimated placing 100 000 men on the Rhine and 200 000 on the Main. To get these forces into combat they figured a minimum of 33 days. This was the danger period. Later in October Moltke rode out into the area around Loetzen in the Massurian lakes region to examine the topography of a war against Russia.[76]

In November 1859 Albrecht von Roon, former regimental colleague of the king, was appointed war minister. Whereas Moltke's relationships with the previous war minister had been formal and subordinate – Bonin had been a general of infantry when Moltke was a 14-year-old student in Copenhagen – his relationships with Roon started off differently. Roon was a contemporary. And they both had special relationships with the king, the one as military comrade, the other through familial contacts.[77]

It is interesting to compare the press coverage at the time with subsequent twentieth-century historical treatment. At the time, Roon, Moltke and Bismarck were often presented as three equally famous men, jointly responsible for German unification under Prussia. Roon, like Moltke, was raised to the Grafenstand in 1871, given a royal grant and appointed general field marshal. Today Roon has disappeared from historical accounts. It is possible that he was no match for Bismarck and Moltke. Or as Eugen Richter, a prominent Reichstag defence critic of this era, put it regarding a later chief of the General Staff, Waldersee without his wife would have been like Wilhelm I without Bismarck. Roon may have been out of his depth: as he described himself, a sergeant in the great company captained by the king. In 1859, he had been the man who played a central role as head of the commission which drafted the new army reform legislation. At the time the then war minister, General von Bonin, was slow to draft this legislation, saying it was foolish to draft new laws when the Landtag would clearly not vote the funds to carry them out. Bonin resigned soon thereafter and Roon replaced him. And clearly the War Ministry was the big loser in the bureaucratic shuffle which accompanied these three wars. In 1857, when he was appointed, Moltke did not even have the right to report directly to the war minister. All orders were issued by the king through the war minister. By 2 June 1866, less than ten years later, Moltke issued all orders and directly briefed the king himself. The War Ministry had been cut out of the command, control and briefing loop.

War Plans for Austria and France

The year 1860 started out with memorandums regarding wars against France and Austria. Against France, a Prussian army would concentrate near Trier, a second on the lower Rhine. Against Austria Moltke wondered what Russia, England and the other German states would do? He assumed only Saxony would ally with Austria, with the south German states neutral. Part of the Austrian Army would remain in Italy. If the X Federal Corps was in support on the west, Prussia could concentrate seven corps in the eastern provinces.[78]

He figured Austria and Saxony could put into the field 220 000 men, leaving 25 000 in her fortresses. The earliest these would assemble along the upper Elbe River was 42 days. To maintain a defensive position, Prussian corps would locate at Delitsche and Halle, at Torgau and Herzberg, at Wittenberg, Jüterbog, Baruth, Spremberg, Streigau and Schweinitz. For an offensive, Prussia would assemble its army in Silesia, with the lead corps near Torgau. In 42 days, 200 000 men would be ready for the approach march south.[79]

Moltke believed the key was that Austria was 46 miles closer to Berlin than Prussia was to Vienna, a two- or three-day march. By remaining behind the Riesen and Lausitz Mountains until the last moment, Austria could keep Prussia in the dark about its plans, seize Silesia and use its rich resources as a base. The first assembly of the Austrian forces, he theorized, would be along the line Prague–Pardubitz, with further movement to Dresden along the left bank of the Elbe River. The main movement would be along the right bank of the Elbe, over the Lausitz Mountains, and, three days after the declaration of war, the Austrians would be on the upper Elbe and Spree rivers.[80] One further day's march would be sufficient to unite these armies between the rivers for a drive against Berlin.

Moltke had to decide whether to protect Berlin directly or indirectly. If Prussia lost a direct frontal battle, it was in danger of losing Berlin and perhaps Stettin. Meanwhile Austria would be able to plunder Silesia at will. Therefore an indirect defence might be better, from a flanking position on the Elbe. Every attack from the west moved the enemy towards the shortest path. If Prussia attacked east to west from the Elbe River, it pushed the enemy back out of the yet unplundered Silesia. If this failed, Prussian forces could take refuge behind the river.[81]

The May 1860 General Staff ride simulated this war.[82] The key point was correct assembly of the Prussian Army in northern Silesia. If the Austrians had already assembled and marched into Bohemia to attack Berlin, this assembly became impossible. How to prevent this? Leave Silesia unprotected? Use it as the basis for a flank attack? They tried to move the Prussian Army behind the Elbe River, as far forward as possible, to push against the Saxons at Dresden. But it did not work. There were too many Austrians – estimated at 134 000 – against too few Prussians, 107 000. How long would this take? What would France do meanwhile?[83] Possible scenarios were drawn up, critiqued and revised.

In January 1861 a Germanic Confederation Railroad Commission was convened, with Austrian, Prussian, Hanoverian and Bavarian officers. Wartensleben was Moltke's representative.[84] The commission rode the railroads, main and secondary lines of the German states and also those of Belgium, the Netherlands, Luxembourg, France, Switzerland and Italy – in 1861 the extent of these lines was not very great. They examined the general track plan, the number of double- and single-track lines, their work capacity, load and offload possibilities. On the basis of this, a railroad transportation plan was written for the German Confederation against France which laid the technical foundation for all further war plans.[85] Here was the first time cut of the French War: eight days from garrison to assembly points, followed by 21 days for the military travel plan up to the border.

That same month, an Austro-Prussian military conference met in Berlin, to outline formalities of a possible war against France. Austria said it could put 46 000 infantry and 18 000 cavalry on the upper Rhine in 28–42 days.[86] This gave Moltke an indicator of what the Austrians thought they could do in a war situation. He did not realize that they were incapable of doing it.

Size, space and time factors were changing. By the royal manoeuvres of September 1861, Moltke's schedule was hurried and compressed. As he wrote to Marie from the town of Dueren, south-west of Cologne, he had been working in the Cologne area for weeks setting up the manoeuvre: liaising with officials in Koblenz and Münster, connecting the railroads and the horses, making arrangements for all the 'majesties, highnesses and excellencies' from 16 states to travel about in the rain, with 170 stable horses, and enough draft horses for more than 200 guests, plus quarters for the changing court entourage. Doing all this every day caused Moltke more grief than the actual manoeuvre itself. Up at 6, 20–30 miles by railroad and wagon. Then at 9, on horseback with the king for two or three hours and after lunch five hours back, and at 6 dinner. Then at 2 a.m. the first dispositions for the next day sent out. And the whole thing begins again. Moltke lamented that he saw a lot of old friends, but only in passing: they had no time to talk. And as soon as the manoeuvre ended, he had only a few days to prepare for the GGS ride to Königsberg![87]

Moltke and the American Civil War

The American Civil War, which began on 12 April 1861 at Fort Sumter, South Carolina, had been under way for nearly three years by the time the Danish War began in January 1864 and finally ended in the year before the Austrian War.

Although the Prussian Army studied contemporary armies with great thoroughness – a French general once complained that the Prussians knew more about his army then he did – some scholars have suggested that Moltke thought of the American Civil War as a struggle between two armed mobs chasing each other around the countryside, from which nothing could be learned.[88] Officers were said to have a low opinion of the mainly conscript American armies, a war fought by amateurs could teach little to professionals, they were thought to have concluded. Though more than 200 000 native Germans served in the Union Army, it is thought that few accounts got back to Germany.

Moltke knew a good deal about the American Civil War for he had followed it carefully from the beginning. For one thing Moltke was kept on track by a circle of professional colleagues. One of these was Theodore von Bernhardi. Scion of a wealthy Swiss family, educated in Germany, Austria, Italy and Spain, he spoke several languages and was known as a learned man.[89] Moltke saw Bernhardi regularly. He was very well informed about the American Civil War, and early on he suggested that Moltke watch it carefully.[90] The first year it had seemed rather conventional, but by 1862 – Forts Henry and Donalson, Shiloh, Antietem – and 1863 – Chancellorsville, Gettysburg, Vicksburg – Moltke became interested. He realized that this was a new kind of war.

Moltke decided to send an observer. He asked his former chief, Prince Radziwill, now chief of engineers, for a suggestion. Justus Schiebert, an engineer officer with excellent English, was chosen.[91] He was sent specifically to gather data regarding the effect of rifled artillery on earth, masonry and iron. But in reality he had wide-ranging experiences between March and August 1863. Schiebert was an eyewitness at 14 battles, including Chancellorsvile, Brandy Station and Gettysburg. He observed and talked with Lee, Stuart and Stonewall Jackson. Upon his return he discussed his conclusions widely, lectured in the War Academy and General Staff and became so well known that he was on special assignment during the Danish War and Bismarck requested his services as a guide through the captured Danish works at Dybbol.[92]

Prussian observers began publishing their impressions of the American Civil War in 1862. They emphasized the advantages of technology: the ferocious impact of artillery, and the great difficulty of storming a position held by rifled infantry.[93]

Almost from the start the American Civil War was a railroad war. In the first battle of Bull Run, 21 July 1861, railroads played a role in strategic manoeuvre. At the battle of Shiloh, 6–7 April 1862, both sides brought

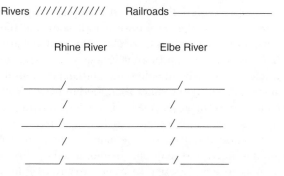

Figure 3.1   Relationship between railroads and rivers in Germany

up forces by rail. It became the single means above all for moving and supplying the huge Union Army which ground away the Confederacy. It was the Military Railroad Construction Corps that allowed Sherman his slow, methodical advance from Chattanooga to Atlanta.[94] In October 1863 occurred the epic rail transport of nearly 80 000 men, 1200 miles from Virgina to Tennessee in seven days! For Europeans, this was equivalent to moving three corps from Berlin to Moscow in a week's time! A feat impossible ten years before, it allowed a permanent Union position to be held and reinforced deep in Confederate territory. With the opening of the Mississippi River, when Vicksburg surrendered that summer, Sherman was enabled to launch his drive from Chattanooga to the Atlantic Ocean, a war-ending strategic move.[95]

For Moltke the revolutionary impact of railroads was clear. And he put this knowledge to good use. Moltke began to look at the German states as a grid pattern. The great rivers which flowed south to north were the unchangeable barrier positions of German defences. The system of railroads east and west, he said, set the main directions of travel for all time (Figure 3.1). It can be enlarged, but not essentially changed. These fundamental relationships conditioned the direction of transport and also outlined the initial concentration format of the Prussian Army.[96]

The Crisis of 1862

The failed mobilization of 1859 – an external crisis caused by the Prussian Army's organizational and command weaknesses – was followed a year later by an internal crisis – the Prussian Landtag's opposition to army reforms aimed at fixing other weaknesses. It was these together that convinced the regent to carry out radical reforms in Prussia's Army.[97]

By 1860 it had become clear that the Prussian Army was much smaller than the armies of her three neighbours: perhaps 100 000 men smaller than the Austrians, 200 000 smaller than the French, and almost half a million smaller than the Russians.[98] The reason for this was that the basic conscription law had been laid down in 1814. In the meantime the Prussian population had tripled. This meant that two-thirds of those liable for military service were never called up. And the first and second reserves, men up to age 40, with a year's active duty, went untrained and unexercised.[99]

To remedy this the army bill of February 1860 called for 60 000 new recruits each year, and specified that the reserves were to be placed under the command of regular officers. The three-year term of service, dating from 1856, was continued. After weeks of discussion, the Landtag committee recommended that it be accepted but only if infantry reserves served two years and the old *Landwehr* format was retained. They were suspicious: putting the *Landwehr* under regular officers was against tradition and made the liberals uneasy.[100]

In spite of opposition, army reorganization went forward, based on assumptions contained in the bill. Certain *Landwehr* regiments were dissolved and their members taken into line regiments. The size of each recruiting class was increased. The three-year service obligation remained. In May 1860 the government put forth what they called an interim arrangement to fund all of this. It was passed.[101]

In January 1861, when King Frederick Wilhelm IV died and the prince regent ascended the throne as King Wilhelm I, it was the first change of sovereign under the Constitution of 1850. A new ceremony was called for: instead of feudal vassals exchanging traditional vows, a more symbolic ceremony, without feudal connotations. But at the coronation, at Königsberg, 18 October 1861, the new king greeted the Landtag as advisors to the crown, rather than as a legitimate and independent political body. Furthermore the army delegation included commanders from the new line regiments created on the basis of the interim funding arrangement.[102] Six months later, the king's speech to the Landtag brushed aside the need for regularly voted budgetary provisions supporting army financing. Opposition increased. Early December 1861 elections returned a Landtag with 260 out of 325 against the army bill.

Fearing a revolution, sealed orders were sent out to troop commanders in the Berlin region. Special telegraph lines were strung connecting major Prussian cities with the same object in mind. When the so-called 'liberal Landtag' met, nothing happened. And after a while, the orders were torn up.[103] However, in March 1862 this Landtag called upon the government to break down the budget bill so that they could clearly see that it contained no secret provisions continuing army reorganization. The king countered by appointing a conservative government.[104]

With a major constitutional crisis under way at home, Prussia found itself facing a renewed challenge over the German question from Austria and the smaller German states. It had to do with the Germanic Confederation. Who was going to be in charge and within what political framework?

When Saxony proposed a plan for a stronger Confederation, Austria lined up all the smaller states to oppose this. Prussia meanwhile had negotiated a new trade treaty with France, designed to keep Austria out of the Customs Union. Austria now gathered all the smaller states together to oppose this treaty.[105] Under the threat of this double-barrelled attack, Prussia declared a state of 'war readiness' on 15 May, ordering IV Corps (Magdeburg) and VII Corps (Westphalia) to begin preparations for mobilization. General von Shack was nominated commander-in-chief and plans were set for advance into Hesse.[106]

During all this, Moltke had been away working on coastal defence problems in Hamburg. He got back late and had to make rapid decisions about what to do next. One possibility was a two-front war against Austria, her German allies and France. In that case, Prussia, with no allies, would send four corps against the west and south (Bavaria), and five corps against Austria and Saxony.[107] It was improbable, he hypothesized, that Bavaria would do anything until France came to its aid. If Saxony was neutral or allied, then the advance march against Prague could go forward. If this march encountered resistance from Austria, then Prussia stood on the edge of a quite unpredictable war.

The advantage for Prussia, said Moltke, would come by seizing the initiative. Prussia could complete its mobilization before any of its German opponents.[108] That France was expected to mobilize faster than Prussia was not decisive here. France already had troops in Italy and Mexico. This reduced her power. War would be ordered in response to mobilizations among the German states or if Austria protested against the Prussian advance into Hesse.

But it all came to nought. At the crown council of 23 June 1862, the king and his ministers decided not to continue military actions. By August things looked even worse. With the Zollverein Treaty in jeopardy, facing a two-pronged Austrian attack in the Germanic Confederation, unwilling to capitulate to the liberal opposition in the Prussian Landtag or to stage a *coup d'état*, King Wilhelm considered abdication. In both foreign and domestic policy, the Prussian monarchy appeared to be boxed in.[109]

4

The Danish War, 1864

Preliminaries

Otto von Bismarck was appointed minister-president of the kingdom of Prussia on 22 September 1862. Ten days later Moltke was requested to explore the possibilities of a war with Denmark.[1]

Bismarck's social class and career pattern put him as an elite royal bureaucrat on a different level from Moltke. Moltke had been a soldier for 40 years, but neither by office nor actions was he a dominant player in Prussian military affairs. Bismarck, meanwhile, had been envoy to the Germanic Confederation, Tsarist Russia and Imperial France, ever travelling. Bismarck was a count and an estate owner, Moltke a landless noble. Bismarck had attended university and travelled about on his own. Moltke was a professional soldier, educated at the Cadet Academy, War Academy and in the Ottoman–Egyptian War.

Bismarck was ebullient, gregarious, moody, and considered brilliant. He had held independent appointments and stuck out in each one as outspoken, unique, a hereditary east Prussian Junker of status and character. He did what he wanted. If he wanted to take a leave, he left. If he wanted to travel, he went. Bismarck was unruly, apparently undisciplined. Men did not fully trust him. But they recognized a special individual with unique powers. When he and the king met on the shore of Glienicker Lake at Bebelsberg Palace in mid-September, the king gave up his ideas of abdication and appointed the man who convinced him he might save the Prussian monarchy.

Moltke was quiet, reserved in social relations and only daring in his mind and in war planning. His life was orderly, placid, routine. Superficially demure, taciturn, accepting, only in his ideas, and the war plans which illustrated them, was he a wild man, someone whose methods and processes would dominate the entire next century: the Darwin–Marx–Freud of twentieth-century war.

The Bismarck–Moltke relationship has been used to illustrate the tension between political and military goals and methods.[2] But until late September 1870 there seems to have been little tension between the two men. A more interesting question is whether Bismarck recognized the unique strengths of the Prussian Army of the 1860s. Virtually none of the many biographies of Bismarck deal with this question. If the strengths of the army were a surprise to the Austrians and French, why not to Bismarck? On the other hand, would he have accepted the risks taken without a secure understanding that the instrument chosen to accomplish these momentous political changes was far superior to others of its day? Or did he finally trust Moltke's judgement on these matters? Clearly he recognized that Moltke was unique. Bismarck wrote that Moltke was a completely rare human being, who methodically – 'ein Mann der systematischen Pflichterfüllung' – fulfilled his duties, a man of singular, original nature, always dependable, with a cool heart and very restrained personality.[3]

American Ambassador George Bancroft, who knew them both, said they were the perfect foil for each other: Moltke of tranquil mind and exact observation, calm, logical and unhurried, in contrast to Bismarck's swift intuitive judgement, vehemence and intensity.[4] In September 1862, at the time of this request, Bismarck hardly knew Moltke, a lesser bureaucrat in a minor subsection of the Prussian government. Bismarck asked War Minister Roon to request from Moltke a plan for a war against Denmark.

Moltke knew Denmark well. He had grown up there, gone to its schools, served in its army. His father had died as a Danish lieutenant-general. Several of his brothers and sisters still lived there, as did his wife's family. He travelled there often.[5]

To attack Denmark without a fleet, he replied, winter was the most favourable season. The freezing of the coastal waters would limit the Danish navy. Above all they must avoid a frontal assault against the Danewerk, the ancient earthwork and stone defence line – the symbolic bulwark against foreign aggression – just north of the German border. They should attack it on both flanks, encircle Dybbol and Fredericia and seize Jütland as a basis for negotiations.[6]

To test out these ideas, Moltke ran a hypothetical test. Assembling a Prussian army of two divisions, he transported it via Hamburg and

Lübeck and attacked it against a hypothetical 40 000 man Danewerk defensive position. He concluded that at least a 50 per cent Prussian numerical superiority was needed, and more if Swedish aid materialized. Twenty-eight days after mobilization had begun, a Prussian army could be at the enemy position. The high cost of maintaining such an army in the field had to be balanced against the time frame of a short war. Moltke concluded that everything depended on speed, catching the Danes before they were ready. Everything must be kept secret. On the day of the ultimatum everything had to be ready to go – mobilization notices, march orders, railroad schedules. Once we set up the schedule, he said, neither diplomatic negotiations nor political considerations should force us off it.

To back up and 'historicize' this, Moltke turned to research. A cadre of officers worked up the Schleswig-Holstein War of 1848–49 as a military history project. Moltke himself edited it and wrote the first section. What did they find? The war had been indecisive. There were wasteful and ineffective frontal attacks, slow timing patterns and a lack of follow-up. The Danes were pushed back, but not destroyed. German battlefield victories were insufficient to decide the campaign. A long-lasting and indecisive war, whose final outcome was a stalemate. The Danes held out and won.[7]

Why in 1862 had Bismarck asked for a military appraisal of a war against Denmark? And what did the minister-president have in mind? The Duchies of Schleswig-Holstein touched upon several passionate political sentiments of the times, especially nationalism and ethnic politics. Although dynastically tied to Denmark and legally inseparable, Holstein had a German-speaking majority and was part of the Germanic Confederation and Schleswig had numerous German communities. After the turmoil of 1848–52, the European Great Powers had signed the London Treaty, formalizing the duchies' status with the King of Denmark, who promised not to annex Schleswig or change the duchies' legal status without consultation. In March 1863, Danish King Frederick IV unilaterally imposed new constitutional orders on Schleswig. When he died eight months later without an heir, the Great Powers supported the claim of Prince Christian of Schleswig-Holstein-Soenderborg-Glücksburg, who succeeded to the throne but agreed to carry out the new constitution. Challenging him was the German Duke Christian August of Augustenburg, who had succession rights to the duchies and was widely recognized in the Germanies as the Duke of Schleswig-Holstein. Now a groundswell of popular opinion engulfed the German states, demanding recognition of the duke, the separation of the duchies from Denmark and their entry into the Germanic Confederation. The duke won the support of a majority of the Confederation. Against this majority stood Austria and Prussia, who supported King Christian, providing he adhered to the treaties of 1852. In adopting this position, Bismarck had joined two separate but related issues in a conditional relationship. He kept Austria in play by assuring Austrian Foreign Minister Rechberg that Prussia would follow the London Treaty, but, in order to retain a pretext for intervening in the duchies, he made this assurance conditional upon Denmark keeping her promises to respect the constitutional status quo in the duchies. As William Carr writes, this allowed Bismarck to 'run with the hares and hunt with the hounds'.[8]

In spite of mixed feelings, members of the Confederation finally voted sanctions against Denmark. The Danish king ignored this. Meanwhile Austria and Prussia moved towards a common policy but with very different motives and goals. Rechberg wanted to use the Danish issue to lay the foundations for conservative Austro-Prussian domination of liberal–national forces in the Confederation. Bismarck, on the other hand, was attracted by the idea of annexing both duchies to Prussia, using them as a tactical pawn while he waited to see what would develop with Austria in foreign policy and in the Prussian Landtag with regard to the domestic political crisis.[9] In both cases he sought to use the forces of popular nationalism against those of popular liberalism.

Bismarck agreed with Moltke: they had to defeat Denmark quickly, before the Great Powers intervened on Denmark's behalf. Meanwhile, Bismarck would cooperate with Austria without committing himself as to the future of the duchies.

As the political situation gradually heated up, specific details were added. By spring 1863 the king tentatively decided on 70 000 men as the minimum Prussian force.[10] And that autumn such a force level was tested out in the field. Manoeuvres between III Corps, commanded by Prince Friedrich Charles, and the Guard Corps, commanded by General Count Groeben, were conducted north-west of Berlin, to check out the transportation system in the exact direction they would move if they went to war. Moltke was the field judge.

In November Moltke went to Frankfurt for a military conference of the Germanic Confederation, as it prepared to go to war with Denmark. It was his first official working together on state business with Bismarck. They negotiated the details of military cooperation between Austria, Hanover, Saxony and Prussia. Before Moltke returned to Berlin, he stopped off in Leipzig to review the railroad mobilization plans which his colleagues Wartensleben and the younger Bronsart von Schellendorff had worked out with officials of the Ministry of Trade.[11]

When the Danish War began Moltke was at first not directly involved. The king appointed Field Marshal von Wrangel, the 80-year-old veteran of the Napoleonic and 1848 Wars, commander-in-chief. The politics of this appointment are revealing. Prussia had requested that a Prussian officer command the overall force. The Austrians agreed, but stipulated that it be someone with war experience. The only Prussian officer who qualified under these conditions was Wrangel. After appointing him, King Wilhelm briefed Wrangel on Moltke's plan: hold the Danish Army at the Danewerk but do not attack it frontally. Send forces around the flanks – at Missunde and Arnis on the right and at Treene and the Schlei on the left. Do it quickly before the Danes know what hit them.[12] Privately Moltke had repeated: our only chance is to hold the Danes in Schleswig and destroy them there, before they can withdraw to fortified positions further up the peninsula. Moltke tried everything to get this plan across. He could not. A long and difficult campaign, full of mistakes, followed.[13]

The Danish War

It began with honour in a season when wars were usually not fought. Two days before Christmas the Germanic Confederation began to move 12 000 soldiers from Hanover and Saxony into Holstein to take up an ancient land claim. Danish regiments retreated to the Eider River, just north of the frontier.[14] On Christmas Day the Danish government resigned, unwilling to make war. But a new one wanted to fight. A week later envoys from the Confederation presented an ultimatum. Wrangel formally offered the Danish commander-in-chief Christian Julius de Meza the 'opportunity' to leave Schleswig. De Meza, born when Napoleon was still an anonymous captain, showed up at Wrangel's headquarters, catching the Prussian in his dressing gown. 'When the Marshal is ready to fight, so am I', he said.[15] Combat could now begin. The bridges were mined. Soldiers on guard duty no longer saluted their enemy.

Wrangel tried to run things like the old days. Business was conducted verbally. He refused to look at briefing documents: I make war with the sword not with paper, he told his staff. Commanders' conferences were formal affairs – with officers in full dress, plus swords, hat held correctly in their right hand – with brief memorized presentations to the marshal.

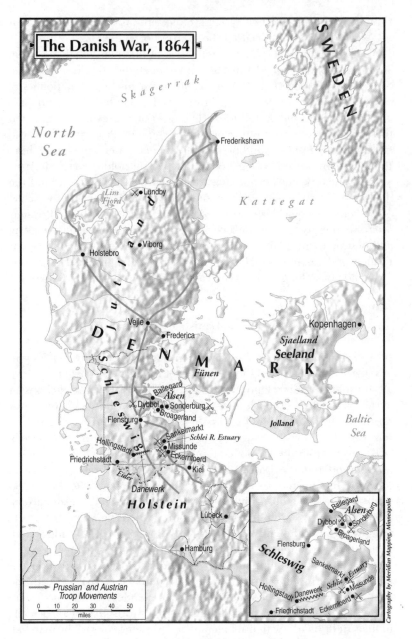

Figure 4.1   The Danish peninsula (Philip Schwartzberg © Meridian Mapping).

More than once Wrangel interrupted, reminding them this was a report not a lecture. His orders were sparse. 'On February 1st, I want to sleep in Schleswig!' They called him 'the old one', responded 'Zu Befehl' and did what was decided by a group of men headed by Prince Friedrich Charles and his chief of staff Blumenthal, who was in daily communication with Moltke.[16]

Both of these commanders had fought here before. On Easter Sunday 1848 Wrangel's First Guards had stormed the Danewerk and in two weeks his forces were in Jütland. When the Danish navy began to shell Prussian cities on the Baltic Sea, Wrangel sent the Danish commander a message: for every house destroyed by the Danish navy one village in Jütland would be burned.[17] De Meza, who had been chief of artillery on the fortified island of Alsen, held out to the end. Both of these old fighters believed in the sanctity of their war experience, validated as it was by death and honour.

Denmark is a peninsula, sliced by deep fjords and a collection of islands. Its only large city, Copenhagen, sits just across from Sweden far to the east. Narrowing to 25 miles in places, some of the fjords go miles inland. Swept by ocean tides and sea winds, in order to grow crops above any potential waterlines, it is covered with 'knicks': ten-yard square hillocks built up of soil, held in place by grasses, used for planting, to buffer winds, and to prevent soil erosion. Denmark is littered with medieval fortifications and her military mentality was fully in tune with the romantic notions conjured up by this built environment. Hamlet would have been thoroughly at home, not only at Elsinore, but far south on the Danewerk and in the ancient fishing village of Missunde.[18]

The weather during the first half of the Danish War was miserable: heavy snow on the ground, snow every day, temperature 20 °F (-6 °C), now an icy drizzle, now a cold fog blowing in from the Baltic Sea to the east and the North Sea to the west. This undoubtedly slowed combat operations, although it does not seem to have affected the battles much, except for the first attempt to besiege Alsen Island, when a blizzard came up and halted all activities for several days. As Moltke had predicted, the weather restricted the Danish navy, which sent only a single ironclad steamship against Prussian land forces, and that without much result.[19]

At 7 a.m., Tuesday, 1 February 1864, Prussian advance units crossed the Eider River with loud 'hurrahs'. The purpose of 'hurrahs' – so strange to twenty-first-century observers – was to give a clear auditory signal to all neighbouring units that an infantry attack was under way so that, hearing the shouts, they would join in. It was so important to Prussian tactical–operational methods that the 'hurrah' appeared in Moltke's June 1869 'Instructions for Large Unit Commanders'.[20] By 11 a.m., lead platoons were on Eckernfiord Bay. An enemy ship moved into range, and Prussian gunners, set up on the beach, opened up with six pounders. Stationary guns could hit targets, even moving ones, moving guns could not. The ship backed off. A battalion of Brandenburg infantry entered the city of Eckernfoerde at noon: the first Danish city was liberated! Jubilation by German residents![21]

As Hans Delbrück reminds us, the Danish War may be broken down into three phases.[22] At first, the Prussians tried to go east around the Danish left flank but were repulsed with heavy casualties at Missunde. The next day the Danes evacuated the Danewerk and retreated north. Moltke went up for an inspection tour, reported to the king, and then Prussia and Austria negotiated the further strategic goals of the campaign.[23]

After that Prussia began a desultory advance to Dybbol midway up the east coast, while the Austrians moved simultaneously up the west coast. But it went slowly. Frontal attacks against entrenched infantry led to high casualties. Austria, on a tight leash from Vienna, feared British intervention. Finally Bismarck convinced the king that Prussia needed a clear-cut battlefield success: the kingdom had not had a military victory since Waterloo! Something had to happen at Dybbol, the ancient fortified hill position. Moltke, meanwhile, was in daily contact with Blumenthal, chief of staff to Wrangel, and he could not see how the capture of Dybbol would end the war. Moltke and Blumenthal finally concluded that artillery, not infantry, might bring this victory. Soon thereafter heavy siege artillery was ordered up from Berlin. By 23 March the big guns were in place. They mounted a slowly intensifying 25-day artillery barrage, the likes of which would not be seen again in Europe until the spring of 1915. At the end of the barrage Dybbol was stormed in 20 minutes. The position had been almost totally destroyed. Its shell shocked defenders had neither the will nor the material to continue: 4800 Danes were casualties there.[24] They saw no reason to continue. Phase one ended.

Although the soldiers knew it was not over at all, there was a big celebration in Prussia. The king travelled to Schleswig to take the salute from the victorious soldiers and hand out medals and decorations.

At this point there were sudden and unexpected changes heralding the second phase. An armistice was declared from 12 May to 20 June and negotiations were opened in London. Wrangel was retired. Moltke became chief of staff to the new commander-in-chief of the joint force, Prince Friedrich Charles. Ten hours after his appointment, Moltke arrived in Flensburg. After viewing the situation on the ground, Moltke sent a memo to the king. Inflict upon the Danish Army, assembled and concentrated, a destroying annihilation that would force them to sue for peace. Seize Alsen Island on the east coast and occupy all of Jütland.[25] Attack the Danes only where we can be successful. Use every advantage of technology. Moltke readied operations to carry out his plan, confident, after the bloodletting of phase one, that Prussians and Austrians were ready to try something new. But the Austrian commander-in-chief Ludwig Gablenz raised both technical and political opposition. Above all, he feared foreign intervention.[26]

During the armistice, the Danes evacuated everything as far north as Fredericia and Alsen Island, which gave the impression of a Germanic Confederation victory while covering up a lack of any real military success. But the Danes felt in no way defeated. They held all the big islands and the largest part of Jütland. They believed they could hold out at least until neutral Sweden or Britain weighed in on their side.

The third phase began with a conference between Austrian Emperor Franz Joseph and Prussian King Wilhelm I at Karlsbad. Moltke's plan was agreed upon. Four days after the armistice ended, Alsen Island was in Prussian hands as a consequence of a stupendous night-time cross-channel amphibious invasion. Only then did the Danes begin to feel defeated. Now they feared similar attacks on Funen Island, perhaps against Zeeland, maybe even on Copenhagen itself. Their will to resist was broken and the ongoing debate in the British Parliament showed that neither Britain nor any other European state was ready to save Denmark from its fate. Denmark declared itself ready for definitive peace negotiations. A second armistice began on 20 July, the preliminary peace treaty was signed 1 August and the final treaty on 30 October.[27]

How can we understand the Danish War at the turn of the twenty-first century? Theodor Fontane wrote that the Danish reserves, half of their army, was comprised of men who were too old or too young: the elderly had forgotten how to fight and the young had not yet learned. Officers and men lacked training and unit cohesion. Morally and physically they were no match for the Prussians.[28] It was a clash between an ancient agricultural elite army, fighting for its honour with traditional close-order, muzzle-loading bayonet charges, and an industrial mass army, armed with rapid-firing breech-load rifles and rifled artillery. A clash of technology, organization and leadership, with plenty of old-fashioned bravery, and terrible bloody carnage in the snows of the Danish winter and spring. And heroes and great sadness and much suffering.

As illustrations of this let us look at the battles of Missunde, 1–3 February, Sankelmarkt, 6 February[29] and Dybbol, 18 March–18 April, the cross-channel amphibious invasion and seizure of Alsen Island, 29 June, and the battle of Lundby, 1 July.

The Battle of Missunde, 1–3 February

Missunde was an old fishing village – 40 houses and a church – fortified as the eastern anchor point of the ancient Danewerk, the hill and stone barricade stretching across the narrowest 25-mile land neck of the peninsula. Backed up on to the Schlei River basin, which opened behind it into a series of lakes, flowing out to the Baltic Sea on one side and south-west across the neck to the small city of Friedrichstadt on the other. West from Hollingstadt to Friedrichstadt was a frozen swamp.[30] Behind the Danewerk was a half-finished railroad line. It snowed every day. Landscape and towns were blanketed under feet of snow. Now a thaw and fog, then drizzling rain, but not enough to melt ice in narrow or shallow waters, with rain refreezing.[31]

Missunde commands an estuary on the narrowest point of the Schlei River. It consisted of five forts, arranged in almost geometric formation, rising on both sides of the water.[32] Twelve-feet deep palisaded counter-scarpment, 18-feet thick trenches, blockhouses on the breastwork between cannons, crenelations four to six feet thick and three to four feet high, powder magazines, grenade cannons and cross-fire positions. The Danes had taken down the only bridge across the Schlei River estuary. In short a medieval fortified position.

The Danes had no rifled cannon. Their guns' range was thus about 1000 feet, with 100 charges per gun in the Missunde forts.[33] Prussian rifled siege guns hit targets at 3000 feet. Danish rifled muzzle-loaders were the Danish underhammer, ranged at 1200 feet. At .69 calibre, it did great damage if it hit a man, tearing holes straight through at 150 feet. The many motions of loading single charges, standing up, took more than a minute.[34] The Prussian needle gun could shoot five shots during this time, with 43 per cent accuracy at 700 feet.[35] And it could be reloaded lying down. Danish troops were tall, strongly built and earnest, somewhat phlegmatic, evincing no elation or enthusiasm, disposed to do their duty, well armed and equipped. With a certain heaviness, awkward in movement, they were mainly recruits just called up from the reserves, but well controlled by their officers.[36]

To defend Missunde the Danes had 2000 men and 20 guns. Prussian forces at the start were two brigades, some 6000 men and 64 field guns. During the battle another 19000 soldiers and 20 guns arrived. Air temperature was 25 °F (-3 °C) with thick fog. Visibility was nil, with great banks of fog rolling across the position from the Baltic Sea.[37]

The Prussian advance guard, a battalion of the 24th Brandenburg infantry regiment, accompanied by a *Jäger* company, a squadron of Zeiten hussars and two howitzers, marched straight down the main road to Missunde.[38] The route had been carefully prepared by the Danish defenders: fire paths marked out with bales of straw, knicks entrenched and shaved bare of foliage like earthen forts. At 10 a.m. the 9th and 10th Prussian companies attacked in thick fog. Five men abreast, 20 columns deep. They were shot down on the road and stopped dead.

Meanwhile, on the right 12 Prussian batteries moved up.[39] Taking casualties, they moved to within 250 feet and poured a deadly fire into the fortification. Danish defenders had now moved back behind the stone palisades and battlements. By 11 a.m. 24 Prussian six-pounders moved up again. Three howitzer batteries set up and began to fire. Four mounted batteries with 16 guns began to shoot. In the thick fog, the Danes could not see that their few artillery pieces were firing high. At 12.30 three Prussian companies moved to within 1000 feet, 'hurrahed' and stormed. They got within 100 feet of the fortifications, found no cover and would have been destroyed except for the increasing Prussian fire superiority.

The Danes were now taking heavy casualties. They had lost their captains and lieutenants and had begun to disintegrate. But their rifles kept firing.[40] By 2 p.m. Prussian howitzers moved closer, firing at point-blank range. But they lost their lieutenant, 30 men and 10 horses. At 3.30 p.m., in thicker fog, visibility dimmed and the day began to darken into night. In the gathering darkness Prussian commanders broke off the attack, moved their forces back to a line Eschelsmark–Cosel–Holm and put out advance guards.[41]

In five and a half hours, the Danes and Prussians shared nearly 500 casualties, nearly 100 casualties an hour, with little change in the military situation.[42]

At that point, Moltke suggested they go across the water further east. There the Schlei narrowed to 50 feet. They could circumvent the fortifications and take it from the flank. This plan was discussed, war gamed, discussed again, then orders issued.[43]

Two days later, during a heavy snowfall, 25 000 troops assembled for a 4 a.m. crossing. There was a foot of snow on the ground with more falling. The troops, waiting to attack in 20 °F weather, were ordered to build no fires and there was no straw. Silence was in effect. Then out of the blue, a local pastor came by and told them the Danish troops had left. An NCO rowed across the Schlei and found no soldiers. An hour later, a fisherman confirmed this. The advance guard got into boats and by 7.30 the first regiment was across. By 9.15 there was a pontoon bridge across the river. With water temperature at 20 °F (−6 °C), 20 000 troops crossed in the next eight hours.[44] Prussian brigade commander Freiherr von Canstein placed himself on the north side of the pontoon bridge and was cheered with loud jubilation as the troops passed by.[45]

At that point the Danes evacuated the entire Danewerk. As de Meza had said, they could hold it for six days, on the seventh they would leave. This was taken as a great victory in Germany, and covered up the fact that the assault at Missunde had failed. In fog and snow, 300 men had died and been wounded, but the Danes had escaped north. And Sankelmarkt, a violent footnote to this battle, was fought the next afternoon.

The Battle of Sankelmarkt, 6 February

As the Danes retreated north, the Austrians were urged to attack them. At 3.30 p.m., 6 February, a mixed brigade under Austrian command ran into the rearguard of the Danish 3rd Infantry Division. As a train column was in the midst of leaving a village, Austrian hussars pushed into it, killing many, then they themselves were attacked from two sides. The Danes then evacuated and set up defensive positions outside the village. One brigade set up and allowed others to move between it. The road there runs through low hills, forested and snow covered, backed up against the village of Sankelmarkt. The Danes drew themselves up in ranks, behind knicks. The Danish rifled musket, the Underhammer, whose main advantage was safety for the eyes from the exploding cap, was still a ferocious weapon. With a muzzle velocity of 2000 feet per second, in half a second it penetrated 14 inches of oak plank.[46] Remembering a legendary battle there in 1848 between Danes, Brunswick cavalry and Hanoverian infantry, Austrian commander

General Ludwig Gablenz ordered an immediate frontal attack. He thought to catch the Danes retreating.

It was dusk and growing dark. The Austrians were tired, having spent three nights in makeshift housing. It was snowing and cold. Four companies marched forward on slippery roads. *Jäger* in front attacked straight ahead, with two companies going around the side. Danish riflemen shot them down from the knicks, Austrians charged and recharged, finally closing with rifle butts and bayonets. As quickly as the Danish front lines were taken, the survivors slowly retreated through and beyond the village outskirts into the woods, until the two Austrian companies which had gone around the side attacked them from behind.[47]

Sankelmarkt was a disaster for both sides. Without operational or strategic implications, over 400 Austrians killed and wounded, almost 1000 Danes, in a fight which lasted only an hour until darkness came. One dead or wounded soldier every three seconds. There was no help available for the wounded, and many died in the deep snow and cold of night. The roads were ice covered, it continued to snow, drifts covered everything, burying the wounded and the dead. Deep trenches at the roadside made movement treacherous. In the snow the wounded were a terrible sight: Austrians, in their white uniforms with shot off heads and limbs, dead horses everywhere. Bodies, weapons, cartridge bags and equipment littered the scene. Ten loads of Danish dead were taken off. A smith lay beside his shop, dead lay around it on both sides of the road in a wide circle: many wounded, seeking shelter in the storm, had died there in the night. Austrian and Danish dead lay on top of each other. A deep stillness lay over the land. A soldier of the Prussian Guard Regiment passing by the next morning wrote that it was too much for his young heart to bear.[48]

The Siege of Dybbol, 11 February to 18 April

Dybbol is a scalene triangle, roughly a half mile across its land side.[49] An ancient hilltop position, whose western land side slopes gradually down 100 feet, and whose other two sides are water, the Wemmingbund, an open sound of a mile, and the Alsen Sund, a narrow channel of several hundred feet. Inscribed laterally across the sloping hillside from water to water were the rude outlines of seventeenth-century bastion system. Walls crouching low to the ground almost merging with massive banks of earth, partially lined by masonry-retaining walls and sloped turf.

Along the bastion were planted nine blockhouses, small diamond-shaped fortifications. Joining them was an open parapet, an infantry position running around the outer rim of the wide ditch behind the wall. Although the classic forms of the bastion – the glacis, a clear fire-swept zone which descended gradually to open country, palisades and counterscarp – were not fully developed, here and there some of these were built.[50] Two hundred feet across the channel bridge is Alsen Island, with its town of Sonderburg. The island is 12 miles long, and two to four miles wide. Sonderburg, an ancient and prosperous fishing village of 4000, nestled in a protective cove tucked into Alsen's south-west coast. The rest of the island was covered with dairy and sheep farms. It has a high crown, with cloud-touching meadows. Dybbol fortification was the war front, guarded by several thousand Danish soldiers. Sonderburg was the home front, where a small hotel, warm housing and food for men and officers, a market and church provided a semblance of normal civilian life. For a while.

Moltke saw the siege of Dybbol as a waste of time and manpower which, even in the best case, would only gain Prussia a small advantage.[51] However, Bismarck overruled him. Prussia needed a clear-cut military victory to ensure domestic support and to stem increasingly urgent British requests for an international conference.[52] Therefore Moltke reformulated the operational methods for attacking Dybbol. He wanted to use heavy siege artillery to force the Danes to give up Dybbol by destroying first its fortifications, then its supply base, reserve area and camp at Sonderburg.

But Wrangel went his own way. At first he thought only in terms of the traditional infantry storming attack. Two regiments were set out to do this job. It was a disaster. They were shot down with heavy casualties.

Next came a classic siege: a network of trenches, laterals and parallels were dug and gradually troops and guns were moved forward against that segment of the fortifications nearest the Wemmingbund, the open bay to the south.

Then, in a heavy snow storm, with haze so thick they could not see a quarter mile, they tried another infantry storm. This time they were shot down and bombarded: the Danish ironclad steamship *Rolf Krake* came right up to the shore and attacked the Prussian flank. No Prussian artillery battery supported the attack and reserves did not arrive in time. The Prussians did not have sufficient force. The Danes counterattacked, capturing men and ground.[53] On the road back to Sonderburg, young, beardless boys of the Prussian 18th Regiment bore their capture with apparent unconcern.[54] The Danes shook them by the hand, called them 'Comaraden', slapped them on the back, raised bottles of schnapps to their lips, stuffed cigars into their hands, bade them cheer up. Two Prussian officers held themselves aloof from this civility.[55]

Meanwhile Moltke had ordered up the heaviest siege and fortress equipment – 24-pound rifled guns and 25-inch mortars – which took almost a month to transport by rail.

The Attempt to Invade Alsen Island, 1–2 April

While awaiting the arrival of the guns and setting up the huge supply mechanism to feed them, they tried Moltke's original idea, an amphibious invasion of Alsen Island. As Alfred Vagts reminds us, landing operations across water are shockers: the attacker intends them to be exactly what the defender fears most. The psychological shock of the water landing may be as great as the actual battle casualties caused after the landing. This description fits the Danes in this situation well.[56]

Between 12 March and 2 April, a great deal of effort was expended in preparing a cross-channel invasion. Separated by a channel roughly half a mile at its widest point, but narrowing to 200 feet here and there, the island side has a wide open shoreline, without forests or rocky promontories. In planning, they weighed a northern against a southern invasion. Whichever way, troops about to cross had to march their columns out in the open on the mainland side to get on boats, thus informing Danish forces of their whereabouts. If they went to the north, near Ballegaard, they would land in a sandy beach area, but the channel there was 700 yards wide. Due to the limited number of boats, they could transport only 1600 men at a time and it would be a long time before a second group could land. If they crossed south near Satrup, about 3000 feet north of the Dybbol entrenchments, they had only to cross 300 feet of water, but Prussian forces might immediately confront reinforcements from the Danish main camp and artillery park at Sonderburg.

The tiny Prussian Baltic Sea fleet assembled in Stralsund under the command of Admiral Prince Adalbert. The plan was for it to appear suddenly one morning in the Alsener Fiord loaded with troops. Just behind the beach, artillery would be set up to protect the crossing. When the project was first laid before him, Moltke cautioned that working together with the fleet was difficult and not to be counted on. Danish armed warships controlled the open water and the Prussian fleet was no match for it.[57]

The Prussian fleet assembled in Stralsund and was expected to appear near Alsen on the morning of 2 April. Two days before this, ocean storms were so strong that the ships could not go out on the high sea. A telegram informed Prince Friedrich Charles that he could not count on the fleet any more, and asked him if, under these circumstances, he wanted to risk the venture. The prince decided to go.

During the evening of 1–2 April, long wagon columns moved the six miles from their positions besieging Dybbol north to Ballegaard. Behind the beach two naval officers had assembled a veritable fleet of wooden boats, collected from the harbours and fishing villages of the Prussian coast and brought up by rail and wagon.

Meanwhile a terrible storm came up. As the morning dawned, the sea was high and churning: the naval men declared it impassible. If the boats did not fill with water, they would be impossible to steer. Everybody hunkered down behind the dunes so as not to alarm the Danes, to wait and see what the next day might bring. But the weather on the second day was worse, so it was called off.[58]

On the morning of 3 April the Danish high command had become aware of the situation, but did nothing. They concluded that a crossing was impossible. Moltke urged Blumenthal not to get depressed over the temporary setback. 'Remember Philip II and the armada, don't take your forces against the elements, but only against the enemy.'[59]

The Siege of Dybbol

By this time the Prussian king was becoming dissatisfied with the way things were going in Schleswig: everyone procrastinated! He felt the bombardment of Dybbol unjustified if they had no intention of storming it with infantry.[60] They turned again to the siege of Dybbol. General Eduard von Hindersin, the father of modern Prussian artillery, came up to direct it.[61] He worked with Prince Kraft zu Hohenlohe, an artillery officer on Wrangel's staff who had the king's ear. Many guns had already arrived and in the next few days the number constantly increased. In the end, there were 122 in all: one every 12 feet across the whole defensive line.[62] Estimates of the rain of firepower are various. Rüstow says more than 8000 artillery rounds in 24 hours: every ten hours 100 tons (2000 Zentner) of iron rained down upon the Dybbol defenders.[63] Dicey, who experienced this war on the Danish side, says 136 000 shots in all and sometimes they fired all night.[64] One thing is certain: firing escalated roughly every three or four days: if they fired 3000 shots per day on 8 April, by the 15th this had doubled or tripled.[65] Danish historians count over 4000 shots per day in the final weeks of the siege.[66] Each Prussian battery was given a specific, mathematically and cartographically defined location on which to drop its fire. For example, on the right wing of the Danish position, Prussian battery No. 13, 18 guns, directed its fire at Danish blockhouse fortifications Nos. 8 and 9 and the terrain between them.[67] The supply system to feed these guns for more than a month exceeded that initially used to deliver the original 13 divisions: more than 40 trains and several thousand wagons weekly.[68]

While the artillery barrage went forward against the fortifications, Prussian engineers continued to push forward a system of classic entrenchments: a series of four lateral trenches, 100 yards long, and, every 50 yards, two 400-yard vertical connectors. In front of the foremost parallel, 100 feet from the main bastion wall, were a series of four storming trenches. All of this between the Wemmingbund Sound to the south and the village road, where they judged the terrain broken up and more favourable for an infantry rush. According to one account, the Danes allowed the Prussians to pursue the erection of trenches, parallels and batteries without molestation. Orders were not to fire upon earthworks in preparation, within range and in full view of Danish batteries.[69] Agricultural elite warriors held back, honouring their enemies' work? In reality, the Danes did not have the guns or ammunition to respond. Equally important, as soon as a Danish gun fired, giving its position away by the smoke, within a few moments answering Prussian guns had put it *hors de combat*. Prussian artillery totally dominated.

In April the weather was cold for an English January but both armies were well fed and clothed. The sun was not powerful, winds came fresh from the Arctic regions. In the shade it froze all day long, the ground as hard as iron, ponds and ditches coated with ice. Every few hours there was a pelting storm, powdering the countryside with a fresh layer of snow.

The siege went on. Prussian rifled heavy siege guns were so superior, they fired at will from a safe distance, taking the lives of their enemies without exposing their own.[70] The Danes lay in their trenches, unable to respond, waiting for the shells to arrive. They counted: it was ten seconds from the departure of a shell at the Prussian artillery position on Broagerland to its arrival at Dybbol.[71] Every other evening, about dusk, the Danish troops relieved each other at the batteries and evacuated the various camps and posts on the eastern slope of Dybbol hill. The relieving soldiers had to march from their Alsen Island farm quarters through the town of Sonderburg, across the open bridges and up the exposed hillside. From the moment they crossed the summit of Sonderburg hill they were under fire.

After a while even Sonderburg village became a war zone. The great open space in front of the castle, which the troops had to pass every morning on their way to the front, was filled with carpenters making coffins. Still the Danes fought on. In late March a regiment of Copenhagen Guards arrived. With tall bearskin caps, they looked a race of giants and had that professional air which was not shared by the rank and file of the army.[72]

English newspaper correspondent Edward Dicey walked across the long bridge from Sonderburg to Dybbol. A young Danish soldier walking to battle, fell in with him. He was a boy, toiling under a heavy knapsack. He said he had not changed his clothes in a week, spending night after night in the trenches, till five or six in the morning, then a long trudge home, and by nine he had to be on parade. And yet there was no discontent. It was all in a day's work.[73]

Danish casualties mounted to 100 per day. Even on Alsen one could not get away from the war. Ambulances crowded the roads, as did powder trains and long files of wagons loaded with military stores. In every village, in almost every house, soldiers were quartered. Small Danish flag pennants waved in front of farmyards, denoting the presence of some officer in command. The roadside hedges far and wide had been cut down by the Danes in order to make fascines for the fortifications.[74] Fascines, familiar to Roman soldiers, are long cylindrical bundles of small sticks, bound together. They are used in raising batteries, filling ditches, strengthening ramparts, and making parapets and revetments.[75]

Meanwhile Prussian laterals and storming trenches pushed ever closer to the fortifications. And as the half-circle around Dybbol got smaller, the political situation heated up. Britain tried to set up a conference to save its protégé. Sentiment was that a bad impression would have been made if Prussia and Austria had had to appear at the conference, nine weeks after the evacuation of the Danewerk, without having accomplished anything against the small kingdom.

Prince Friedrich Charles convened a war council to ask if they should try storming from the third parallel.[76] The two leading professional soldiers, artillery general Hindersin who had taken over technical leadership of the siege and Blumenthal, Friedrich Charles' chief of staff and

Moltke's daily correspondent, spoke against it. The prince decided instead on three more days' bombardment and then to take another look. Through the diplomatic ability of Bismarck and the natural slowness of the German Confederation, the conference was put off. An aide came to headquarters with this information and the king's request to get the job done quickly because he could not put Lord Palmerston off for ever.

By this time there was no longer any town for the soldiers to take refuge in. As long as Sonderburg remained the headquarters, the troops were cheered by each other's company. And by the consciousness that they formed part of a force which was still considerable. After weeks of continuous shelling, 100 shells in 15 minutes, 10000 in a day: except for one or two buildings, the town was destroyed and the army dispersed in small detachments all over the countryside outside of artillery range.[77]

The Danes in the fortifications were not numerous enough to make a sortie. But they had to keep forces close to their bastions and block-houses in case the Prussians attacked on foot. Marching to and fro, they waited. Daily casualties were kept secret. But Dicey met the daily train of sick and wounded, being carried by cart to Hoerup-Haf to be shipped to Copenhagen. Forty carts, with four men per cart, with a similar train coming daily from Augustenburg.[78]

By 14 April, many thousand shells a day were dropped on to the Dybbol fortifications, as 18 batteries of field artillery and eight companies of heavy siege guns fired almost continuously.[79]

That day, after a night of continuous bombardment, a Danish council of war was held. Among the officers the wisdom of exposing the army to this hapless slaughter was gravely questioned. There was a strong desire to end the war. They believed Danish honour had been satisfied.[80]

The morning of 17 April there was a brief truce. At the great inn in the centre of Sonderburg, untouched by shells, in the charge of a single bar-maid, the cellar was exhausted, with the exception of a few barrels of beer. The rooms were all shut up, the only inmates a half-dozen soldiers, loi-tering in the taproom and paying court to the barmaid, whose love of admiration exceeded her fear of cannon balls. The only sign of life in the town was the making of coffins. Military undertakers had been driven out of their spot in the open space in front of the castle, and now carried on their trade in a sort of sand pit, close to the high road at the brow of Sonderburg hill. There army carpenters hammered busily away at a great number of coffins. Others were painting them a dull deep black colour. Elaborate and cumbersome boxes. The demand exceeded the supply and the stock in hand was low. Though it was Sunday, the work continued.[81]

Troops became more and more unwilling to cross the bridge. Desertion became common. On the Dybbol hill, the forts most exposed were completely silent, their guns dismounted and destroyed.[82] At 2 p.m. Prussian firing grew brisker. Everybody at Sonderburg had got used to the crash of artillery and the sound of shells, but there was no doubt that this was different. More than 1000 shells fell in an hour. The roar of artillery was incessant. Prussians firing from new positions acquired on the 17th from Avn-Bierg on the Wemming Bund, through Dybbol and Ragebol villages to Sand-Bierg on the Als Sund. Suddenly a white puff of smoke from the castle of Sonderburg, at the entrance to the Als Sund harbour. The first shot was put down to deviation of a gun aimed at Dybbol bastion. But then, at one-minute intervals, shell followed shell. Evening came on, guns continued. Every shot seemed to take effect. Two Wemming Bund batteries were shelling the lower part of Sonderburg. The Danish batteries were silent.[83]

As the dusk deepened, blood-red patches of flame appeared on the hillside of the town. Barracks which had been run up for the troops were burning and the fierce cold winds fanned the flames into a devouring fire. The centre of the city had three sections: from the bridge to the town, a crooked narrow thoroughfare, then a broad straight section from the town hall to the military post office, with all the main shops and houses, and a third, steep winding alley from the post office to the windmills and open country. Up to then the first and third of these sections were untouched. The deadly fire of the Prussians had concentrated on the middle section, the main official and business section, the Regent Street of Sonderburg. Most of the windows had been broken and there were great chasms in many roofs. But still the houses were open and several occupied by soldiers.[84] Now this whole quarter became a mass of bare walls, charred rafters and tottering chimneys, enveloped in a dim haze of a smouldering smoke. The remaining walls looked near to toppling over. Brick and lath and plaster were laid bare to the elements, gutted. Heaps of blackened bricks lay everywhere. The bare walls of the town hall were standing, but the roof and flooring had disappeared. The streets were covered with shell fragments, tiles and rafters. Fifteen hundred shells had wrought this havoc.[85]

The next day, 18 April, having opened a fourth parallel, the Prussian 'storming' took place. It was completely successful in less than 20 minutes. Two days later, Lord John Russell, British prime minister, called the London Conference for 1 June. In the battle for Dybbol there were almost 5000 Danish and 1000 Prussian casualties. In 26 intense days the

Danish Army had sustained over 100 casualties a day, the Prussian Army almost 20. Military men did not think this a particularly successful operation but it was greatly celebrated in Berlin as the first Prussian military victory in 50 years.

Moltke as Chief of Staff

In the six weeks between the taking of Dybbol and the beginning of the London Conference, the allies did nothing.[86] Wrangel and Gablenz wanted to seize Jütland and then attack Alsen. Moltke argued against this, saying that Jütland was only defended by 3000–4000 men, against 9000 Prussians; that Frederica was held by 6000 men, against 20 000 Prussians, that on Alsen Island were only 11 000–18 000 Danes against 22 000 Prussians. Moltke convinced King Wilhelm and the king convinced Austrian Emperor Franz Joseph. In a sudden and unexpected move Wrangel was retired and sent back to Berlin.[87] Moltke was appointed chief of staff to Prince Friedrich Charles, new commander-in-chief. They would go forward on two fronts simultaneously: seizing Alsen Island and occupying Jütland.

From 12 May to 30 June there was an armistice. The London Conference followed. It seemed to some that the Danes would be willing to negotiate, having lost at Dybbol. However, in reality the Prussians and Austrians had not gained anything worthwhile. For ten weeks the allied powers had fought, but their tiny opponent still held the island of Alsen, a large piece of Schleswig and most of Jütland. The Danish regime believed itself in no way defeated.[88] It was not ready to renounce the whole of Schleswig and could not decide upon a line of division. So they had to fight again.

The Amphibious Invasion of Alsen Island, 29 June

For the cross-channel attack and seizure of Alsen Island, the troops took up war positions on 20 June. Six days later the armistice ran out. Although the entire land side of Alsen Island, from south to north, was a fortified entrenchment covered with breastwork and trenches, Danish equipment was outdated.[89] West of Kjar village, lay a deep bay which divided the coastline into two parts.[90] Along this coast were 32 batteries, in all 64 guns. But many were canister guns and blunderbusses: short guns with large bores and bell muzzles capable of holding a number of balls. These were military shotguns, obsolete in 1864. The Danish defenders, roughly 18 000 men, did not expect or anticipate an invasion, although they had thought about it in theory and placed troops at various positions. Across from Ballegard, the most likely spot, were six regiments. Between Satrupholz and Sandberg were four regiments and between Dybbol and Rackbull two more, with a two-regiment reserve near Ulkebuell, where headquarters was located. In an hour reserves could theoretically show up at any point. However, the Danes believed themselves impregnable. They were convinced that a cross-channel invasion was impossible. Their confidence was total, their preparations for invasion nil. Even after Prussian troops had landed, the Danes could not believe it was happening.

Prussian forward planning for this operation was extraordinary.[91] During the entire period of the armistice two former Schleswigers, a ship captain and a boat builder, assembled a flotilla of 140 boats near Rendsburg. The largest could hold 40 men, the smallest ten. Two pontoon bridges were prepared by the engineer and pioneer corps.[92] Twenty-seven artillery batteries were set up: over 70 guns faced the channel, ready for both Danish naval intervention and shore units straight across the water.[93]

At first they decided to go across at Ballegard and moved the main forces there, but they found out that the Danes had prepared for it, so at the last minute, on 27 June, they shifted the force to the area between Schabeckhage and Satrupholz, closer to Sonderburg, where the smallest contingent of Danish troops was billeted.

Moltke was on hand, with his staff – Quartermaster General Ferdinand von Podbielski, adjutant Major von Kleist, engineer officer Colonel Karl Friedrich von Mertens – at the launching of the cross-channel attack. They left Alpenrade, where the headquarters was located, after finishing their game of whist at 10 p.m.[94] The weather was quiet and still but he had a sense of the whole of Alsen Island laid out before him from the top of fortified blockhouse No. 10 on the peak of Dybbol hill. Moltke watched everything: the crossing, the shore batteries opening up, the appearance of the Danish ironclad steamship *Rolf Krake* and its retreat at the shelling by Prussian 24-pound shore guns, the Danish use of underwater mines.

It was 2 a.m. on a dark black night, air temperature 20–30 °F (-6 to -1 °C). There was no moon, one could not see ten feet. Crossings began at 2 a.m. at four points. The most westward 30 boats were sent against

Ballegard as a decoy: to convince the Danes that the crossing would be mainly there. No convincing was needed: the Danes were asleep, with pickets and outposts unmanned.

Eleven minutes across the 850-foot wide Alsensund. It was 2.11 a.m., Column A opposite Arnkiel, landed first, led by fishermen and ship captains. The water depth was even, with a gradual fall off for 100 yards. In the first boat was the Prussian flag. Prussians landed, assembled and readied for the storm. They moved close to the entrenchments, finally came the first shot, then loud 'hurrahs' and the charge was on. Shore firing broke out all along the line, many boats were hit, a few sank. The men were good swimmers and made strongly for shore. The defenders retreated, a Prussian flag was planted on the breastwork, and enemy guns were captured which had not fired a shot.

The 5th Company was the first up the bank. With 'hurrahs' they broke the silence and charged against the fortified trenches. In ten minutes the position was taken: 50 prisoners were ferried across the water. The Danes fled to Kjar and Bagmose. The Prussians halted and awaited orders.

At another point, the Prussians were in the water an hour. By this time, artillery from both shores lit up the sky. As the boats neared the shore they were met with bullets and canister shot. The bank was eight feet high, they sprang over it, but met very weak resistance. Behind them came another wave of 37 large boats. At 200 feet they began taking fire. The 64th regimental band began playing the 'Storm March'. They hit the beach, and sprang forward, with club, bayonet and sabre, moving into the trenches, capturing men, guns and horses. By 3.30 a.m. they had moved with 'hurrahs' to Roenhof, Kjar and Bagmose.[95]

In an hour the Sund was crossed and the enemy shoreline defences defeated. The Prussians moved inland. The Danes were completely unprepared; they had not expected this. One encounter battle tells the story.

An hour after it began, in the freezing pitch dark, it became known at Danish headquarters that the enemy had landed and was attacking across the island. The Danes counterattacked in uncoordinated lines, singly and without overall leadership. Colonel Carl Faaborg, brigade commander at headquarters, took command of the nearest four companies, led them northwards, arriving on the extreme left flank of the 64th Prussian Regiment. Faaborg's four companies and the 3rd Company of the Prussian 64th Regiment were marching on parallel roads, when Faaborg's forces abruptly turned 90 degrees west. Neither saw the other until the last 100 feet, when sounds from the forward skirmishers alerted them. Immediately the Danes readied to charge with bayonets. Their route was narrow and constricted by a series of knicks. The Prussian company quickly organized, and met the four Danish companies from behind knicks with quick fire, firing as fast as they could shoot. The compressed Danes were mowed down. Colonel Faaborg, hit by many shots, fell from his horse and the attack dissipated.[96] He died the next day. Alsen Island was under Prussian control by dusk. The ratio of Danish to Prussian casualties was 8 : 1.[97]

The Battle of Lundby, 1 July

Meanwhile, 40 miles to the north, the occupation of Jütland moved forward. Twelve days after seizing Alsen Island, the Lim Fjord was taken in two places at once: the Austrians occupied the western part, the Prussians the eastern end. Lundby is a village on the eastern point, a mile from the Lim Fjord. On 1 July three Prussian reconnaissance units approached it, the first to the south-west, the second to the south-east and the third directly south. Only the third fought. And of its three elements – at Soender-Tranders 90 hussars and 20 infantry, in Lindenborg 71 infantry, at Lundby 124 infantry – only the last one – the first company of the 50th Regiment of Lower Silesian Infantry – engaged. At Lundby Captain von Schlutterbach's half company were in the village, they had stacked their weapons and were resting. It was 4.30 a.m. He himself had gone north on reconnaissance. As he returned, he saw Danish forces – a regiment of infantry and a squadron of dragoons, roughly 200 soldiers – approaching atop the hillside ridge line from the south. An advance scout section of the enemy was about to begin shooting. It was a critical moment.

The Prussians picked up their weapons and in running march took up positions behind a dozen knicks that were planted in the gardens south of the village; 64 men were there, with 48 in reserve hidden behind houses to the rear. At 600 feet, up on the heights, three companies of Danes formed into a column and advanced, 12 men abreast and 20 deep.

The young Prussian soldiers wanted to seize the moment and open fire, but their cool commander quieted them: let them come closer. I will tell you when to fire.

The Danish troops halted at 300 feet and readied their weapons to fire. They were disquieted and unsettled – made restless by the deep and

absolute silence from the few defenders confronting their overwhelmingly superior force. The Danes, out of breath and in extreme anxiety,
awaited the first shot. Prussian fingers on the triggers were itchy, 'Herr
Captain, shall we go after them now?' 'Not yet, children, wait.' The
Danes moved to 250 feet. There was absolute silence.[98]

The command rang out, 250 feet, stand ready, now in God's name
fire! Both sides fired, the first line of 12 Danes against 64 Dreyse rifles
behind tall sand knicks. The first salvo crashed through the Danish
lines. The smoke cleared, two officers and many men had fallen, but the
Danish units were standing fast. They moved forward to 200 feet and
began to reload. Again the Prussian command rang out and again a
Prussian salvo rocked the Danish lines. Smoke cleared, great gaps in the
Danish lines, whole rows on the ground.[99] The Danes moved to 150 feet,
laboriously reloading. A third salvo roared forwards, hitting and scyth-
ing across those Danes still standing. As the Danes, now 60–80 feet away,
reloaded for the final assault and bayonet charge, the Prussians opened
up with quick fire: each man fired as rapidly as he could reload, 60 men
firing a shot every 15 seconds, almost 400 shots a minute. Half of the
remaining Danes were killed or wounded on the spot. The column
broke apart and retreated, seeking shelter from this firestorm.[100]

In 20 minutes, while three Prussians were hurt, more than half of a
force of 200 Danes were killed or wounded. One every nine seconds.
Most Danes were hit with three or four bullets, some by seven or eight.[101]

For example, Danish First Lieutenant Conrad Betzholz, from the
Swedish Guard Regiment 'The Queen's', shot first in the shoulder, nevertheless sprang forward and stayed with the moving column. Shot
again, shattering his left arm, he was knocked to the ground. As Prussian
troops tried to take him to a field medical station, he forbid this, got to
his feet, staggered back to his troops and tried to lead them again in
fighting. His left arm now hanging in ribbons and bones, he sank help-
lessly to the ground, asking the nearest Prussians to end his life. Don't
bother with me, he said, take care of your own.[102] Prussian surgeons at
first hoped for the best, but he got infections in his lungs and brain. He
was much visited by Prussian officers and his spirit won all hearts. A
Danish nun from the Munster Sisterhood brought him flowers and
stayed with him day and night. His sister was a lady-in-waiting to the
Swedish royal family and his funeral in the village of Holbro attracted
hundreds. There was a torchlight procession at 9 p.m., and a wooden
coffin with hundreds of coloured ribbons in Danish and Swedish colours,
two Danish flags and a Swedish banner. On a silver plate were engraved

the words, 'Conrad Betzholz, born in Stockholm 1827, wounded near Lundby, died in Holbro, 28 July 1864. All Danish hearts honour his memory.' The streets were covered with flowers and fresh leaves. Danish and Prussian officers attended. In front of the city hall, a Lutheran pastor gave the benediction, and the city choir sang the final goodbye.

Betzholz's silver dagger, a gift from the King of Sweden, had been taken by Captain von Schlutterbach as a memento of the battle. When his family requested it back, he readily gave it up. Officers of the Swedish Guard Regiment 'Queens' sent Schlutterbach a beautiful dagger in return.[103]

When the war had resumed on 26 June, things happened in rapid fashion. In four days Alsen Island fell, thereafter Austrian and Prussian ships, aided by their land forces, occupied the west coastal islands of Denmark. Meanwhile other forces pushed north to Frederikshaven on the northern tip of the peninsula. On 20 July a new armistice was signed, and on 25 July a peace conference was opened. No Prussian–Austrian concessions were forthcoming and a preliminary peace was signed on 1 August. The Treaty of Vienna, signed at the end of October 1864, handed over Holstein, Schleswig and Lauenburg to the King of Prussia and Emperor of Austria.[104]

Two of the king's adjutants, princes Hohenlohe and Metternich, came up to Denmark to distribute medals. Moltke was given the Crown Order 1st class, with sword, and the Grand Cross of the Order of Leopold, War Decorated, two cordons to add to his dress uniform, and a nice handwritten letter from the king.[105] Moltke and Prince Friedrich Charles and their staff played whist.[106]

On the way home Moltke and his wife rode part of the way in an open carriage. They were recognized and repeatedly cheered. Marie was embarrassed. With the campaign ended, Moltke thought about retiring. He would soon be 65. His position as chief of the GGS was at the lieutenant-general grade, to get promoted he needed a corps command. Neither of his predecessors had been promoted. There was talk of Moltke taking the VII Corps. But he had been too long away from troop duty to do these things, he did not have the eye for detail. With the conclusion of a victorious war and the full confidence and praise of the king, it was a good time to retire.[107] Finally he went to see the king and spoke with him about it. The king interrupted him in mid-sentence. Stop, I need you in all of your present duties.[108]

5

THE AUSTRIAN WAR, 1866

Opening

Prussia fought Austria and her allies from 14 May to 22 July 1866. For
Europe it was the last act in 100-year struggle for supremacy and leadership among the German-speaking states. For world military affairs it
was a benchmark in war-planning processes, validating 50 years of invisible development with a startling upset victory. And certifying Moltke as
a planning genius of the first order.

Finally, it brought the kingdom of Prussia more than $1 billion in
war indemnities, killed and wounded 52 000 men – 20 per cent of the
Austrians engaged – and destroyed 7000 horses.[1] For individuals and
units involved came lots of undifferentiated chaos: death and destruction
to which duty and fate delivered some and spared others.

The whole affair was a sudden, even unexpectedly astonishing, surprise. As a world-renowned military critic wrote before it began, it would
be very surprising if the superior leadership, organization, tactics and
morale of the Austrians did not prevail.[2]

Moltke had the whole Austrian War in his head several years before it
happened. As an artist he was constantly imaging the world. As a soldier
he was constantly thinking about future war possibilities. As chief of the
General Staff, Moltke had almost ten years of war gaming, staff rides
and manoeuvres worth of looking at possibilities. Possibilities on paper,
at the sand table, possibilities riding through the countryside with two
dozen officers or with the king and two divisions or corps. Moltke
thought in terms of constantly changing scenarios. His mind imaged
war possibilities as a director images shots in a film: with the whole film
in mind. Possibilities came and went. Each one inevitably suggested

others. Each door closed opened others not apparent before. The trick
was to balance and relate the separate individual moments to the pro-
jected image as a whole. No one else in Europe or the world looked at
war in this way in 1865.

Except perhaps Ulysses S. Grant. By autumn 1865 Moltke knew a
great deal about the American Civil War. How could he not? Moltke was
a professional soldier. This was the biggest war – by far – going on in the
world at that time. Casualties were over a million. Forces engaged were
several million. The stage was many hundred thousand square miles.
The audience of observers was vast. The word got out. Rifled artillery
barrages that levelled cities and decimated ranks of soldiers as at
Gettysburg and Petersburg, rifle fire that swept away attackers as at
Malvern Hill in 1862, causing 5000 casualties in two hours.[3] Railroads
that carried 80 000 men 1200 miles in time to change the course of battles as at Chattanooga in 1863. Coordination by telegraph of units separated by vast distances of time and space. The American Civil War was
over for more than a year by the time the Austrian War started: ample
time for Moltke to understand and incorporate some of its novel principles of industrial mass warfare. And so he did.

The Two Armies

In 1866 the kingdom of Prussia had four important but invisible advantages over the Austrian Empire. Invisible because, like Frederick Engels
quoted above, no one saw them.

The General Staff organization, after a half-century of slow development, was the only one of its kind in the world. Austria, in contrast, had
something called a 'General Staff' but it was not one. Little serious work
was done in it, ranking and able officers shunned it and the top command
structure did not use it. This had immense ramifications. All the way from
the fact that Prussia could mobilize and concentrate in half the time it took
Austria, to the command and control of forces once mobilized, to a certain
uniformity among divisions and corps when they – in combat, separated
and out of touch with their command and control headquarters – decided
what to do. The Prussian system was established, tested and practised.

The second Prussian advantage was with respect to commanders-in-
chief. Again reality was the opposite of what most people at the time
believed. The Austrian commander, Field Marshal Ludwig Benedek, was
a tested combat veteran from a dominant superpower, universally considered one of Europe's top field generals. Moltke was an unknown general

who headed an obscure agency within a subordinate kingdom aspiring to central European leadership. His only combat experience had been in the far-off and unknown Ottoman–Egyptian War. At age 66 – retirement age – he was not widely known even in his own army. As one of the king's adjutants described the situation: 'The king in command, at the age of 70, with the decrepit Moltke at his side! What will come of it all?'[4]

Beneath the veneer of fame and obscurity, each man's approach to risk was diametrically opposite, and this was the third advantage. For one thing Benedek had spent nearly his whole career in Italy: he lacked confidence in the novel terrain to which he was now assigned.[5] As the most recent account of the Austrian War says, Benedek was a hesitant, weak-willed pessimist.[6] At home leading a corps, he was lost with anything larger. Benedek was cautious and slow to respond to developing battlefield situations. From 11 a.m. to 3 p.m. on the battle day of Königgrätz [Sadova], 2 July, the 'zero moment' period of the war, the transition from crisis to catastrophe, Benedek did nothing and his army lost their chance. Of course he had no instrument to help him decide: no competent staff and no clear lines of communication and control back and forth to his corps. In the thick of the battle he often had to go and see for himself what was happening and then often drew the wrong conclusion. As he himself recognized, he was way out of his depth. Of his two chief advisors, one, Krismanic, was a rigid conservative, cautious to the point of timidity, the other, Henikstein, cynical and hypercritical, believed Austria could not win.[7] Henikstein had not read Engels.

Moltke, in contrast, was a strategic virtuoso, cool and self-confident. He had a competent staff, both at headquarters and out in the corps, plans which had been worked out and war-gamed for months, clear lines of communication out and back, but, above all, a certain attitude towards risk. Moltke differentiated uncertainty – the inability to know for sure what would happen – from risk – those factors that could be quantified by size, space and time.

However, there was a problem. Within the Prussian high command few understood his ideas.[8] Moltke and several dozen colleagues had adopted modern war-planning processes. Few others had: not in the king's entourage, not at the highest command levels of the army. Here and there were chiefs of staff who knew what was going on in Moltke's head, but a certain number of Prussian general officers were agricultural elite warriors, traditionalists of the old school.

For example, one of the king's closest advisors, General Gustav von Alvensleben, wrote Moltke three letters late in June 1866, warning him his plan was too much of a gamble to pull off. The assembly of forces on the eastern side of the Silesian Mountains was just what the Austrians wanted, he said. The Austrians would defeat one Prussian army and then turn on the other two. Even the Bavarians might attack the widely dispersed Prussians, unable to help each other out. Alvensleben counselled Moltke to concentrate all his troops on the western side of the mountains, seize Dresden, then secure Hanover and north Germany. That way, he said, Prussia would risk nothing, and gain strength and support. This is not just a more conservative risk projection, it is virtually risk free, except that it left unaddressed the only serious, lethal opponent, Austria.

Moltke did not respond to these letters. How could he? In terms of pure logic, Alvensleben was right. But Moltke had already gone to the next level: beyond pure logic to risk calculation. He figured two Prussian armies could withstand the numerically superior Austrians long enough for the third to show up. 'Long enough' meant a maximum of four hours. Then they would move from tactical–operational weakness to strategic strength.[9]

A final Prussian advantage was in weapons and training. The bolt action Dreyse gun could be loaded and fired from the prone position four or five times faster than the Austrian muzzle-loader which had to be armed standing up. The Austrians had drawn the wrong conclusions from their experiences against France seven years earlier. Beaten by French shock tactics – the bayonet charge – Franz Joseph decided never again to trust to fire. Only the momentum of attacking bayonets would do it. Prussian infantry was trained to do the opposite. Whereas Austrian recruits hardly fired a dozen rounds in a year, working at cheap, traditional shock tactics, Prussians fired a lot. Austrian sights were fixed by their NCOs. Prussian soldiers adjusted their own, all the while practising movement and support.[10]

So whatever surface appearances seemed at the start of the war, realities were very different. In spite of this the outcome was by no means preordained. On the contrary, Prussia made many mistakes and opened itself up at the zero moment time to possible catastrophe. Austria made more mistakes, but above all its commander refused to act at the zero point of the battle. Cumulatively over time these pluses and minuses added up. So did casualties. As casualties mounted, morale changed.

History Lessons from 1864

What did Prussia learn from the Danish War? Moltke wrote these lessons down in the July 1864 *Militär-Wochenblatt* and in the GGS History of the

Figure 5.1 The Prussian Royal War Council, 1866 and 1870. This was the decision-making group, roughly equivalent to President John F. Kennedy's 'Ex Comm' group during the Cuban missile crisis of 1962. Prussian King Wilhelm I seated at the left table end, Moltke seated in the middle of the table, Count Otto von Bismarck, Prussian Minister-President, seated at the right side. Crown Prince Friedrich is standing beside the king, his father, and War Minister von Roon is standing at the right table end, behind Bismarck. Behind the king's chair and closest to Moltke is his staff officer Julius von Verdy du Vernois and behind the crown prince is his chief of staff Karl Leonhard von Blumenthal. Note the seat placement the king at one end, Bismarck at the other, and Moltke in the middle, symbolizing the balance of power between politics and the military during these three wars. Note the standees: Roon over Bismarck's right shoulder – he and the king had served together as young lieutenants, and they were drinking friends; Anton von Werner, the Berlin artist who did this scene, has given Roon a speaking part here not representative of his actual weight in wartime deliberations. The other standees are the crown prince, animated as usual, and the two staff officers, both highly treasured by Moltke and well respected by everyone at the table (Courtesy Ullstein Bilderdienst, Berlin)

Danish War.[11] First, that the Dreyse breech-loader had unimagined strength in a defensive position against attacking muzzle-loaders. Second, its obverse, a frontal attack across open land against defending, protected troops was to be avoided at all costs. Third, that artillery preparation before an infantry attack could be very effective. Fourth, that a defensive position which forced the enemy into a frontal attack, followed up by a Prussian counterattack, worked. Fifth, that company-sized units would no longer do: battalion and even brigade firepower now began to be emphasized in troop exercises.

What did Prussia learn about the Austrian Army in the Danish War? Its generals were swashbucklers from good families who dashed ever forward. Its staff officers were young and conservative, lacking judgement and independence. Its cavalry was praiseworthy, its artillery not as good as it had been. Its line infantry was very mixed: language differences between the dozen or so ethnic contingents worked against tactical cohesion.Prussian commanders realized that to get troops to work hard in battle, officers had to appeal to their spirit. This the Austrians seldom could do because they, like the troops they commanded, did not know each other's languages. Austrian operations were slow and dense with heavy casualties assumed.[12]

Moltke now took these observations to the next level. Just prior to the autumn 1864 GGS ride and royal manoeuvres, he had published an essay on 'march depth'. Moltke saw two separate fundamentals from military history coming together. One derived from the increased size of armies, the longer ranges of rifled artillery and the use of railroads. The size and scope of strategic planning and control were suddenly much larger. Operationally, this change necessitated another: the explicit division of this larger army during the approach, then a uniting at the point of battle. Joined together these observations became the famous slogan known throughout the army: 'march separately, fight together'.

Although Moltke did not realize it at the time, this concept was firmly grounded in transportation theory.[13] Specifically, on the degree to which distance impacts spatial integration: the beginning of a 'space–time convergence'. Moltke stated this theory nicely when he said that Prussia could send troops into Denmark faster by railroad than the Danes could get them there by ship and on foot. A corollary to this relates transportation costs to specialization of labour. High-cost transportation – defined as slow, fatiguing and scattered – and illustrated by walking or animal power – resulted in relatively low specialization of labour divided between many small local organizations. Low-cost transportation – defined as fast, economical and concentrated – and illustrated by railroads, allowed maximum specialization of labour within a few large units.[14] In military terms this meant the possibility of increased specialization of labour within each corps. Examples of this during the

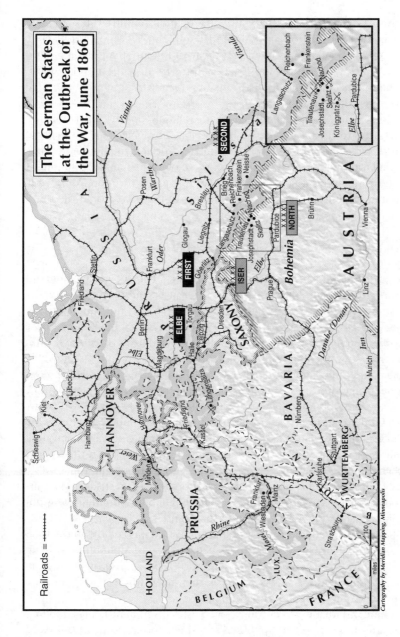

Figure 5.2 The German states in 1866 (Philip Schwartzberg © Meridian Mapping)

Danish War were the artillery–infantry relationship at Dybbol and the sea–land coordination at Alsen Island. Specialization of labour depended on enlarging the military market to more than half a million men, which allowed this much larger force to meet the novel requirements of specific combat situations over a much larger spatial range within the time limits imposed.

Moltke joined theory and practice so closely that his ideas may be compared to fractal geometry. It describes real objects in the natural world. Or, stated more closely to Moltke's working methods, it is concerned with making spatial intuition more objective.[15] Moltke's thought patterns remind us that the more perfect the artist, the more completely separate in him will be the man who lives in the present and the mind which creates for the future.[16]

Changes, 1864–66

In the 19 months between September 1864, when the army command returned to Berlin, and April 1866, when it began to mobilize for the Austrian War, there were many changes.[17] Moltke now attended the king's council when strategic matters were on the table. A three-phase supply system was put in place. Soldiers were given three days' 'iron rations', supply columns followed with three days' supplies, movable magazines came later with heavier goods. War games and field exercises dramatically shortened mobilization times. In the autumn of 1864 they knew it took too long. The army was made up of 34 per cent regulars and 66 per cent reserves. How could this mix be combined better? One conclusion was that Prussian garrison troops were too concentrated. They spread them out – again grounded in transportation theory and specialization of labour – increasing garrison cities from 234 to 330. Only engineer and supply units had single city garrisons. As war-mobilized strength now rose above 600 000, mobilization time was gradually reduced to 30 days, then into the twenties.[18]

Railroads speeded this up. A Railroad Section was created in the GGS with Count Herman von Wartensleben in charge. Moltke intended to use his advantage here. As he wrote in April 1866, against Austria we can concentrate in three weeks, whereas they need twice as long because they have only a single railroad line in Bohemia.[19]

There was further decentralization. District commands, local military headquarters, were set up based on their connections to railroads, telegraph and corps headquarters. GGS officers now oversaw the districts and by doing this the GGS gained immediate influence over mobilization preparation. By spring 1866, with the exception of the Guard Corps, which was recruited from the kingdom as a whole, each corps was stationed in the region from which its reserves came. Within each corps, district commands slowly assumed more and more prominent roles. In peacetime they kept muster rolls, tested out alert procedures, held courts of honours and carried out other administrative roles. In war, district commands organized mobilization.[20]

Finally the GGS was enlarged and divided in two. The Secondary Bureau, a specific technical competency whose product – maps – was widely used outside the military in the burgeoning industrial economy, was split off and given its own quarters and administration. Certain General Staff officers, whose knowledge and competency were unique, were exempted from troop rotation duty, giving more continuity to planning processes. The GGS and War Academy both expanded.

All of these together meant that the Prussian Army was entering a period of intense change.

The Austrian War

Soon after the end of the Danish War it was clear that Austria did not want any part of Schleswig or Holstein. Prussia was willing to buy it, but Austria wanted to swap it with Prussia for land elsewhere, perhaps along the Silesian border, or to sell it to a third party. From the moment when this was clear, Bismarck began thinking about war.[21]

In January and February 1866 questions over what to do with the Danish provinces strained relations between the two German Great Powers. Bismarck soon began negotiating an alliance with the Italians: he assumed it would be needed for a war against Austria. On the day this secret alliance was signed, 8 April, the Prussian delegate to the Germanic Confederation presented Bismarck's reform plan for this body, designed mainly to infuriate Austria more. Within two weeks news of Italian troop movements forced an Austrian partial mobilization.[22] As we will see below, counter-mobilizations were essential in causing the war of 1866. But, as William Carr says, the Austro-Prussian War was essentially a power struggle for mastery of Germany, an eighteenth-century war fought with nineteenth-century weapons. Austria wanted to keep the balance of power as it was. Prussia wanted to alter this balance in favour of herself.[23] Bismarck, drawing upon the new forces of nationalism,

Prussian war processes and his colleague Moltke, the first modern war planner, brought it about.

King Wilhelm was very reluctant to fight his brother emperor to the south-east. Habsburg Austria had been the dominant Germanic Great Power for several hundred years. Wilhelm had grown up under this ancient power lineage. Moltke, raised in Copenhagen, had no 'such sentimental attachments. As a professional soldier he had begun a year before thinking about, talking about and planning this war.[24]

Fourteen months before it began, on 29 May 1865, a royal council straw vote showed four pro-war, one hesitant and two against. The king asked Moltke: What is the feeling in the army? Moltke said he believed this was a war they could win.[25]

War Plans

During winter 1865, Moltke sketched out a number of scenarios. Then he gave each one a 'stress test': subjecting it to worst-case hypotheticals and war games.[26]

His ideas had changed from the previous decade. He had a much better sense of Prussia's strengths and Austria's weaknesses. He estimated that Austria could put 240 000 troops into northern Bohemia and that 25 000 Saxon troops in Dresden would join them. Should Prussia concentrate in the north-west in the Lausatian region or in the south-east, in Silesia? Silesia was the indirect and long way, but, if Prussia threatened Vienna and Prague, Austria might advance on Berlin. Clearly if Prussia could arrive sooner and in greater strength at the battle area, that was the thing to do.[27] What if the south Germans mobilized 80 000 men at Bamberg to augment the Austrian Army on the Elbe River? This would take a long time and Prussia's VIII Corps could deal with this situation. All told, Moltke figured 300 000 Prussians or as many as the largest number Austria might raise. His initial deployments were at Mainz (52 000), Torgau (94 000), Goerlitz (99 000) and Schweidnitz (54 000).[28]

Since the mobilization of 1859, Moltke's war plans were drawn up with built-in periodization. Each segment of the plan was 'phased'. The number of phases depended on the strategic objectives, the training and war game experiences and the size, composition and quality of force levels. At that point the 1865 war plan had five phases: (1) war alert, (2) mobilization, (3) military transportation plan, (4) advance march, and (5) attack formations.[29] Each phase was numbered in days, and certain segments were divided into four-hour blocks. A part of the war plan against Austria was 'stress tested' in the September 1865 autumn manoeuvre around Merseburg, east of Leipzig, close to the railroad lines used by the Second Army in 1866.[30] It is important to recognize that the autumn 'royal manoeuvre' was not just military. Although the General Staff planned, coordinated and judged it, it was also a social and political event: the formal and official visit of the sovereign to the province. There was always a large parade, a troop review, an exercise against marked enemies and a three-day manoeuvre, with two corps competing against each other. The king gave a banquet for the army corps, another for the provincial officials, an evening dinner with the commanding generals and a special reception for the leading nobles of the province. One or two parades came in the middle of these activities, and the king made it a point to see and be seen by every man in each corps.[31]

A second test came in the October 1865 GGS ride between Weissenfels and Naumburg in the Reisen Mountains borderland of Saxony, just slightly north-east of the Magdeburg–Halle rail line, the main route of the First Army in 1866.[32] At that point, Moltke strategically imaged the whole Austrian War: Russia and France neutral, active assistance of Italy. Only the south German states posed an extra danger. Decisive operations would be launched against Austria on the direct line northern Silesia–Vienna.[33] One corps to hold and contain southern and western Germany, eight corps against Austria, building a numerical superiority at Brunn and Olmütz with sufficient size to threaten Vienna. The exact location for the concentration of the army in the Lausitz, with simultaneous attack marches in Saxony, was still unsettled but he continued to think in terms of the coming together of three armies – one moving south-east from Dresden, a second attacking due south from Goerlitz, with a third force wheeling south-west through the Silesian Mountains from Schweidnitz.

Moltke assumed Austria would attack: marching across Bohemia in short rapid marches to try to reach Berlin and split Prussia in two.[34] This assumption, coupled with poor or latecoming intelligence about what was really happening, proved unsettling in the actual war, because it was exactly what the Austrians did not do.

Counteractivity

Counteractivity is a key aspect of modern war and it began in February 1866. It means each side responds to the other's moves or presumed moves: what they know or think they know about their potential opponent's actions. Although formal, public war mobilizations – defined as those with public notices accompanied by highly visible large-scale troop movements – did not begin until late April, secret, preliminary moves began much earlier. As these moves were observed by each army, counteractive thinking also began.

At the 28 February Prussian royal cabinet meeting, the question was raised whether war with Austria was coming.[35] Moltke reported Austrian troops movements into Bohemia but he emphasized that Austrian units in Venice were not yet in the stage of war readiness. Moltke knew from the quality of the reports that there was no immediate danger. And he emphasized that there had been no signs of horse purchase.

Horse purchase was a fundamental element of nineteenth-century mobilization. The horse was an ancient symbol of military prestige and political power. Its imposing bulk and appearance, however, concealed a delicate and sensitive nature. A horse eats roughly ten times what a soldier eats in a 24-hour period. Horses are sensitive to climate change. They are prone to disease and, in combat, are easily wounded since they are the largest targets on the battlefield. Horses were critical but not because cavalry was a decisive aspect of war fighting. In reality cavalry was a leftover from agricultural elite war, of less and less impact in industrial mass war. But this leftover was still essential for transportation. These many hundred thousand-man armies could not move without tens of thousands of animals. Horses were graded according to use: cavalry, trains, field artillery and heavy artillery. And the numbers were large. In 1866 more than 120 000 horses were mobilized for war.[36] In 1870 the man to horse ratio was 4 : 1 : 250 000 horses were mobilized by Prussia and 300 000 by France. When several hundred thousand horses are mobilized – the horse purchase plan – hardly anyone fails to notice it.[37]

On 2 March Austria began limited mobilization and three days later Moltke reported his time anxieties to Roon. It was not the absolute number of troops, he said, but the time in which they are assembled that is important. A week later Prussian war plan phases began: phase one, alert and supply: commanders were made aware their units might be going to war, provisional fortress supply began for Dybbol, Sonderburg and Kiel and heavy gun placement was begun in the Silesian forts.[38]

Moltke again stress-tested his assumptions about the south German states. After an indoor war game, he concluded that if Bavaria used the Nuremberg–Prague–Dresden railroad, it might speed up Austrian mobilization. At that point he figured simultaneous mobilizations. Each day that Prussia did nothing, while Austria mobilized, decreased Prussian operational time.[39] A few days later the GGS began drafting mobilization orders. VI Corps, of the Silesian Army, was first up. On 23 March fortresses at Cosel, Neitze, Glatz, Torgau and Wittenberg were brought up to war strength and equipped with munitions and supplies. VI and I Corps were brought up to 'march ready' status, one notch below mobilization.[40] Artillery horse teams were placed 'in readiness' for these corps and for the 6th, 7th and 9th divisions. Horse purchase began for half of the field artillery and 155 reserves were added to each of 75 artillery battalions.[41]

At the 28 March ministerial conference the king was unconvinced that war was necessary. Bismarck's argument that it was better now than waiting until Austria moved into an advantageous position was not convincing.[42] Moltke suggested they bring in Italy. Then Austria would have at most 240 000 troops to fight us, we will have the same, plus 50 000 to deal with Bavaria. Bismarck convinced the king to send Moltke himself to Italy to complete negotiations.[43]

The next day the king signed orders to mobilize the 'war shield': five divisions to guard the Austrian and Saxon frontiers and to fully arm the border fortresses.[44] By 2 April, Saxon war preparations were reported. On top of this Moltke was concerned about VII and VIII Corps in Munich. If they pushed north-east to Prague, what then? Worse, alliance with Bavaria gave Austria access to a second railroad line into Bohemia. He cautioned the king that every day Austria mobilized before Prussia was dangerous.[45] The king saw only the numbers, Moltke also understood the time factors.

At this point Moltke made a critical decision. He changed the force structure and distribution. Prussian mobilization was dependent on railroad line commands. Five railroad lines stood ready to operate in the very favourable Lausatian region, and, for that reason, two Prussian armies were to assemble there. But they had also to protect Berlin. The most critical province in this respect was Silesia. Silesia had three advantages. For one thing it flanked Bohemia and offered the chance to attack a Berlin-aiming enemy force in the flank or rear. For another Silesia was a quicker way to the enemy than the Lausitz: hit the enemy on the side, cut the Austrians away from their reinforcements, finally attack their operational base point, Josephstadt–Königgrätz, from the flank or rear. Finally, and most important, Silesia was served by two main rail lines as far as Breslau, with three trunk lines extending many miles further south-west into the mountain foothills.

Therefore making Silesia a strong point of the concentration made sense. A 200-mile extension was added to the advance march from Liegnitz and Breslau south to Landshut, Frankenstein and Neisse, each one the last station on the railroad lines in the foothills of the mountains separating Silesia from the Bohemian plains. This force was then reinforced with twice as many troops as the Elbe Army, and one-third more than the First Army. It was to be the hammer that crushed the Austrians against the anvil of Elbe and First armies to their front.

Prussia's three armies were now positioned – on paper – exactly astride three main and six secondary rail lines. The Elbe Army moved on the Berlin–Dresden–Friedland railroad, the First Army on the Frankfurt–Goerlitz–Liegnitz line and the Second Army on the Stettin–Breslau–Langashutz–Reichenbach–Frankenstein and Brieg–Neisse railroads.[46] After short marches which were different for each unit, trains would begin delivering the field army to their jump-off points, more than 150 miles south of Berlin.[47]

As we saw above, on 8 April came the Prussian–Italian alliance. It opened a 90-day window: in the event Prussia declared war on Austria within the next three months, Italy would join Prussia. This flagrant violation of Article 11 of the Federal Constitution, which forbade members to enter into binding agreements directed against other federal states, weighed heavily on the king, who thought of it as a slur against his honour.[48] Wilhelm I wanted to fight an agricultural elite war. His General Staff had already turned the page.

On 9 April Theodore von Bernhardi, who had just returned from Vienna as Prussian emissary, had a lengthy conversation with Moltke. Austria's war plan, he said, was based on the experiences of the eighteenth century, especially the Austro-Prussian War of 1778–79.[49] It risked nothing and had very limited goals. It assumed Vienna was not a main object of the war, that a Prussian attack would be directed at Dresden on the one hand and at Prague on the other. One Austrian army was oriented to the north-east, the other to the north-west in the direction of Linz. In that case, Bernhardi argued, the two halves of the Austrian Army north of the Alps could not come together. If so, Prussia's two armies could unite near Mautern above the Strom River, threatening Vienna and the railroads as far as Soemmering. The Italians, meanwhile, had to hold and keep busy an important part of the Austrian Army. To do this, Bernhardi emphasized, Italy must position troops at Ancona and Ferrara and place its fleet on the lower Po and Etsch rivers.[50]

Moltke believed Austria would be much stronger than Bernhardi thought and would try an attack into the heart of the Prussian monarchy.

He apparently discounted Bernhardi. Or did he? If true, it confirmed his strategy: what appeared risky and incomprehensible to the Prussian war elite, looked very different if Bernhardi was right.

Counteractive mobilizations now began to force both sides along a path neither monarch desired to go. At some point in time, technical considerations would begin to override ancient loyalties and historic memories.

On 14 April Moltke sent a long memorandum to the king, laying out his preliminary troop dispositions.[51] The seven eastern corps would have assembly points at Herzberg, Calau, Goerlitz, Liegnitz, Landeshut, Schweidnitz and Neisse. The two western corps would assemble either at the Main River or above Hanover and Kassel at Halle-Weissenfels.[52] Austria, he noted, already has an army in Bohemia and the Saxon Army will assemble in Dresden shortly. As our forces remain in their peacetime garrisons, our enemies will be moving to their mobilization points. However, as long as Bavaria does not mount through trains on the lines Regensburg–Pilsen and Nuremberg–Prague, Austrian forces can mobilize only along a single railroad line.[53]

Prussia, in contrast, will move against Austria on nine railroad lines. At a 9:1 transportation ratio, a time will arrive when we will have numerical superiority. At that moment Prussia will concentrate for a decisive battle. It will come sooner if the Austrians move into Saxony or push forward into our territory. If they go on the defensive, assembling their forces near Pardubitz or Olmütz, giving up Saxony and a great part of Bohemia, the numbers would be about equal and the battle would occur later.

On the twenty-fifth mobilization day Prussian strength would be between 118 000 and 200 000. On the thirty-second mobilization day 182 000–223 000. Thus, from the twenty-fifth to the fortieth mobilization days, a 15-day window, Prussia can expect a numerical superiority. Even after that the Austrians will be able to add only one brigade to the battlefield every 48 hours. That is the moment, he said, when we will fight the decisive battle. It must fall within the area of Pardubitz–Königgrätz–Josephstadt.[54] The most dangerous part was the movement of the Silesian Army through the mountains. If they meet a strong enemy force at Josephstadt–Königinhof, they would have to retreat.

In short, 75 days before it was fought, Moltke envisioned the whole war scenario, virtually as it later came about.

As Moltke said to Doering, one of his section chiefs, we can use our forces advantageously only if we concentrate in Bohemia. That would be impossible if the enemy gets there first. This moment cannot be waited for, we must seize it.[55] Austria is the fulcrum to the whole Germanic

Confederation edifice.[56] In order to eliminate resistance in the rest of Germany, we must defeat Austria.

For a short time counteractive mobilizations paused. On 18 April the Austrian council of ministers authorized withdrawal of Austrian forces from the Bohemian frontier, if Prussia did the same. Things seemed to be cooling off when two days later came the news of threatening Italian troop movements.

On 21 April, at the insistence of his generals, Franz Joseph ordered mobilization of the southern army and on 26 April Victor Emmanuel ordered general mobilization. On 27 April, when he learned that Italy had an alliance against Austria, Franz Joseph mobilized against Prussia.[57]

Resisting full mobilization, King Wilhelm on 3 May allowed only the second phase of war readiness, reserve call-up. The war plan at this point had seven phases: war alert, reserve call-up, mobilization, military travel plan, concentration march, advance march, attack march.[58] The next day the king, again rejecting general mobilization advice, ordered five army corps on 'war footing'. Three days later came partial mobilization orders for the rest of Prussia's forces.[59]

It was ten more days, 14 May, until the king agreed to full war mobilization. Balanced against the disinclination of the Austrian commander to attack and the desire of King Wilhelm I to avoid war entirely was the coercive power of counteractive mobilizations.[60]

Moltke and his colleagues expected Benedek to mount an overwhelming invasion through Silesia. In reality, neither he nor his advisors were thinking of anything of the kind. As Bernhardi had told Moltke in April, they feared being overrun by a Prussian army which, they realized, could mobilize much faster than they. The memory of Frederick the Great attacking Bohemia from three sides in 1757 and 1778 dominated their thinking.[61] They worked to assemble an army under the protection of the Olmütz fortress and await the advance of the Prussians into their territory. Moltke did not know this, but his systematic overpreparation, his stockpiling of extra time, size and space meant that Benedek's moves complemented his own.

Eleven days later Prussian forces were advancing across a 200-mile arc in northern Lausatia and Silesia from Torgau (46 000) to Goerlitz (93 000) to Breslau (115 000).

On 1 June, Moltke warned the king that Austria was several weeks ahead of Prussia in mobilization. He emphasized the risks: our theatre of operations is deep and able to give very little help in case Austria moves directly north against Berlin. The neutrality of Saxony must be negotiated with Austria, not Saxony.[62] The key is Austria: after defeating her, the smaller German allies will fold.

Moltke and Operational Warfare

The next day, 2 June, Helmuth von Moltke as GGS chief, became effective war commander of the Prussian Army: he took over the issuing of orders. That he was only promoted to general of infantry six days later suggests to us that, instead of a simple promotion as reward for a job well done, rather it had to do with power, respect and efficiency within the military organization. To make the system work, Moltke needed to be a full general. Hitherto orders had always been issued by the king, with advice from his closest military advisors, the military cabinet, through the War Ministry; a lengthy process which could take days. This was a momentous change, both bureaucratically and in terms of the professionalization of armies. It signalled confidence that Moltke – the war planner extraordinaire – was the single individual in the system who could best direct Prussian armies in war fighting. It signalled that speed in order issuing was important all by itself and cut out four bureaucratic steps in the process: king, closest advisors, military cabinet, War Ministry.

In so doing, the king now shared operational authority in a way few Prussian chiefs of state ever had. Frederick the Great had commanded his own army. A hundred years later, Wilhelm I used technical specialists. The change put operational and strategic control squarely into the GGS, realigning command and control. It speeded things up: Moltke used a simultaneous combination of telegraph and aides-de-camp at first, then as headquarters moved following the forward edge of combat, he used dispatch riders, usually close colleagues of his, sometimes two or three simultaneously, to communicate to army commanders. There was a sense of urgency about this: Moltke's war plans and orders were timed to specific four-hour blocks. What kind of a staff did Moltke take with him to war?

Called the 'mobile General Staff' it was comprised of Lieutenant-General Podbielski as deputy chief and three department heads, plus the railroad coordinator Major Count Wartensleben, who was married to one of Podbielski's daughters. The first department was operations, the second was intelligence and communications and the third was supply and railroads. There were also a number of adjutants and a cadre of message runners, a group of *Jäger* supported by infantry.[63]

Moltke frequently sent staff officers out to confer. Army and corps chiefs of staff just as frequently checked in with Moltke at his headquarters to confirm, clarify or spell out an order they had received. His old friend Quartermaster General von Stülpnagel from the First Army came back from Kammenetz to Gitschen to have Moltke clarify points in the march order which had been delivered to his headquarters.[64] Moltke also sent telegrams, written orders and personal letters. He always requested confirmations and asked that locations of subordinate commands be reported daily by wire.[65]

Drafting orders was taken to a high art form in the Prussian Army, beginning right at the start of an officer's career at the War Academy. Orders were to be clear: logically arranged, short sentences, using universally understood expressions and railroad time designations – 0700 for 7 a.m. and 1900 for 7 p.m. Orders were to be precise: subordinates needed to be made acquainted with the intentions of their superior. Orders were to be complete – distinguishing the part that each unit was asked to perform. Orders were to be short. The rule was that they should never contain a single word by the omission of which their meaning would not be suddenly and completely affected.[66] For example, the most common orders, for march and order of battle, spelled out the aim and object of the march, number and composition of the various units plus the names of their commanders, departure and arrival times, possible routes and march destination.

The quantity as well as the quality of communication between the mobile GGS and army and corps chiefs of staff was truly remarkable. Communications went in both directions: orders down, reports back up. Each commander was required to keep a diary of the war from the first day of mobilization.[67] Their purpose was to have an accurate record of all important events and occurrences, to collect practical experiences, and to furnish a narrative of military operations from the point of view of each unit concerned.[68] Diaries recorded such information as marches, engagements, outpost duties, nights bivouacked or quartered, the state of the weather. After-action report content was spelled out: circumstances and time action began, including strength and position of friendly and enemy forces, orders issued, decisive phases of the engagement, results or outcome including next steps proposed or taken. Finally a casualty list and 'enemy trophy' description: men and material taken from the enemy, with attention drawn to any distinguished actions performed by individuals, regiments or corps.[69] All generals holding commands and all officers commanding corps or regiments were expected to forward these war diaries to higher command.

With this information stream, mobile General Staff and *Auftrag* orders, Moltke was forging a new chapter in military history, by defining and illustrating 'operational warfare'.[70] Operations – defined by size, space and time differentials – were set apart from tactics and strategy to define a range of activities between these two levels.[71] Note that the size and space of battlefields had been getting larger: from Austerlitz (1805), roughly eight miles wide and four deep, to Solferino (1859), 11 miles wide and five miles deep, to Königgrätz, initially 60 miles wide by 15 deep.[72] As the war market space expanded, specialization of labour within armies increased.

Combat: the West

As units left Berlin the officers assembled at the Königswarder memorial, and the generals and commanders went to the palace to be received by the king. At 5 a.m. the next day, first light, the king was on hand at the Brandenburg gate to see them off.[73] Forty military trains in each 24 hours concentrated Prussian forces around Bohemia during the first five days of June.[74]

Meanwhile in the north-west, Prussian forces moved from Schleswig, which it ruled, south into Austrian-controlled Holstein. The Holstein Estates were prevented from meeting by armed guards with bayonets at the door of the assembly hall. Denmark was not going to become a threat. Austrian commander Gablenz withdrew his X Corps south of the Eider River and then to Hamburg. As he left his headquarters in Kiel, the Austrian national anthem was played by the Prussian Marine Band.[75] The Austrian corps retreated home across the south German states to join Benedek's army. In three weeks his corps fought and won at Trautenau.

At noon on 15 June, Prussia issued 12-hour ultimatums to Saxony, Hanover and Hesse-Cassel: stand down your forces, and join the new Prussian state otherwise Prussia would declare war. At midnight Prussia invaded all three. A day later Austria declared her willingness to help any state invaded by Prussia. This was interpreted in Berlin as a declaration of war. Two days after this Italy declared war. Her declaration came at nearly the last possible moment: only hours ahead of the alliance deadline.[76]

The army of the kingdom of Hanover, two divisions or 19 000 men, found itself mobilized only because 15 June coincided with summer manoeuvres. They barely escaped a Prussian invasion from Minden by moving south to Göttingen, abandoning their supplies and equipment. Prussian commander Falckenstein – a well-connected courtier and wealthy seigneur with huge Silesian estates who despised Moltke, the *Kammerjunker* who had replaced Falckenstein in Denmark two years earlier – ignored Moltke's orders.[77] On 18 June, arriving in Hanover a few hours after its army had left, he declared a day of rest. Replying to the king, not to Moltke's urgent requests to press on immediately south-east against the Hanoverian Army, he reported he had found 700 wagons of abandoned food and war supplies. The Hanoverians would starve before they reached Bavaria, he told the king. Meanwhile their prey had stopped in Göttingen to rest, requisition and reorganize.[78]

Moltke, realizing that the Bavarians might move north-east to link up with Hanover, four times ordered Falckenstein to attack the Hanoverians. A fifth order came from the king. Finally Moltke intervened directly: he temporarily suspended Falckenstein's command, and issued orders directly to his divisional commanders: General Eduard Flies to mobilize fortress troops from Frankfurt and move to Gotha, General Friedrich von Beyer to move from Göttingen to Eisenach and General Count von Groeben's force to go north towards Cassel.[79] At Langensalza the Hanoverians awaited help from the Bavarians and the VIII Corps to the south-east. Both, however, had decided to let Hanover go to its fate. On the night of 26 June Moltke issued a seventh order to Falckenstein to put an end to the Hanoverian Army.[80]

Meanwhile Flies, with 9000 troops and 22 guns, was directed to await the arrival of Beyer and Groeben. Moltke advised him to sit tight and prepare to hold Gotha and the Werra valley against the anticipated Hanoverian breakout. But Flies, with seven elderly *Landwehr* battalions, hungered after glory. He attacked the well-entrenched Hanoverians at Langensalza. Forty-five per cent of his army fled, hundreds pretended to be wounded or concealed themselves on the field. The remainder were chased all the way back to Gotha. It was a disaster which accomplished nothing.[81]

Meanwhile, the army of Saxony, 25 000 strong, moved south but neglected to destroy the railroads behind it. Instead of twisting the rails and burning the ties, as was done in the American Civil War, they merely took them apart, stacking the iron and wood beside the roadbed. Prussian engineers reconstructed it and in 48 hours, Prussian troops reached Dresden.[82]

The South German Federal Army, the Bavarians and VIII Corps, commanded by Prince Karl of Bavaria and Prince Alexander of Hesse, hesitated to venture out of their camps. Southern Germany comprised a formidable defensive position: with its headquarters at Munich south of the Danube River, the Main River across its front, its eastern flank protected by the Bavarian Woods and its western flank by the Hessian and Black forests. On 16 June the commander of VIII Corps said he would not take a single step forward to aid the Hanoverians, until Frankfurt had been secured as his base. His forces were scattered across south Germany. His allies – Nassauers in Wiesbaden, Württemberg's two brigades in Stuttgart, the Badenese in Karlsruhe and Austria's Neipperg Brigade, 12 000 garrison soldiers drawn from the Germanic Confederation's Rhine fortresses in Aschaffenburg – had not even begun mobilization.[83]

Meanwhile, a single Prussian division overran Hesse, seizing its commander-in-chief's home, before they could mobilize. Kassel's brigade just barely escaped Prussia's 3rd Division and retreated south on the railroad to Fulda. Like the Hanoverians, Kassel's troops abandoned their supplies, their commander was captured by the Prussians, and they arrived at Frankfurt without ammunition for their rifles.[84]

In other words these smaller states, promising perhaps 150 000 troops in support of Austria's 240 000, never got off the ground.

Strategically this meant that by 29 June, nearly 72 hours before the main battle against Austria at Königgrätz, Moltke knew he would not have to worry about anyone coming to Austria's aid from this direction. He expected Austria would get no relief from the south: Italy had fought Austria to a deadlock at Custova, on 24 June, and, after that debacle, Archduke Albrecht's army was in no position to move north against the Prussians.[85]

Naumann and Tactical Encounters: the Stress Factor

How can combat at Königgrätz be understood? Part of the answer is the reticence of the Austrian commander-in-chief. Part is in the command and control processes. Part is reconnaissance and timing. But the bottom line is often tactical encounters. Company, battalion and regimental combat.

A famous nineteenth-century guide to tactical encounters is the von Naumann tables.[86] Naumann, a Saxon lieutenant, tried to answer the question: why do troops retreat before an enemy? He initially hypothesized three answers to this question. Either they were exhausted, in confusion or frightened. In many cases all three. The sudden appearance of the enemy where he was not expected, or where his presence was dangerous, always had a disturbing effect. A flank attack generally created terror.

But the main cause of that panic which preceded defeat seemed to Naumann to be the losses caused by enemies' firearms. The impact of killed and wounded on their colleagues' morale was the heart of the matter. The question then became, at what point would men be induced to change their minds about attack or defence and retire or surrender?

Naumann laid out a scale of values, arrayed in a matrix. For one thing it depended upon the specific and unique circumstances. He called them 'favourable' or 'unfavourable' conditions. 'Favourable conditions' were that the company was attacking; that it was on the side which in general had been more successful in the war up to that point and that its losses were spread over a longer span of time, many hours or half a day. 'Unfavorable conditions' were that the company was on the defensive, that it was the side which in the war thus far had been the loser, and that the losses were suffered in a short period of time, a few hours or less. Under favourable conditions, a company could lose 40 men, 16 per cent, and not flinch. In all but exceptional cases a company that lost 60 men, 24 per cent, under unfavourable circumstances or 90 men, 36 per cent, under favourable circumstances, had to be considered shaken if not lost. A loss of 120 men, 48 per cent, even under favourable conditions, put a company out of action and losses of 150 men, 60 per cent, meant its complete destruction.[87]

War game umpires applied this formula as follows. After an action, when called upon to decide if a company should advance, halt or retire, they asked four questions:

1. Were the troops tired?
2. Had they been moved for any length of time at more than their normal pace?
3. Were they in good order and good morale? Had they received contradictory orders?
4. What was the impact on them of enemy fire?

Applying the formula, war game conductors used specific details to reach their final calculations: number of firing units, range, total time of fire, condition and situation of target, number of units fired at, and the degree of protection or cover these units had. They concluded using a set of tables which mathematically estimated the casualty impact of one squad of infantry firing for one minute at various ranges, force densities and coverages. A Dreyse equipped infantry company of 250 men could fire 1250 shots per minute. They estimated the killing zone at various ranges: 100, 150, 200, 250 and 300 feet.

Combat: the South

Can we apply Naumann's formula to combat in 1866? Let us try, by examining the battles of Nachod and Trautenau, 27 June, Skalitz, 28 June and Königgrätz, 3 July.

On 27 June, three Prussian corps moved south-west through the Silesian Mountains separating Silesia from the Bohemian plateau. These corps, roughly six to ten miles apart, were the Guards at Eipel, I Corps at Trautenau and V Corps at Nachod. The first and third of these were victorious. The second was not.

Battle of Nachod, 27 June

Nachod was a small city of 3000 perched on the western slopes of the Silesian Mountains. It stood near the heights of Branka, a high wooded ridge in the middle of the mountains, in the centre of which was a pass through which most of the traffic between Silesia and northern Bohemia passed.[88] Nachod is two-thirds of the way through on a winding east–west dirt road which follows a steep mountain ravine, sided with rock and forest. A mile south-west of the city the west-sloping mountain foothills begin to open up. There is a wooded plateau, overlooking a broad rolling area of several square miles sloping gently down to the west. From there a plateau carried the road west. After a quarter-mile, there was a basin of perhaps 10–15 feet in depth, running perpendicular for perhaps 200 yards, forming a naturally protective shelter below the plateau itself. After another 50 feet or so the terrain began to drop down the south-facing gently sloping hillside. Running across the slope of the plateau in a north–south direction were four significant points: flat farm land, a small wood, the village of Wenzelsberg and another small wood. Each of these four points would be fought over.

June 27 was a warm midsummer day. Air temperature was 70 °F (21 °C) and a cloudless sky allowed full sun. It was 'torrid'.[89] The battle took place three hours before and two hours after noon. For most of it roughly 21 000 Austrians, under Lieutenant Field Marshal Freiherr von Ramming, fought roughly 10 000 Prussians commanded by General Karl Friedrich von Steinmetz.[90]

On the evening of 26 June units of the Prussian advance guard occupied the city as the first units of V Corps came out of the mountains behind it. The next morning, six half battalions of infantry and half a *Jäger* company of Prussians arrived just after dawn; by 9 a.m. they were set up along the plateau and through the woods. Their centre was a walled churchyard, with right and left wings to either side in woods. Behind them in Nachod were the rest of the six companies of infantry. Moving slowly out of the Silesian Mountains behind them came the rest of V Corps, another 15 000.

Ramming's VI Austrian Corps had been marching for days without rest, 150 miles through badly marked dirt roads.[91] Responding to a late-arriving order – it took six hours to travel 15 miles – Ramming's brigades were awakened at 1.30 a.m. and sent off helter-skelter, some at 3.30, some at 5 a.m., before they had any breakfast fires started. The final 12 miles' march put the 1st Brigade – two regiments or 6000 troops – on the Nachod flat road, looking across two-thirds of a mile of rising hill, with a depression in the centre. Prussian troops were arrayed carefully across its top ridge line. At 9.30 a.m. Austrian infantry were sent against this ridge in columns: five ranks abreast, 20 columns deep. Through high grass and brambles on a gently upsloping rise, they faced several thousand Dreyse rifles and five field guns firing shrapnel and canister. By 10.30 eight battalions had been shot down by quick fire or were forced to seek refuge in the culvert depression at mid-slope. Austrian *Jäger* got as far as the churchyard. Attacked by two battalions of the 37th Prussian Regiment, they fled. By 11 a.m., six Prussian half battalions of 1000 men had beaten back an Austrian brigade of 4000.[92]

Another Austrian brigade, the Jonak, arrived, reached a point opposite to the battle and was thrown in, ascending into the withering fire. Meanwhile, Ramming, their commander, was in Skalitz, 3 miles away where he could see but not direct the fight. Now a sixth Prussian battalion arrived and began firing from a position on the flank of the attacking Austrians. Two shattered Austrian battalions – one had lost 50 per cent of its men, its commander and 66 per cent of its officers – reached the plateau and entered its covering woods. During the ensuing 90-minute fight, Austrian battalions got mixed up, lost nearly all their officers and NCOs, and were finally pushed out and back to the village of Sonov, their starting point. Some Austrian units panicked during this retreat, their flight covered by a Hungarian battalion which moved out of the woods, opening itself up to Prussian quick fire. It was scythed down like wheat. The second Austrian attack had failed.

By now it was nearly noon and the Austrian commander felt he had no choice but to commit the rest of his forces to avoid losing those already engaged. Ramming ordered in an infantry brigade and five squadrons of cavalry. Fighting all the way, they finally got to the village of Wysokow where only the churchyard remained in Prussian hands. Meanwhile, the Prussian main force and reserve had still not arrived. It looked as if the Austrians might roll up the field.

At this critical moment – the zero point of the battle – Ramming believed it had been won. He halted his infantry and sent in his cavalry to mop up.[93] In a cavalry mêlée of more than an hour the Austrians were unable to push the Prussians from the field. The Austrians retreated. Meanwhile, the Austrian infantry companies in the central depression, in the village and elsewhere had begun to collapse from hunger, tiredness and wounds. They had not eaten anything or rested properly in 24 hours. It was noon. Ramming paused to collect his forces.

During this pause, Steinmetz's artillery and his 10th Division came out of the mountains and drew up for battle. When Ramming resumed his attack, at 1 p.m., it was met with a 42-gun barrage and a counterattack from the fresh, newly arrived Prussians.

An hour later, having lost 7372 men to the Prussians' 1120, Ramming withdrew. The Prussian commander, Steinmetz, did not pursue.[94] The battle of Nachod lasted roughly five hours and, during that time, Austrian casualties were roughly 19 men per minute or one every three seconds. With less than half as many men engaged, Prussia lost just over three men per minute. As Alfred, Count Schlieffen later wrote, Nachod was a battle of open order against closed, of lines versus columns, of fresh soldiers against exhausted ones, and of breech-loaders against muzzle-loaders.[95]

Applying Naumann's formula, Austrian forces had suffered almost 36 per cent casualties under mixed circumstances. They were attacking with clear orders, but were tired, hungry and hard pushed. They suffered horrendous casualties, but over an extended period of five hours. Shaken, further action would have destroyed them completely. They were withdrawn.

The news of Nachod was telegraphed to Berlin and the war suddenly became popular. Bismarck found cheering crowds wherever he went. Happy throngs besieged the palace and citizens' groups bombarded the king with fulsome messages of support and affection.[96]

Battle of Trautenau, 27 June

Twelve miles north-west of Nachod is Trautenau, a town of 5000 noted for its cotton textiles. In the western foothills of the Silesian Mountains, sited along the northern bank of the Aupa River, it nestles in a basin almost surrounded by mountains. The ground was wet and marshy. It was the entry point to the Silesian Mountains at this point. Immediately south of the town three large hills, covered with woods and tangled brush and criss-crossed by ravines, rise up to dominate the area. Nowhere was it favourable for the actions of cavalry or artillery.[97]

Moving north-east from Olmütz on the upper Elbe River towards the 'gates of Trautenau' was Field Marshal Lieutenant von Gablenz's X Austrian Corps, which had left Kiel on 8 June serenaded by the Prussian IX Corps band.[98] It was 24 000 strong and nicely balanced between infantry, cavalry and a 72-gun artillery. Arriving in camp near Jaromirz on 26 June, they sent a single brigade ahead as advance guard. Brigade Mondl arrived in Trautenau at dawn, looked through the town, then withdrew to the heights south of it to await the arrival of their corps. They arranged themselves among the three large hills which towered to the south.

When at 10 a.m. the Prussian advance party entered Trautenau, they looked around, saw no Austrians, and settled in to eat, rest and wait for the rest of I Corps to arrive. I Corps was East Prussians, and its ranks contained some of the most famous Prussian regiments. The plan was to secure Trautenau, then push on to Pilnikau, a village three days' march from Gitschin, where it could make contact with the First Army. I Corps commander was Adolf von Bonin, a veteran courtier but a greenhorn commander. He focused straight ahead, forgetting to watch his flank and secure the hills that protected it.[99] No reconnaissance patrols were sent out, no pickets, no guards. Soon soldiers from Gablenz's brigade in the hills stole into the outskirts and opened fire. By noon the Prussians had chased the Austrians off the hills. When an aide-de-camp arrived at 12.30 p.m. from the 1st Guard Division, some 8 miles south-west, he was told I Corps needed no help, the Landshut Pass was secure.

Soon thereafter 12 000 more men from the Austrian X Corps arrived. With 72 guns, Gablenz now began a steady attack across the Prussian positions.[100] Ten Prussian guns could not respond and, after an hour-long cannonade the likes of which Bonin had never experienced, he retreated, leaving a small guarding force to protect his rear. For the next three hours, four Prussian battalions held off virtually the entire X Corps, inflicting horrendous casualties from strong defensive positions.[101] At 5 p.m. one more Austrian brigade arrived and was thrown into a flanking bayonet attack against the Prussians, losing almost 1000 men, but finally forcing their enemy down into Trautenau where the Prussians followed the rest of I Corps back up the Aupa River.

Trautenau was an expensive and pyrrhic victory for Austria. The Prussians were not defeated, rather I Corps hardly engaged: 11 battalions plus two batteries fought for half a day. Fourteen battalions plus nearly the whole of the artillery did not fire a shot. Prussian forces did not lose because of casualties, they were mishandled. Austrian troops were shaken, but their casualties, which might have led to their defeat, were spread over a long time period and only approached the danger threshold of 24 per cent at that point when the Prussians withdrew. Austria had almost 5000 casualties or 20 per cent of those engaged and nearly four times Prussia's 1300. After the battle the hills around Trautenau were covered with dead and wounded, left to die from shock and exhaustion in the hot dry weather.[102]

Meanwhile the surprised Prussian I Corps commander was inactive and out of communication for the next 24 hours. Prussian corps on either side were left with a huge hole where I Corps should have been.[103] Crown Prince Frederick Wilhelm, meanwhile, never dreaming that Bonin had lost contact with Gablenz, ordered the Guard to advance through the pass at Eypel, taking Gablenz in the rear while expecting Bonin to attack him in the front.[104]

Gablenz saw this coming. He abandoned Trautenau and returned quickly to Josephstadt to avoid being encircled by the Prussians approaching from three sides. As in the Danish War, Gablenz succeeded tactically in a fight without operational or strategic implications, but with heavy casualties.

Between 1866 and 1870 Moltke studied and restudied Trautenau. It was the only outright Prussian battlefield defeat of a corps-sized unit in the war against Austria. His conclusions were passed along in the *Militär-Wochenblatt:* poor leadership and command, no reconnaissance, poor response during the battle. In spite of this four Prussian battalions gave a good account of themselves during a four-hour defence against overwhelmingly superior forces.

Battle of Skalitz, 28 June

The battle of Skalitz, 7 a.m. to 3 p.m., 28 June, pitted 14 000 Austrians against 70 000 Prussians. It was the bloodiest battle of the war for the former, whose casualties topped 33 per cent. Although Prussian losses were much less, several attacking Prussian battalions lost all of their captains and several generals fell leading their brigades.

The Austrian commander, Archduke Leopold, made the wrong assumptions at the start, issued few orders before the battle and gave no direction during it. Steinmetz, the aggressive Prussian commander, risked a bold attack and Prussian subordinate commanders all the way down to company level, pushed forward in front and on two sides, marching to the sound of the guns.[105]

Skalitz is just five or six miles down the road from Nachod. Both lie along the Aupa River, and the twisting mountain road through the Giant Mountains, separating the Bohemian plain, where the Austrian Army was waiting, from Silesia, through which the crown prince's army was approaching. It is a famous military region filled with the sites from the wars of Frederick the Great, a century before. Half a dozen of Frederick's most famous battles – Mollwitz (1741), Hohenfriedberg and Soor (1745) Leuthen (1757) and Liegnitz (1760) – were fought within a few miles of this location.[106] Prussian officers knew it well from history, war games and manoeuvres.

The town itself, with a population of 4000, is built upon a 30-foot high plateau which backs up against the Aupa River, flowing north and south. To the north is a plateau stretching half a mile, to the left front is a wood, to the right front are open fields sloping gently down, with a railroad coming in from the south, turning east and running along a high embankment past a wood. An hour before the Prussian attack began, the Austrian commander-in-chief, Benedek, surveyed the site on horseback, accompanied by his staff. One of his commanders requested he move his corps to Skalitz to join the fight: he knew of the approaching Prussians. With the artillery of a corps and cavalry superiority, Skalitz would have been impregnable.[107] Benedek did not believe Steinmetz would attack and he refused, instead sending these forces west. Archduke Leopold was left by himself: ill, unsoldierly, thoughtlessly assuming everything was OK.

It was not. The woods, filling up with Prussian troops even as Benedek looked on, came to within 700 feet of his front lines, and his flanks were unprotected. A single narrow bridge lay to his rear.[108] The battle had three major turning points: the occupation of the Dubno woods across from the railroad embankment on the left flank of the town, the seizing of the railroad viaduct running alongside the woods, and the storming of the Aupa heights, including the rail station and the centre city.[109]

The Prussian forces got to the outskirts of the town first and they arrived there without Austrian forces being aware of them. Once noticed, half an hour past noon, two Austrian regiments with bands playing rushed at the Prussians in Dubno forest, ending with a bayonet charge. In an hour of quick fire 3000 Austrians were shot down at the rate of 50 per minute. Their commander was killed. Five battalions came to their aid. To do so they had to cross an open field in front of the railroad embankment, at which position a Prussian regiment had arrived first. Two Austrian waves were shot down by the Dreyse. After a fresh Prussian division arrived, still the Austrians died in reckless, uncoordinated attacks. By the time the orders came to withdraw, these units had been decimated. Casualties were estimated at 5500 Austrians and 1365 Prussians.[110] Finally Prussian regiments pushed on to the town itself, the railroad station and the bridge. By 2.15 the streets were filled with Austrian stragglers, men drowned trying to cross the river any way they could, or were burnt to death in house-to-house fighting. Austria's forces had suffered nearly 800 casualties per hour. That is 13 per minute and nearly 40 per cent of the force engaged: Naumann's threshold between 'shaken' and 'out of action'.

The Battle of Königgrätz

Some have called 1866 'the captain's war', implying that there was little strategic or operational command and control, but instead that the battle was won and lost completely at the tactical level based on company grade officers' orders and leadership. In a general sense one can say that all wars are 'captains' wars': it is tactical level leadership or lack of it that wins or loses on the combat battlefield. Without captains, lieutenants and sergeants, wars are not fought at all. However, it is strategy and operations which places the companies and squads into fighting position and in 1866 Moltke was in command and largely controlled things from 2 June right through to 3 p.m. on 3 July, by which time the battle turning point – the zero hour – was passing.

Moltke, the first modern war planner, practised the art of operational warfare. Strategy described the war goal. Tactics was a means to that end dealing with the lowest military units – regiments and companies. Between these was operations; Moltke frequently used the term 'operative' in the sense of intermediate level actions to be combined for decisive battle.[111]

To accomplish this Moltke issued several different kinds of orders.[112] The Prussian invention in these matters was the *Auftrag* or 'mission type' orders in which the will of the commander is spelled out but without restricting the lower commander's freedom of action.[113] This assumes lower commanders, uniformly trained in the Prussian war system, have more knowledge about the specific operational situation, and thus can best apply this knowledge to their own circumstances. Mission type orders assume respect in both directions. It allows the subordinate to assess his situation for himself and to execute the commander's goals the best way he can.

The most common orders were 'directives'.[114] They described briefly and generally what Moltke had in mind to chiefs of staff and commanders who were well known to each other, who respected each other and who in general had discussed and agreed to the strategy and operations to achieve it beforehand. Directives allowed commanders a great deal of latitude in carrying out Moltke's wishes.

The second kind were 'order commands'. Generally these were not issued by Moltke, but by corps, divisions and lower headquarters. But Moltke occasionally issued them. When the conditions for directive orders did not exist, when subordinate commanders did not understand or respect Moltke's position or ideas, or when they made mistakes which threatened to disrupt and endanger, Moltke issued the more restrictive commands. For example with Vogel von Falckenstein against the Hanoverians.[115] But Moltke cautioned again and again against these kinds of orders. High commanders, he said, should order only what is absolutely necessary: constantly changing situations cannot be fully understood from far away, and subordinate commanders' confidence will be shaken and details will clutter up the main objectives if orders are too specific.[116]

And Moltke did command and control in 1866. Let us be clear about at least 11 of Moltke's operational directives during this battle.[117] Each of these was sent out and returned by telegraph, when possible, and by special courier, sometimes two in tandem, who left and came back at all hours of the day and night.[118] Where did Moltke get his information? We do not know for sure but it was probably roughly similar to General Fred Franks, American VII Corps commander during the Gulf War of 1991 with Iraq: 20 per cent from his staff, 40–50 per cent from what he was seeing and hearing himself and from his commanders and the rest from his professional knowledge, training, education and experience.[119]

On 28 June Moltke wired the First Army – Prince Friedrich Charles with chief of staff Voights-Rhetz – reporting victory at Nachod and Bonin's setback at Trautenau and pointing out that the successful crossing of the mountains by the Second Army would depend on the First Army's progress.[120]

The next day, 29 June, at 8 a.m., Moltke wired the First Army again, urging speedy advance south-east. Meanwhile the king and headquarters moved to the front on six trains, arriving at Reichenberg, then Gitschen on 1 July. Moltke's orders were: Second Army – the crown prince – to maintain itself on the left bank of the upper Elbe, its right wing to unite with the left wing of the advancing First Army near Königinhof. First Army – Prince Friedrich Charles – to advance without pause in the direction of Königgrätz. Elbe Army – commanded by Herwarth von Bittenfeld – to attack enemy forces on the right flank of this advance.[121]

At the 2 July, noon, war council, the king, Moltke, General Adjutant Alvensleben, Voights-Rhetz from the First Army and Blumenthal from the Second Army were there, but no representatives from the Elbe Army. No one knew exactly where Benedek's forces were. They each proposed possibilities. Some felt the Austrians had withdrawn behind the Elbe River and concluded it was time to unite the armies. Moltke disagreed: keep the armies separate until we know for sure where Benedek is.

Meanwhile Prince Friedrich Charles at Kamenetz had sent detachments to reconnoitre the Bistritz creek valley. They bumped into Austrian hussars. Quickly they sent uhlans to reconnoitre. They met Austrian cavalry patrols, captured some, interrogated them: four corps were there. The prince issued orders to attack these corps and dispatched Voights-Rhetz to headquarters to report what they had seen. He arrived at midnight, getting Moltke out of bed. Moltke did not countermand Friedrich Charles's orders, that would have made for confusion, instead he confirmed them and sent orders to the crown prince to make immediate preparations to come to the assistance of the First Army.[122] As Moltke drafted his battle orders, his operational assumption was that the whole of Benedek's force lay before him. He sent them off with his aide-de-camp Fink von Finckenstein to the crown prince's headquarters at Königinhof. Finkenstein rode into Königinhof at 4 a.m. and the crown prince's staff began drafting the orders for the battle that was about to take place.[123] Meanwhile Moltke and his staff rode from Gitschen to Horsitz and at 5 a.m. the king and his entourage arrived. By 7.30 they were assembled, and by 8 came the first sounds of the battle.[124]

At 8 a.m. Moltke ordered the First Army to attack along the whole Bistritz creek line. Friedrich Charles did not like this, for he realized that his forces would not play the decisive role in the battle that he envisioned. These orders reflected Moltke's belief that the battle would be decided on the flank.[125] Friedrich Charles's role was to pin and hold the Austrians, so they could not escape the coming flank attack from the Second Army. At 10 a.m., when Bismarck questioned this, saying that the First Army's commitment was too great, and that more could be achieved by pulling back and enticing the enemy down into Prussia's strong defensive positions, Moltke said no, the important thing was to hold the enemy for a battle of the whole. He feared the Austrians would escape.[126]

An hour before noon the battle was entering its zero moment period: a four-hour phase of maximum danger before the arrival of the crown prince's forces. Moltke, along with his staff, Bismarck and the king and his staff, was atop the Roskosberg, a low hilltop near Horsitz, little more than two miles from the main fighting to their front. They could see and roughly identify troop units with a telescope.[127]

At 11 a.m., one of the king's adjutants was sent to talk with Fransecky, 7th Division commander and point force for the First Army at the centre of the battle for Königgrätz. When Freiherr von Loee returned, he told the king that Fransecky should be reinforced with fresh infantry. The 7th Division was heavily outnumbered. While the king considered this, Moltke interjected against it. No reinforcements, not a single soldier until the crown prince has begun his attack. If the Austrians begin an offensive, the only thing we have to counter it with is III Corps, our reserve. We have already sent a cavalry brigade to help. I know Fransecky and he will stand firm. The king agreed with this.[128]

At 1.00 p.m. Prince Friedrich Charles ordered General von Manstein to begin commitment of III Corps, the army's reserve. Moltke countermanded, pointing out that it was important to hold the enemy, not punch him back out of the vice closing around him.[129] At 1.45 p.m. Moltke sent two messages to the Elbe Army. Advance and attack. The crown prince is at Zielowes and the retreat of the Austrians to Josephstadt is to be cut off. It is of the greatest importance that the Herwarth corps advance against the wing opposed to it while the Austrians are still making a stand in the centre.[130]

At critical operational points in this battle, Moltke intervened with acts of commission or omission. His vision would be played out. By 2 p.m. advance elements of the crown prince's army began coming out of the Silesian Mountains to the north-east and launched themselves against the right flank of the Austrian Army laid out in front of them.

The climactic battle of nineteenth-century German history took place in a land area which changed with time. On 6 June, the day of Prussian mobilization, it was 200 miles square. By 23 June it had narrowed to 50 miles square. On the eve of battle, 2 July, it was an area roughly five miles deep and eight miles long, which got smaller as the battle developed. Key bastions from noon to 4 p.m. were within a two-mile square. Benedek, meanwhile, after moving his army north along a single rail line, advanced it across the river in three parallel columns. To get it back together again for an attack took three days. Meanwhile he considered what to do. Attack one of the two Prussian armies within arm's reach to the north or west? When did he realize that a third Prussian army was about to break through the mountains to his north-east? His personal reconnaissance trips soon convinced him that this was the case and he dispatched forces to deal with it before it became a problem: as we have seen, two small but lethal forces to destroy the Prussians as they came out of the mountains at Skalitz, Nachod and Trautenau. Two of these Austrian forces were defeated, and the third, though initially victorious, turned back when confronted with superior numbers.

Meanwhile Benedek concentrated on the two armies immediately facing him. He concluded that the tactical advantage of strong defensive positions was more valuable than the 24 hours available to him to attack one of the Prussian armies to his front, before facing the danger of a third Prussian army on his flank. He chose a safe known strength rather than a riskier but potentially greater advantage.[131] Meanwhile at the forward edge of the battle, the Prussian Dreyse gun was causing enormous Austrian casualties. Benedek, giving up any thought of attacking, now gave up command and control as his forces were steadily being ground down.

Moltke conceived of this battle as one of encirclement. But he could not get his forces to close the noose. Faulty communications at the start, generals who did not follow orders and finally a huge confusion as the troops of the crown prince's army ran into the advancing front of the First Army, entangling both and causing further delay.

In the confusion Benedek, whose casualties by 3 p.m. already totalled over 25 per cent, backed out of the noose. As dusk came on he tried to withdraw his forces southwards across the Elbe River.[132]

Prussian King Wilhelm's earlier hesitations about making war on his ancient Germanic brother had disappeared at the firing of the first shot. He was now eager for a prompt and vigorous pursuit, to crush the Austrians and impose upon them a punitive peace.[133] Moltke, believing Benedek still capable of offensive action and fearing reinforcements from the Italian war theatre, was more cautious. Just at this point Moltke and the king became separated as the latter wandered off to distribute congratulations and decorations. Moltke's 4 p.m. plan for a speedy advance that night and the next day – which might have succeeded against the demoralized, shaken, disorganized Austrian forces – by 6.30 p.m. had been dropped in favour of a day of rest. Benedek thus extracted more than 150 000 troops from the battlefield. But it was a painful, chaotic extraction.[134] Extreme chaos prevailed among the Austrians who saw themselves being chased across the river by the onrushing Prussian legions. There were not enough bridges. No one had thought to put up pontoons. The men who rushed towards the protection of the ancient fortress of Königgrätz found it closed. Worse, the fort commander, expecting Prussians, had closed the city gates and opened the sluice-ways of the Elbe and Adder rivers. As dusk came on, 60 000 Austrians, with guns, wagons and the flotsam and jetsam of defeat, trying to enter the city on the narrow causeways, found themselves suddenly in a sea of water.[135] It was closer to midnight when the town commander realized that his own troops, and not the Prussians, were at the gates. By this time the chaos had got out of hand.

Prussian forces had also taken a beating. Moltke rode across the battlefield. In many places the ground was layered by the bodies of men and horses. Terribly wounded men whom no one could help. As Moltke's party passed, one badly wounded officer begged them to shoot him dead. Moltke's horse walked gingerly over the horrible kill. Three days later dead Austrians and Saxons lay in many places unburied. Men were busy digging huge graves for mass burial. Fires from seven burning villages smoked across the fields. Those houses still standing were filled with wounded. Long lines of wagons carried off the dead. Further on, fewer bodies, but more signs of a terrible fright and wild flight – thousands of knapsacks, bandoliers and sabres covered the field. In front of the small fortress of Königgrätz – whose commander had a few hours to consider whether to enter the battle and finally declined to fire upon the advancing Prussian forces – stood thousands of wagons of all kinds: munition wagons full of shells and grenades, ambulance wagons with slings, bandages and medicine bottles, officers' baggage carts. Weapons by the hundreds were piled at street corners.[136]

As Moltke and his staff rode towards Pardubitz – a small city on the Elbe River a few miles south-west of Königgrätz – they came upon two or three columns – several miles long – of munition and food wagons. In the handsome ancient market square, covered with straw, bivouacked the Prussian 1st Guards Regiment. The Elbe River bridge was burned and smoking. Through the narrow city entrance gate streamed an indescribable mass of thousands of wagons – troop units on the march, stragglers, prisoners, looters and camp followers.[137]

It was the afternoon of the second day before a victory proclamation was drafted. Moltke and his staff were billeted in the home of a local countess who cooked for them herself using a very good local wine. But writing to Marie he noted that the 27th Regiment had lost 30 officers.[138]

Casualties

Casualties from Königgrätz were 64 000 Austrian killed, wounded and taken prisoner. That is 8000 per hour or 133 – more than half an infantry company – each minute. And 9000 Prussians: a ratio of about 7 : 1 or about the level of the most efficient Prussian company, whose soldiers fired the needle gun four or five times a minute to their opponents' single shot.[139]

In sum, although there were many dicey moments for individual soldiers and units, 1866 was in some ways nothing like the 'near-run thing' so close to the hearts of military romantics.[140] Moltke's risks and Benedek's inactivity sealed it.[141]

Two days later the French emperor proposed an armistice and the beginning of peace talks.[142] Against royal desires to advance to Vienna and impose a draconian peace treaty, Bismarck realized that once Napoleon III had taken this step, the French ruler could not permit it to be disregarded without a loss of face. While negotiating, Bismarck was ever mindful: there was always the chance that ambition or wounded pride would tip the French emperor into invading the Rhine provinces, a serious affair with the Prussian Army fully committed so far to the east. And he had to watch Austria, lest it negotiate a separate peace with Italy, then detach its Italian armies north to reinforce Vienna.

Negotiations went forward as the war continued. Prussian forces approached the Danube River and prepared to cross it as a preliminary to a march on Vienna. On 19 July the French envoy proposed an immediate five-day armistice. At that point Napoleon III indicated that France was willing to allow the exclusion of Austria from Germany as well as the formation of the North German Confederation under Prussian leadership. South Germany was to remain independent. Bismarck continued to negotiate. Three days later the emperor said that he would not object to Prussia acquiring as many as 4 million new subjects: in other words, Schleswig, Holstein, Hanover, Frankfurt, Saxony and a few other principalities. This was more than Bismarck had been expecting. He immediately accepted and the armistice began. The peace was signed on 26 July.[143] At the ceremony in which the preliminary treaties were signed the king made Moltke and Roon Knights of the High Order of the Black Eagle – which put them eighth on the court precedence list, after the principal chamberlain, the minister-president, general field marshals and the top four court officials – but before cardinals, the heads of the 41 princely and imperial families and everybody else down to number 62.[144]

Theodor Fontane closes his two volumes with nearly 100 illustrations of the memorial tablets, statues, grave sites and plaques to the dead of this war. He noted that, although the victorious army and the defeated enemy were safe at home and the wounded were healing in sheltered hands, those who died on foreign soil remained alone, separate and isolated in alien lands. Only their memorials remained as silent witnesses and pilgrimage shrines to patriotism and bravery, while their sad and dutiful death embedded itself in the minds of their families. Their graves were decorated with symbols of love and sympathy, the visible memorial of the lifeblood of their children.[145]

6

THE FRENCH WAR, 1870–71

Thinking about the French War

By the summer of 1870 deep future-oriented war-planning processes had been developing in the kingdom of Prussia for over 70 years. Three, almost four, generations of officers had wrestled with this novel technology. But little showed outside; 1864 did not reveal much. Denmark was a minor kingdom, a small war in the snow. And 1866, though a major surprise upending power relationships in central Europe, did not catch everyone's attention.

Austria, after all, though the important German power, had been at the apex of her power in the early eighteenth century. Austria was not among the rising industrial, imperial or colonial powers the likes of Britain, France or even Russia. Britain was the arbiter of the world's oceans, largest colonies and most successful manufacturing. France was considered the world land army par excellence. Napoleon Bonaparte's legacy and teaching were followed in Russia and the United States, Egypt and Vietnam. Her army was toughened by 30 years of colonial wars, breeding a string of battle-tested commanders – Bugeaud, Canrobert, MacMahon, Bourbaki – who, it was supposed, carried on Napoleonic traditions. France had carried off the honours in the Crimea in 1856, and had won in Italy in 1859. For nearly 80 years France had given the law in military affairs to Europe.[1] Even Russia, with its huge Eurasian land mass stretching east to China and south to India, was more significant. Defeating Austria, while momentous for the kingdom of Prussia, was for the rest of the European Great Powers more like slaying a mythological dragon whose powers, even in fairy tales, had waned. So they did not pay that much attention.

But even if they had, the novelty was difficult to see and even harder to figure out. For it was essentially the modern twentieth-century way, hardly recognizable to nineteenth-century minds – the systematic use of organized knowledge applied to the practical skills of war. It was in their applied knowledge that Prussia had an advantage over other armies. It was their processes – organizational, representational, educational and analytical – that enabled them successfully to field, command, control and supply the first industrial mass armies in Europe. Technology and process – and opponents lacking these – gave Moltke a chance few commanders ever have: to plan a war in his mind, then carry it out pretty much according to this mental scenario.

Moltke becomes Famous and a Widower

If Europeans did not understand the process and methods, if they tended to discount the Austrians, they understood a military victory and gave credit to a single individual. By the autumn of 1866, Moltke had become famous, a celebrity.

When he and the GGS went on their annual rides, they were likely to find, as in Silesia in 1867, a continuing celebration: church towers covered with flags, roads surrounded with flowers and tourists. At night, towns were illuminated and towers filled with Bengali torches, Moltke's picture was here and there, and there were poems for kindergartners to learn – 'He thought up the war plan, then carried it out, Moltke got it right.'[2] During Moltke's early morning rides in Berlin everyone took off their hat and bowed. Restaurant windows were filled with people who wanted to greet him.[3] Prussians had not experienced a military victory for three generations. Although in years afterwards Moltke often travelled in civilian clothes, without a servant and carrying his own small handbag – so that he was sometimes not recognized – as soon as people realized who it was the most characteristic response was repeated over and over. It was typified by the arrival of Moltke at a choir concert in Berlin: the entire audience and the performers rose and stood silently until he had taken his seat.[4]

As he travelled with the royal entourage people wanted to meet him. In June 1867 at the invitation of Napoleon III, Moltke travelled with Kaiser Wilhelm I to Paris. He met the Russian tsar, attended the Parisian Exhibition, had long talks with French marshals Neil and Canrobert and received the Grand Cross of the French Legion of Honour. Whether this was primarily personal, or represented an assessment of the invention and development of Prussian war processes and the man who had proved they could work, is hard to say.[5]

Even at home he was honoured. In the autumn of 1866 Moltke, already a knight of the Order of the Black Eagle, was raised one level in the Prussian nobility – to Freiherr or duke – and received a royal grant of 200 000 Prussian thalers.[6] Following the July 1867 General Staff ride, he purchased a country estate outside Schweidnitz in Silesia: the fabled 'Kreisau' of World War II resistance fame. Here he gathered his family. Later some talked of a dynasty. But this smacked more of circumstance than plan. He and Marie were childless. When his nephew, Helmuth von Moltke the younger, became chief of the GGS in 1906, it was more because the nephew was the last close friend of Kaiser Wilhelm II in top governmental circles.

In winter 1866–67 plans were set for a new General Staff building on the Königsplatz. Helmuth and Marie worked on it, especially the choice of historical figures from the Prussian Army in Moltke's study. Busts of kings and generals were planned. The crown prince also worked on the building and, at his personal suggestion, both the Moltke and the Burt coats of arms were put on to the parquet floor and main doors, in honour of the first inhabitants of the building. This was very unusual and demonstrated the couple's acceptance and general popularity in royal circles.[7]

In spring 1867 Moltke and Marie went to Wildbad for a cure. In November they attended the silver anniversary of Moltke's sister Jeannette. Back home in Berlin at a charity bazaar Marie caught cold. Soon rheumatoid arthritis set in. On 6 December she went to bed, sleeping only with the help of morphine.[8] A few weeks later she gave a Christmas ring to her husband and died early on Christmas morning.[9] A public, official funeral was held in the GGS building, an unusual honour for a foreign private person. Queen Augusta led a large group of mourners. Moltke accompanied the body to Kreisau where Marie was laid in the small Catholic chapel on the grounds of the estate.

When Moltke returned to Berlin his life changed. For the first time in a quarter century he was single. Although his family circle changed – his sister Auguste and older brother Fritz moved into Moltke's apartment and his nephew Henry Burt was appointed adjutant – he also became much more of a social personage.[10] Although commentators have sometimes remarked that he did not like this much, Moltke was often out and about with the top leadership cadre around King Wilhelm I. How did this play out?

For one thing Moltke now advanced on the court order of precedence. Although he was not elevated to field marshal and count until 1871 – which position was second on a list with 62 rankings – knights of the Order of the Black Eagle, the highest Prussian decoration, were eighth and active generals of infantry and cavalry were twelfth – so that by Christmas 1866 Moltke was much closer to the head of the line.[11] He was now in position to see and be seen. Who saw and what did they say?

The most famous memoirs of this period are those of Baroness Hildegard von Spitzemberg, sister of Württemberg's ambassador in Berlin and daughter of a reigning family in south-western Germany. Outgoing and loquacious – the antithesis of Moltke which is why they got along so well – she was a famous and sought-after woman of this era. Always seated next to the host at dinner because her conversation was engaging, intelligent and lively, she was an attractive woman with a bright mind full of ideas. At state and private occasions, Spitzemberg often sat next to Moltke on one side with the king on the other. What did she say?

She liked and respected Moltke and fully appreciated his unique contributions to the Second Reich.[12] In the 290 pages of her famous memoirs, Moltke is mentioned roughly every ten pages, which leaves no doubt as to his visibility or Spitzemberg's opinion, which could be caustic. In Moltke's case she was cordial, respectful and endearing.

Her reaction is confirmed by that of George Bancroft, American ambassador in Berlin 1867–74.[13] Bancroft had apparently sent Moltke a copy of his *History of the United States* in 1866, but he first met Moltke in January 1868 at a banquet sponsored by Count van der Heyde, Prussia's aggressive minister of finance at the time.[14] It was a large dinner with over 50 guests. Bancroft had never met Moltke and he made it a point to look him up. They had a long chat – Moltke's English was excellent after more than a quarter of a century married to Marie – apparently about the events of 2 July 1866.[15] Bancroft remarked that Moltke was a quiet, unassuming man of modest demeanour. Older than Grant and with 'less fire and more silences'. Moltke and Bancroft were both born in October 1800, and both died in spring 1891. They discovered they were soul mates of a kind, often riding in the Tiergarten in the early morning. Moltke was grieving in 1868. Before this Marie had frequently remarked that she did not want to survive him. Now he was asking why? Life held few attractions for him. He was known as Moltke the silent, but with Bancroft he talked at length. On parting, he pressed Bancroft's hand cordially.[16] Moltke and Bancroft became good friends, riding often and having dinner regularly.

Among other things his friendship with Bancroft got Moltke into the American Civil War at a new level. Moltke was already a long-time student of it, now Bancroft sealed this knowledge. He knew all the players: Lincoln, Chase, Seward, McClellan and on and on. And he had first-hand details and stories about people and events that Moltke had only read about.[17]

Management and Experience

Many men who fought in 1864, fought in 1866 and again in 1870. Although this is invisible at the point where it arguably counted the most, the NCO corps, at top command levels it is very evident.[18]

The management team from 1864 and 1866 was still in place. Moltke, who had entered the Danish War decisively only at midpoint, was fully in command in 1870. Also remaining were War Minister Roon, Minister-President Bismarck and King Wilhelm I. Moltke's 'demigods' in the General Staff – Podbielski, Brandenstein, Paul Bronsart von Schellendorff, Verdy du Vernois, Veith – remained on Moltke's personal staff of about 15 during the 1870 War.[19] More to the point, many commanders and chiefs of staff of armies and corps continued: Blumenthal was chief of staff to the crown prince in 1866 and 1870, Voights-Rhetz was chief of staff of the First Army in 1866 and corps commander in 1870, Prince Kraft zu Hohenlohe commanded the reserve artillery of the Second Army in 1866 and the Guard Reserve artillery in 1870; Wartensleben, Moltke's old friend, became a high staff officer of the First Army; and Stiehle was chief of staff to Prince Friedrich Charles. At army command elite level, the crown prince, Prince Friedrich Charles and General von Steinmetz had participated before. At army and corps command levels, again many repeaters. A few, like Steinmetz, who distinguished himself in 1866, were removed from command in 1870, but more often it was the steady move up of men who experienced combat. If they survived, they were promoted and saw combat again and again.

Just a few examples make this point. Frederick Wilhelm von Wittich (1818–84), chief of staff to V Corps in 1866, became commanding general of the 49th Brigade in 1870. Albert von Rheinbaben (1813–80) commanded the 1st Cavalry Brigade in 1866 and the 5th Cavalry Division in 1870. Alexander von Pape (1813–95) led the 2nd Guard Infantry Brigade in 1866 and the 1st Guard Division in 1870. Albrecht Ehrenstein Gustave Manstein (1805–77) commanded the 6th Brandenburg Division in 1864 and 1866, and the IX Corps in 1870. Bernhard Heinrich Alexander von Kessel (1817–82) commanded the 1st Guard Infantry Regiment in both 1866 and 1870. Wilhelm von Grolmann (1829–93) was chief of staff to the 10th Infantry Division in 1866 and commander of the 4th Guard Regiment in 1870. Ferdinand von Danenberg (1818–93) was chief of staff of the Guard Corps in both 1866 and 1870. Rudolf Otto von Budritzki (1812–76) commanded the 4th Guard Grenadier Regiment in 1864, the 3rd Guard Infantry Brigade in 1866 and the 2nd Guard Infantry Division in 1870. Albert Karl Friedrich Wilhelm von Boguslawski (1834–1905) was a company and regimental officer of the 50th Infantry Regiment in 1864, 1866 and 1870. And on and on.[20]

By 1870 the war experience of the previous six years had begun to accumulate in the Prussian Army. It accumulated both negatively and positively. There were officers who wanted to repeat the successful victories they had participated in, using the same tactics and operations they had used against one opponent, in one terrain, under one set of circumstances. They had won, been decorated, promoted and eulogized as a result of their actions on that most competitive stage, the combat battlefield. They would do it again, exactly the same. There were others who wanted to avoid any repetition, any repeats of their prior costly experience. There were those who wanted to repeat the successes and avoid the mistakes.

Combat experience, that rare commodity that few soldiers generally have, puts those who have it in a unique category compared with those who do not. Phrases such as 'the baptism of fire', tell us that no amount of military schooling, peacetime drills and manoeuvres, and rifle range practice can make up for combat experience. In a 'kill or be killed' situation, one never knows how the human animal will respond.[21] No amount of reading about, thinking about or practising for, can substitute for real bullets and shells which kill, maim and mangle the body and compress, shock, reduce, dehumanize and destroy the spirit. Breaking up squads and platoons into pools of blood, body parts and pitiful cries for help. Causing men to lose sight of plans, orders and ideas in hopes of stopping the pain and keeping themselves alive.

Combat tends to increase the normal separation in armies between high command and fighting soldiers. Between those who must put their bodies in jeopardy and those who do not, between those who see, smell and hear their friends and colleagues hurt and dying and those who do not. Between those who hear the thundering war noises so close up they isolate, enclose, terrorize to the point of freezing catatonia, and those for whom these sounds are only a distant noise or a bad dream.

Again Moltke was unique: he had a fingertip feel for the combat battlefield, a sixth sense. In his most well-known practical instructions for commanders, 'Instructions for Large Unit Commanders' of June 1869, Moltke underscored these distinctions in a fully Clausewitzian way. The fundamental sphere of activity for armies is war, he wrote, but that does not happen very often. The normal state of armies, the largest part of military experience – where armies develop – is peacetime duty. The contradiction between these raises all sorts of questions about the relationships between peacetime training and wartime combat. He concluded that moral values that may be more or less invisible in peacetime become the precondition of victory and the true value of a unit in war. Moltke's memories of Nezib in 1839 remained vivid. He did not forget the experience of losing a war. On 24 June 1857 he wrote to Marie from London that this day was always a difficult time for him. Exactly 18 years before he had fought in the battle of Nezib.[22]

Organization and Process

After 1866 Prussia had 46 months to digest the lessons learned. In the knowledge business, in learning organizations, this is a huge window. So much time to tinker and refine that when Moltke went on vacation at the beginning of July 1870 he did so secure in the knowledge that everything for a possible war with France was prepared and ready. Small details of the war plan that never appeared in 1864 or 1866 were now spelled out.

The Prussian war system expanded to encompass the North German Confederation. Four new corps were created, seven plus the Guards in Prussia, IX Corps in Schleswig-Holstein, X Corps in Hanover, XI Corps in Hesse–Nassau–Frankfurt and XII Corps in Saxony. Each corps recruited men from its own region, including both actives and reserves. Outside Berlin there were 27 equal size infantry divisions and two cavalry divisions. Parallel to this were 217 *Landwehr* battalions organized by district commands. By the summer of 1867 peacetime strength was 312 000, war mobilized over 800 000. Each year 70 000 men were liable for service: ten times the average number of factory workers in German industrial corporations at this time. Universal military training meant three years' active duty at age 20, followed by four years' reserve duty, five years in the *Landwehr* and seven years in the *Landsturm*. The adult male workforce, most of it, was enrolled.[23]

This raised the size of the army to the next level: up more than 1200 per cent over the force that fought in Denmark and up again almost 300 per cent higher than the troops engaged against Austria. The million-man army that engaged France in the summer of 1870 was by far the largest single industrial workforce in the world.

The General Staff itself expanded to over a 100, with several dozen more in corps and divisions.[24] The Second Section was mobilization, the Railroad Section was now a separate bureau. The Central Section did administration and management. Map making and history writing were both exemplified in the General Staff work, *The Campaign of 1866 in Germany*, a one-volume 720-page tome whose 20, four-colour maps would have made the French painter Toulouse-Lautrec envious and whose 46 appendices included killed, wounded and missing down to regimental level. Moltke continued to recruit the dozen top officers from each War Academy class to work under his supervision.[25]

But it was those functions directly concerned with an imminent war against France that changed most dramatically. Foremost among these were mobilization and railroad transportation. To deal with almost a million men, several hundred thousand horses and the accoutrements and supplies to move these from peace to war footing and then to support them in war fighting was a much larger undertaking than 1866. A whole new structure was put in place.

Military Travel Plan

The heart of this structure was the military travel plan. The reason is that, as Moltke saw in the American Civil War and in 1866, it was the only part of the war plan which could deliver continuous, reliable, predictable performance. It was the only segment whose peacetime operation simulated precisely its operations in war. Only the volume increased. Mechanical routinization raised to the next level meant that they could practise in peacetime almost exactly what they would do in wartime. Railroads dramatically speeded up the time of concentration, lowered the cost structure, and enabled maximum specialization of labour in a few large concentrations.

To design a process to make this work for the army was highly complex. But it already existed in the civilian railroad system, where the laws of physics and mechanical engineering imposed certain rules. One was uniform speed. Volume was achieved when trains moved continuously, organized in 'correct speed flights'. Brandenstein, Moltke's railroad planner, set it at 14 mph. The second and third rules were interdependency and discipline. Almost everything in an active railroad network touches immediately and directly everything else. One late-running train causes following trains to slow down and connecting trains at junctions to wait, thus backing up the whole system. Discipline dictates 100 per cent synchronization of time and space, based on huge and steady amounts of information. Everything depended on written directives.[26]

To achieve this a Railroad Commission sat in Berlin, comprised of civilian and military officials. Its executive were two members of the General Staff plus one from the Ministry of Commerce. Three permanent line commands operated in peacetime, at Berlin, Hanover and Kassel. There were 13 at war declaration. Each was a joint military–civilian command. During peacetime each line command created, developed and practised its wartime structure and plans. Line commands, corresponding roughly to corps command headquarters, contained a network of phase stations every 80–120 miles. The whole system was linked by telegraph.[27]

All of this was in place by the spring of 1870, no small task considering there were 15 state railroads, 5 private railroads under state supervision and 31 private railroads. The south German governments signed on in August 1869, so that the uniform system could be practised during peacetime exercises.[28] Brandenstein wrote out the railroad plan for the south German states in his own hand.[29]

The key items in the plans were these. At mobilization all civilian traffic was cleared and the entire system was turned over to the military. In 1866 military forces had abided by civilian train schedules. Now there was no civilian traffic. Military timetables, sent out and practised in peacetime, coordinated the whole system thus created, including route maps and detailed timetables for each military unit. The detail of these plans cannot be overemphasized. The plan as a whole ran for 20 days and was broken down into hundreds of separate parts. For example, there was a preliminary phase during which civilian traffic was cleared, soldiers reported to their units and rail cars were converted to military use. Then came mobilization phases, when units filled up. Followed by the military travel plan itself. Six lines carried the north German corps to the western frontier, three lines conveyed the south German corps. Three divisions were sent for coastal defence to Hamburg and Bremen. Even subsistence was prepared: although troops were told to take six days' rations with them, up to the eighteenth mobilization day,

110 trains were provided for this purpose. Each corps had its own 'travel and march tables' arranged for each day's travel, called an echelon. Travel and march tables, sent out in outline format long before actual mobilization, were practised in simulated war games.

The 'unit train rule' was continued.[30] Military trains carried one kind of unit, for example a single infantry battalion. They were uniformly 50 cars in length, with headroom of one hour on double-track lines, 90 minutes on single-track lines, and a system-wide pause from midnight to 6 a.m. to straighten out problems. German railroads at that time were uniformly overpowered, that is, the ratio of locomotives to rolling stock was high.[31] This enabled them to increase the number of trains immediately and gain time and volume: 24 hours and traffic increases of 5000 per cent on some lines.[32]

For the first time the entire mobilization plan, including station times, train sequences and echelons, was laid out beforehand. This instrument aimed at uniformity and speed. As the chief of the Railroad Section, Herman von Wartensleben, said, each new railroad line gives us the chance to speed up mobilization at the rate of one corps per week. In this way the GGS and its Railroad Section had now taken over the reins of mobilization.[33] Mobilization and transportation were ready. What about content – the army – and format – the war plans? What had been learned from 1866?

History Lessons from 1866

From the Austrian War there were published and unpublished accounts. As Moltke said about the General Staff history of 1866, in publishing a work for the general public so soon after the fighting had stopped – and the dead buried – one could tell the truth but not the whole truth. The image put forth publicly was different from the reality discussed within the General Staff.[34]

One published message was that contemporary war was heading in the direction of larger and more intensive battles. Victory by battle, not occupation of land or seizure of forts, was the major method of war fighting. Battle was the main method to break the enemy will. But Moltke understood that battle was not an end in itself, only a means to an end. If the same ends could be accomplished using other methods, he tried! An encirclement, an attack against the enemy rear, a rearguard action which prevented the enemy from attacking, these accomplished the strategic goal without battle. Moltke esteemed George Washington highly because he accomplished his final goal – Yorktown, the war-ending battle of the American Revolutionary War – with very few casualties.[35]

A second publicly acknowledged theme was that war fighting success depended on numerical superiority, often in a combination of tactical defensive and strategic offensive.[36]

More to the point were the unpublished accounts, the failures of 1866. One category was grouped around failures of command, such as Trautenau and Langensalza. At Trautenau an inexperienced commander-in-chief and his subordinates made serial mistakes. At the start tactical units failed to reconnoitre and patrol properly: they were surprised. At the midpoint the high command failed to take control, responding, not initiating. At the end, most Prussian troops had never engaged. Those that had, such as the rearguard during the middle hours of the afternoon, fought well until overwhelmed by superior numbers. Command and control during the battle went unexercised.[37] Bonin fought briefly, then retreated for two days, all the time affording his neighbouring forces – two Prussian corps – no protection.[38]

Moltke's only public statement regarding Trautenau was mild, indirect criticism of Bonin for waiting for orders from the crown prince: instead he should have moved directly towards the Königgrätz battlefield. Under pressure of a short-term tactical defeat, Moltke said, Bonin forgot his operational–strategic responsibilities to the rest of the army. In his statement, Moltke used the future imperative tense, the same one employed in war game critiques.[39]

At Langensalza inexperienced reserves were thrown into a frontal attack against well-entrenched infantry. Moltke had told them to wait for reinforcements. Moltke had written that such attacks were pointless, given the rifled guns of infantry. Flies, the commander, was removed from command. Casualty figures were classified top secret and not published for 50 years.

A second category was the failure of technology and organization, especially the artillery, which had done so well in Denmark. Of course these wars differed greatly. Denmark engaged 100 000 troops, in a small peninsula in winter. It took for ever to fight, with a six-week pause in the middle. The Austrian War engaged more than 700 000 in two campaign areas separated by hundreds of miles, but the main battles took place within seven days. In 1866 Prussian artillery confronted a well-trained enemy armed with rifled cannon. Prussian 12-pounders were outranged and outshot.[40] At the time only half of the Prussian guns were rifled, and even these had only been delivered shortly before war broke out and gun crews had had only a few days to practise with unloaded grenades.

In this short span of time, half of the artillery never fired a shot, the other half often ran out of ammunition. It moved slowly at the tail of the column, at times it was several days' march behind the infantry. When the guns ran out of ammunition, as they often did, they fell back out of action. Under difficult terrain, in a very shortened time frame, artillery never became a factor, except here and there. Prince Kraft zu Hohenlohe, an important combat artillery officer who was also close to the king, said the artillery did not meet expectations: and it made him feel no better that the Austrian artillery did even worse! They needed more practice: a shooting school for artillery just like the infantry had. They needed to find their shooting positions faster. But the main problem was that they needed to be integrated into combat along with other units: Prussian commanders did not know how to use artillery in war fighting.[41]

How to Fix these Deficiencies?

In a sense 'fixing' bad command after a war is a non-starter. One can never tell exactly how a peacetime officer will respond under combat conditions. During the early fighting of every war there is a process of command change which takes some amount of time. Commanders are relieved and removed – and new men put in their places. Of course the Prussians could not act with the alacrity and decisiveness of Eisenhower and Marshall in 1942–43, sacking officers at will. The Prussian system worked much more slowly, but the same process was used. In 1864, for example, Wrangel was replaced as soon as this became prudently possible. In 1866, in contrast, the fighting lasted only a few weeks, not enough time to make many personnel changes. But when it was over, changes were made.

Fixing weapon employment is quite different. As for rifles, 1870 saw a reverse change for the German armies. In 1864 and 1866 the Prussian Dreyse breech-loader had a three to five shot per minute advantage over Danish and Austrian muzzle-loaders. In 1870 the French Chassepot – the most advanced breech-loading rifle of its time – had 1000-yard range advantage over Prussian rifles, with roughly the same shots per minute. The French also had the first operating machine gun, the Mitrailleuse.These machines were deadly when employed well. But they were not spread around the army and soldiers were not trained to use them. French war doctrine never allowed them to be fully and properly deployed.

Prussian artillery, however, was a different story. By 1870, things had changed.[42] Credit for this went to Kraft, Hindersin and Moltke.

Prince Kraft, son of Bismarck's predecessor as Prussian minister-president, had joined the Prussian artillery in 1845. In addition to his court access, Kraft was a theoretical gunner who wrote the most influential book on artillery in the Prussian Army, *Letters on Artillery*. In it he argued that artillery – masses of guns – should directly support combat infantry, close up in the front lines, firing at enemy guns as well as soldiers. Artillerymen knew how to die just like infantry soldiers, he wrote. Concentration, direct tactical support, and large volumes of shells: all were needed.[43]

Eduard von Hindersin was a maverick and very independent, but fervently Prussian. When his eldest son died of wounds received at St Privat, his response was characteristic: there is no more beautiful way for a young officer to die: with the Iron Cross in one hand and the heart of his mother in the other. Assigned, after the Danish War where he had directed the siege at Dybbol, as inspector general of Prussian artillery, Hindersin, a senior general, often showed up at military science lectures in Berlin, asking questions of younger officers. He spent hours listening to the discussion at the Berlin Artillery School and Artillery Examination Commission to learn the newest research. He feared that if Prussia confronted a power with all rifled guns, his beloved kingdom would lose. It kept him awake at night.[44]

In the great controversy over smoothbores against rifled guns, he became a strong advocate of the latter. In June 1864 he had ordered as many four-pound rifled guns as the Prussian foundries could make. By 1870 all artillery units had been converted. Hindersin's single restless passion was to improve the practical operations of the guns. He could not care less for spit and polish and the traditional superficial showiness of units, it was practical operations that counted. Often showing up in the middle of the night or observing units from afar without letting them know, he believed that planning and organization were everything.[45] Hindersin recognized that the infantry had shot better than the artillery in 1866. He concluded the reason was the infantry had a shooting school. Artillery needed one too. But there was no money. So he created a school of his own, with improvised organization, semi-retired officers and borrowed equipment. After 1866 the budgetary dam broke and the Prussian Landtag quickly approved funds for an artillery shooting school.[46] He did not know which shooting system was best so he spent days and weeks at the new school, watching, asking questions, listening to critiques. Before he changed the official shooting regulations, he had allowed the school to test out many possibilities. Hindersin believed that the firing system had to be both mathematically correct and also easy to operate so men would not become confused during the chaos and tension of battle. Once published and set out, the school then went forward and trained cadres from each regiment, who spread the word.[47]

By 1870 Prussian artillerymen had learned to serve the guns quickly. If their target were attacking infantry, they estimated they had 90 seconds before beginning to receive direct infantry fire. If the target was charging cavalry, they had 30 seconds before the horses would be in among the battery.[48]

Artillery regulations were entirely rewritten. Targets became much smaller, guns were expected to hit them, plenty of ammunition was provided. Batteries fired for prizes. Artillery recruits had eyesight tests, and only those with good vision were trained to lay down the guns. Batteries experimented with three kinds of rounds. Salvo made the fewest hits. Rapid fire made a few more. Slow firing made the most.[49] Elegant drill was thrown out, the only things that counted were timing and hitting the target. Specialization took hold. One soldier ordered the direction and nature of fire, a second sponged out the gun, a third brought up the shell, a fourth fused it, a fifth laid it and a sixth pulled the lanyard. In 1866 losing a gun was considered a great disgrace, so that they would stay out of combat rather than risk it. Not so in 1870.

Moltke read Kraft and talked with both Kraft and Hindersin. Then he changed artillery usage. After 1866 he had concluded that peacetime artillery units were alienated from other arms, commanders of mixed forces only learned about artillery in brief manoeuvre days, and they did not know what to do with it. To overcome this, officers came together in the GGS to learn how to use and integrate each arm for maximum battlefield impact. In the May 1868 General Staff ride, officers practised using artillery at the beginning of battles.[50] By the autumn 1869 royal manoeuvres, artillery units were integrated with infantry units in combined brigades.[51] By 1870 the quantity of guns and supplies had increased precipitously. The main ammunition column of an army now took up more than 20 miles. A corps of 25 battalions had 19 batteries. Kraft figured that an artillery battery in combat would fire five times as much ammunition as an infantry company.[52] If there were 122 guns at the siege of Dybbol in 1864, by 1870 at Sedan there were over 600.[53] Supply was organized to keep these firing.

In 1870 artillery was pushed as far to the front as possible. Rifled steel guns could hit their target at 3000 feet. As percussion shells exploded on impact, the burst showed in a heartbeat what the range was. In 1870 supplies of ammunition were up front. They seldom ran out. In a series of single-day battles during August, artillery contributed importantly. At Mars Le Tour III Corps artillery fired almost 6000 rounds. At St Privat the Guard artillery fired 8000, at Sedan 5000.[54]

A third lesson was logistics. Although the 1866 mobilization transport itself went smoothly (in 21 days moving almost 300000 men, 55000 horses and more than 5000 pieces of equipment), after that it could not supply these forces. From 23 June, when the first formations crossed the Austrian border, to several days after the battle of Königgrätz on 3–4 July, the rail system was unable to deliver food and supplies. Troops outran their supply convoys, materials rotted and connections between railheads and troop units were lost. In 1870, with an army more than twice as large, they tried to do better.[55]

A fourth lesson was intelligence failures. In 1866 Prussian armies approached the war blind. In spite of Bernhardi's description, Moltke did not think he knew the Austrian war plan. What he did not know for sure was the location of the Austrians on the evening before the decisive battle.

By 1870 intelligence gathering assumed new importance and was given a degree of specialization no army in the world practised at this time. For example in Paris two officers, the Prussian military attaché Freiherr von Loee and his young colleague Count Alfred von Schlieffen, were given the assignment of finding out the details of the French mobilization plan. They went to Lyon to observe the transportation of munitions and other supplies from there to the great fortress at Metz closer to the north-eastern border lands. Following this up with a trip north, they went from one artillery garrison city to another and, by judicious but casual inquiry, ferreted out the exact location of extra horses positioned along the route of march, which revealed artillery mobilization assignments. They discovered how troops from Algeria were to be echeloned into the mobilization plan.[56] This was reverse engineering; taking a competitor's product apart to see how it worked.[57]

What Prussian intelligence did not know was that these elaborate plans were seldom war gamed or practised in manoeuvres. The French Army was not prepared to carry out its war fighting ideas.

A final lesson was strategy and operations.[58] After 1866 Moltke concluded that his original ideas had been understated. If he had disappointment – he had no regrets. The psychological reaction to Flies's and Bonin's failures was based on relative, not absolute expectations. He was aware of the fortunes of war and hoped that he had built into his system enough back-ups, buffers and reserves, so that the actual outcomes would end up approximating what he had in mind at the start.

In spite of mistakes, Prussia had won in 1864 and 1866. For Moltke the great moral was not bad feelings over the blunders and mistakes made. For lack of bravery and or hard work he faulted no one. His belief was that with such troops one must and should win, unless commanders performed badly.[59] How then could they do better in the future? Moltke focused not so much on single details as on fundamentals: the consequences of modern fire weapons, the power of flank attacks and surrounding the enemy, the value of the tactical defensive united with strategic offensive, marching separately, fighting together, marching to the sound of the guns.

1870: Working Hypotheticals

Moltke's strategic planning for a war with France began three years before the war started. It went through four stages and was based around three major planning concerns. One was force ratio: how many forces to allocate west against the French, how many south-east against a potential Austrian threat? A second was timing patterns: what happened if Austria, the much slower mobilizing army, mobilized before France? The third was concern for capital cities: Moltke was always measuring the relative distances Austrian and French armies had to travel to Berlin, in comparison with distances for Prussian armies to arrive in Paris or Vienna. This concern was a throwback to agricultural elite war: Moltke included it because he believed that the agricultural elite commanders he was confronting thought in these terms: capture the capital and end the war.

In the autumn of 1866, timing was at the top of his list. On the surface France appeared to be the most dangerous and also the best prepared, quickest mobilizing army in Europe.[60] But Denmark and Austria, recently defeated, were still threats. Moltke was acutely aware that in any war against France, the moment the French appeared to be winning, Austria and Denmark could become dangerous very quickly.

His first plan described a short, sudden campaign, to defeat France rapidly in a single great battle. Meanwhile war preparation continued against the much slower mobilizing Austrians. A long war was much more likely to bring Austria in, a short war to keep Austria out. The key to this was an unhesitatingly rapid mobilization and concentration. A three-corps defence against Austria, and a three-division protection against Denmark, in case they declared war. If they did not, these forces became a second strategic reserve to be sent to the west. *Landwehr* troops, meanwhile, would safeguard the southern border and, reinforced by an active infantry division, protect the North and Baltic Sea coasts.[61]

But Moltke kept thinking about it. In January 1867, he appeared at a General Staff lecture on the campaign of 1814. Some have suggested that the 1814 campaign became a model for 1870.[62] In 1814 three allied forces – Bernadotte from the Netherlands, Schwarzenberg from southwestern Germany and Switzerland and Blücher roughly at the 52nd parallel opposite Paris – advanced together into France. Napoleon had roughly 120 000 troops. The allies had three times this number. Even against by far the best field commander in Europe, if the allies fought well and stayed together, it was only to be a matter of time.[63]

Moltke's memo of January 1867 included several scenarios. Probable allies were the south German states and Italy. The minimum was a neutral Italy. Force size was considered roughly equal: Prussia and the south German states against France–Austria 500 000 each.[64] The space was two widely separate campaign areas. Moltke intended at this stage to build a larger force against one and use it for a quick decision. He considered an offensive against the Austrian capital from Silesia. He laid out a defensive against France along the middle Rhine. He compared the difficulty of fighting a defensive war against Austria with fighting an offensive war against France. Even if France lost a battle, he did not expect them to make peace. These hypothetical cases were tested out in the tactical new year exercises, which also included the protection of Berlin from an attack coming from the south.[65]

Hypothetical case one: France

In March 1867 he laid out two hypotheticals. Case one against France alone concentrated the whole force in six through rail lines into the Palatinate, the area around Saarbrücken. He hypothesized that the French rail net provided France a two-region mobilization, separated by the Vosges Mountains: one French force around Metz, the second around Strasbourg. Between these two the German Army would operate on inner lines in the Lorraine Basin, a well-marched route flanked to the south by the Vosges Mountains and to the north by the Hunsrück uplands.[66] The lower Rhine was protected by the neutrality of Belgium and by the distance of the French Army from Prussian borders. Four armies were laid out: the First Army, 60 000 men in the area of Wittich–Bernkastel on the Mosel River: the Second Army, 130 000 by the fifteenth mobilization day, moving forward to a line Neunkirchen–Zweibrucken, behind them on the nineteenth mobilization day the X and Guard Corps; the Third Army, 150 000, crossing over into south-east France; and the Fourth Army, 60 000 men, moving in the direction of Kaiserslautern to reinforce the three most east-lying Prussian corps.

This assembly would make possible by the twenty-second mobilization day a defensive–offensive battle west of the Rhine, probably with a numerical superiority: 300 000 troops, attacking westward, with 100 000 men of the I, II and IV Prussian Corps standing ready as a reserve.[67]

Hypothetical case two: France and Austria

The key question was against which enemy to defend in order to be as strong as possible in an attack against the other? Prussia had a better defensive position on the Rhine than against Austria. He estimated that a defensive force, supported by 100 000 men, could hold for six to eight weeks on the Rhine. France might try to move across Worms, then go around and through Franconia to Berlin. Only an offensive with superior power could hinder this. Perhaps the Austrians did not want a battle in Bohemia, instead, waiting at Olmütz or behind the Danube River to see what happened with France.[68]

War Plans and War Games

During May and June 1867, Moltke led negotiations with the south German states over plans in case there was a war with France.[69] The problems of integration were great. Each had separate and different war processes. Prussia had defeated each state a year before and knew their weaknesses intimately. Bavaria was the most difficult, because it was the largest. Baden and Württemberg were in fairly good shape. The Badenese war minister was a Prussian general and Württemberg had already intro-duced the Prussian system.[70]

The 'periodization' of the war plan took shape. As for the force structure of each corps once it moved against the enemy, that was clear and standard: advance guard, main force, reserve force, rearguard. Prior to this each corps was formulated into echelons, depending on the phases of the war plan. As early as November 1867, these were six: (1) preparatory phase: war alert; (2) mobilization: call up the reserves; (3) military travel plan, divided into two segments: first move reserves to their regiments, then get units on the trains for movement up to the borders; (4) concentration in which the corps are moved together across the border and gradually linked; (5) advance march, and (6) attack march.[71] Keep in mind that as these corps increased in size and number, things became more complicated. If a war-mobilized corps comprised roughly 30 000 men, to change its order of battle from advance to attack might take 18 hours or more.[72]

These ideas were tested out in the July 1867 GGS ride in Silesia.[73] By the November 1867 war game, the military travel plan took 32 days to position the army to begin its march against the west front. Moltke worried about the defeated armies of Austria and Denmark. Prussia had to put some troops there at the beginning of any war with France. The VI Corps at Neisse, I Corps and a reinforced division of IX Corps at Goerlitz, together 80 000 men, and these, plus the *Landwehr*, can deal with the situation, or at least defend Dresden. The rest of IX Corps can concentrate in the fort at Dybbol. When this had been completed, all the railroad lines would be open and could be used by the other ten corps to move west.

In May 1868 came the second round of discussions with military representatives of Bavaria and Württemberg over the joint movement of German forces in the event of war with France. In August Moltke and Prince Albrecht of Prussia travelled across the battlefields of the Main Army in 1866 and then in August participated in the General Staff ride in Thuringia, ending up near Jlemenau.[74]

By 1869 plans had been in the works, on paper, tested in war games, for three years. Force ratios were estimated at 3.5 (west) to 1 (south-east). Timing patterns depended not only on the military travel plan, but on enemy actions. Mobilization phase periodization for many scenarios were sketched out. At the start, three corps (100 000) for the south, ten corps (300 000) for the west. French Army size was estimated at 300 000.[75]

Timing patterns were tightened up. In November 1867, the westfront travel plan assumed that by the thirty-second mobilization day, these forces would be march ready between the Rhine, Mosel and Saar rivers.

By the winter of 1868–69 the military travel plan had been compressed to 24 days and by January 1870 to 20 days. There were four armies, each comprised of two or three corps. Two armies were in the centre, with two more on the flanks, the right army as flank protection against Metz–Diedenhofen, the left against Strasbourg. The south German contingent was figured at 70 000 men.

Moltke's expectations were laid out as worst-case scenarios. Not until the last moment could the three corps poised for possible action against Austria be turned against France. Moltke's greatest fear was that Austria would mobilize before France. In that case, the timing pattern would force an immediate war declaration on France. As for the south Germans, he did not count upon them exactly. Although he attributed to his enemy France, his own sense of timing, he did not assume his south German allies could mobilize with the speed and certainty of Prussia.[76] Moltke did not expect Napoleon III to go against south Germany or through Switzerland. He expected him to take the offensive through Belgium against the lower Rhine region, then continue the attack south through the Palatinate region. Prussia could flank attack this from the north, forcing the enemy to defend themselves in an unfavourable position on the left bank of the Rhine.[77]

By 1869 Moltke had begun conducting two General Staff rides per year: one in the spring before troop manoeuvres began in June, one in late autumn after the royal manoeuvres ended in September. Two intendant officials, from the supply sections of the War Ministry, now accompanied these rides. This was a major step forward in integrating General Staff and War Ministry planning processes. The spring GGS ride in Saxony went from Stolpen into 'Saxon Switzerland', stopping in Dresden where Crown Prince Albert took part. Albert gave a dinner for Moltke and his officers in his castle Grossenhain. From then on Albert of Saxony was close to Moltke: Moltke gave him a separate command in 1870.[78]

In June 1869 Moltke issued his famous 'Instructions for Large Unit Commanders'. Based upon the painstaking GGS 'post-game analysis' of the strengths and weaknesses of the Prussian Army in the 1866 war, it was prepared as a set of guidelines for the army's senior commanders. Written in large part by Moltke himself, many of the long-term GGS 'demigods' also contributed: Verdy du Vernois, Brandenstein, Wartensleben and Kraft zu Hohenlohe.

Moltke himself did not learn much fundamentally new in 1866, but he recognized that others needed to bring their learning curve up to speed. The 'Instructions' are a mixture of Clausewitzian idealism and post mid-century European realism, of theory that is always dominated by practice, of classical as well as modern ideas. He recognized the novel conditions of industrial mass war: the development of modern weapons had changed the technical and material conditions of war. Today larger and more rapid decisions were to be expected. Victory was mainly achieved by battle, not occupation of territory or conquest of fortresses. Decisive battle was now the great method to break the enemy will to resist. As a consequence of weapons, transportation and communication changes, together with increases in size, certain conclusions could be drawn. Combat success depended on numerical superiority, excellent and brave soldiers, and on leadership which brings Prussian strengths to the decisive point. In doubtful situations, it was always good to seize the initiative: march to the guns. The flank attack, an encirclement which takes the enemy in the rear and the combination of a tactical defence with a strategic offensive were emphasized. But Moltke also considered how to reach the goal without battle. Personally Moltke was intolerant of persistent mistakes in both whist and war, because they tended to make quick victory impossible. Yet the Prussian system was tolerant of mistakes: it allowed for them. Clausewitz's 'frictions of war' were assumed: and by the appropriate manipulation of size, space and time, a safety net of expedients was woven to allow and make up for them.[79]

After four years of work, Moltke believed that Prussian mobilization was prepared to the last detail. Six through railroad lines were ready to transport between the Mosel and Rhine. Travel tables, for every troop unit, day and night were ready.[80]

1870 Counter-mobilizations

In contrast to the Austrian War, where both sides took months to mobilize, the French War burst out suddenly, unexpectedly. France, whose army was not ready, declared war. Prussia and her German allies, who were ready, responded. Both were surprised at what happened next.

France bore a large part of the responsibility for its war with the Germans in 1870. After 1866 the south German states, which had made peace with Prussia, were unable to put together an institutional equivalent of the Prussian-led North German Confederation: therefore they increasingly leaned on Prussia. Gradually all of them, even Bavaria, concluded alliances which, in war, put their armies under Prussian command and control. Confronting this evidence of the process of German national consolidation on its eastern border, Napoleon III increasingly sought compensation. First he tried to purchase Luxembourg, but Dutch popular opinion reacted strongly against this. The Netherlands government, which had initially been favourable, withdrew its support and Napoleon's attempt failed. Next he tried for an alliance between France, Austria and Italy, but Austria wanted only peace whereas the Italians did not trust the French emperor to give them what they wanted: Rome. Napoleon III meanwhile had to endure the disastrous failure of his plans to establish an empire in Mexico while the United States was engaged in the Civil War: memories of the withdrawal of French troops and the execution of Napoleon's self-proclaimed Emperor Maximilian in 1867 were still very much alive in French public opinion.

In 1868 came the Hohenzollern candidate for the Spanish throne. Prince Leopold of Hohenzollern-Sigmaringen, a relative of King Wilhelm of Prussia, was secretly asked by representatives of the Spanish legislature to assume the vacant Spanish throne. Initially neither the prince nor King Wilhelm showed much interest, but Bismarck encouraged both. When the offer became public, French opinion became alarmed. The French foreign minister, the Duke de Gramont, went into the Chamber of Deputies and threatened war if the candidacy was not withdrawn. Inquiries in Berlin brought the reply that the candidacy had nothing to do with the Prussian government, the matter was purely a family affair.

Meanwhile the French envoy in Prussia, Benedetti, negotiated with Wilhelm I in Bad Ems. The Prussian king suggested that France pressure Spain to drop the candidacy; Wilhelm had no objections himself if the Hohenzollern prince withdrew. On 11 July 1870 the Hohenzollern-Sigmaringen family withdrew the candidacy. This should have ended the matter.

However, French Foreign Minister Gramont now insisted on a high-profile, public, diplomatic victory. He instructed Benedetti to demand formal written assurances and a letter of apology from King Wilhelm I to Emperor Napoleon III. The Prussian king met Benedetti, informed him the whole matter was over and, in a friendly way, refused to do anything further. On the evening of 13 July, the Prussian king telegraphed a report of his encounters with Benedetti to Bismarck, saying the minister-president could do whatever he wanted with it. Bismarck edited the telegram and released it to the press. It conveyed the impression that the French envoy had been brushed off in negotiations which had ended in a virtual rupture of formal diplomatic relations between France and

Prussia.[81] The telegram had the impact of a bombshell on French public opinion. Excited crowds gathered in Paris shouting 'to the Rhine'. The next day the French Senate and Corps Législatif overwhelmingly voted war credits.

On 12 July Moltke was on leave at his estate of Kreisau, a three-hour train ride south-east of Berlin. He was taking his dying brother Adolf, and his wife and two daughters for a ride in an open wagon when a courier arrived bringing a telegram. The General Staff reported a high danger of war. They continued, going for a walk, with Moltke showing nothing except that he grew quieter. An hour later at tea, he said he had to travel to Berlin that night. After tea he reportedly got up, hit the table and said, 'Let'em come. With or without south Germany, we're ready!'[82] He took the night train. When he got back to Berlin, the crisis appeared to be over.

The next day Moltke and Roon had dinner to talk over the situation.[83] Two days later as the king returned from Ems, the crown prince, Moltke, Bismarck and Roon met the train at the Brandenburg station and brought the king up to date as they rode the ten miles to Potsdamer station.[84] At the station, they received news of the French mobilization and the voting of war credits by the French Chamber of Deputies. The king decided to mobilize.

The next day Moltke dined with George Bancroft.[85] He expressed distaste and sorrow at being forced into war, praising the former French Defence Minister Marshal Niel, who had tried to reform the French Army but died in 1869. Bancroft says Moltke knew perfectly well the defects of the French Army. He intended to wage war on French territory, with no boasts but implied perfect confidence at the outcome.[86] If this was true, Moltke was not telling his colleagues. For them, he offered a different scenario: several hundred thousand French soldiers invading across the Rhine River, based upon the best railroad system in Europe and the high mythology of Napoleon to wage aggressive war on German territory.

The first day of mobilization was 16 July.[87] Everything was ready, over 11 000 guns, 266 000 rifles and more than 164 000 horses.[88] The complete mobilization calendar, including sequences and terminals, had been laid down in writing and distributed to the troops on 1 April. All lower headquarters knew exactly what had to be done to go from peacetime to war footing by consulting their forward mobilization calendar. These were made up in advance, showing the whole process in detail, every step in sequence and chronological order.[89] Within 18 days, 1 183 000 men, regular and reservist, passed through the barracks of Germany; 462 000 of these were transported to France to open the campaign.[90] The war plan had seven phases. (1) The period preparatory to war had already been secretly ordered in the last part of June. This war alert cancelled leaves and manoeuvres and alerted commanders from top to bottom that their units should be ready. (2) Reserve call-up. The Prussian Army of this date was 40 per cent regulars, 60 per cent reserves. There was a lot to do. (3) Mobilization moved reservists to their units, and the units to their railroad assembly points. (4) The military travel plan began on 20 July. Within ten days the first units – the war shield – were disembarked and ready for action on the German frontier. Three days later troops of the Second Army began to assemble at the border. By 18 July there were more than 300 000 there. Two days later their supply trains began shuttling in.[91] In the first 20 days of the military travel plan, actual arrival time matched planned arrival time almost exactly: they had been practising it for two years. (5) By 25 July concentration marches had begun, followed on 4 August by opening round (6) advance and (7) attack marches. The specifics of the military travel plan are worth noting, for no army in the world could do this at the time.

Military Travel Plan

By January 1870 railroad mobilization had been reduced to 20 days, 260 per cent better than 1867, with a force size nearly three times as large and a mobilization and battle space area seven times larger than 1866. It delivered German forces to the French border like a factory assembly line. And allowed Moltke's timing patterns to begin to dominate war.

Stage One was a 'war alert'. Front loaded to the war plan, it was a preparatory period when commanders made certain their units were ready to mobilize. Troops were returned from special duty, school and manoeuvres, equipment was checked and readied, leaves cancelled, war plans rebriefed, reserve staffs notified to be ready for active duty.

There was a seven-day period of mobilization, to get civilians to their units for equipage, to get units to their railroad collection points and to reorganize the railroad system for military transport.

A 20-day military travel plan began. All orders, requisitions, bills and quarters were ready. They only had to be signed by officials to begin to carry four armies with two or three corps each over six rail lines, at the rate of 18 trains per day in each direction over double-track lines and 12 per day over single-track lines. Volume was building: 1520 trains in a period of 20 days or over 70 troop trains per day.[92]

By 1870 the kingdom of Prussia had 3881 locomotives, 6151 passenger cars and 86 299 baggage cars. Its rail system comprised about 11 000 miles, roughly two-thirds double-tracked.[93] For the 1870 military travel plan, nine lines were used: six for the Prussian armies, three for the south Germans.[94] Only four crossed the Rhine River.[95] A military train comprised 50 cars, loaded with all one kind of unit, for example a battalion of 1000 men, a squadron of 150 horses or three-quarters of an artillery battery or munitions column. Thus each corps averaged 94, 50-car trains, or nearly 5000 railroad cars. Plus 100 trains each for supply, hospital, horse remount, field bakery, etc.[96] There were 12 corps. That is 125 700 railroad cars in all, almost one and a half times the number which then existed in the German states. They moved at a uniform speed of 14 miles per hour, with rest stops every eight to nine hours.

By organizing everything ahead, and reusing trains by double-tracking – outgoing trains ran side by side with returning – the first ten army corps used only 60 per cent the number of cars and 40 per cent the number of locomotives than if each train was used only once. They planned to use three and a half days to move each corps instead of five and a half as had been the case in 1866. This reduced railroad transportation time from 1320 to 840 hours.[97]

Observers have described the awesomeness of the mobilization of 1914. This one, 43 years earlier, must have been breathtaking: 70 trains daily for people who only saw a few each week. On the tenth day the first units disembarked on the French border, by the thirteenth day the troops of the Second Army were assembled there, on the eighteenth day the number was 300 000.[98]

High Command and Mobile General Staff

The crown prince's Third Army, including the south German contingents, was set up at Aachen. The crown prince paid immediate visits to the kings of Bavaria and Württemberg, ceremonially important but also finalizing their integration and participation in Prussian war plans. Prince Friedrich Charles' Second Army, six corps plus two cavalry divisions, moved into the centre. Steinmetz, 74-year-old victor of Nachod in 1866, commanded the First Army in the south.[99]

Royal headquarters was something else. It comprised the king and his entourage, Bismarck and the civil and military cabinets, plus important members of the foreign affairs chancellery. Roon and his War Ministry staff were there. Plus a host of privileged spectators, newspaper correspondents and military attachés. Crowds of princelings with grooms, horses, valets and cooks attached themselves to this army as if attending a fashionable sporting event.[100] All the paraphernalia of agricultural elite warfare.

As one can tell from reading Verdy du Vernois' memoirs, the Berlin General Staff was a close body of men who knew each other well from years of working together. During the 1870 War the mobile General Staff spent more than six months in the field together. There was not the least amount of tension or conflict. They lived and worked together as a group of friends. Moltke's spirit pervaded everything and with him there was no tension or competition. Moltke got along easily and, as he was the operative field commander, so did everyone else. They had cemented their relationships in Berlin and on staff rides and it continued exactly the same, even under the immense tension of a major war.[101] But how was it set up to operate in the field?

Aside from Moltke, there were roughly a dozen GGS officers, plus a staff of 70. Podbielski was quartermaster general. There were three department heads: Bronsart von Schellendorff operations, Verdy du Vernois intelligence and communications, and Brandenstein supply and railroads. Each had several captains and a number of adjutants. The most senior staff major acted as office manager: he was in charge of incoming communication, apportioning the paper flow and outgoing communication. Moltke's first adjutant, Major de Claer, was in charge of food, lodging and supplies for the staff. There were ten draftsmen and seven clerks. How did the GGS command and control this horde? Very closely, as one learns by comparing two images of 1870: one at the command top, Verdy du Vernois, one of Moltke's demigods who during the battle of Sedan liaised between Moltke and his army commanders, another at the army operational level, Bernard von Blumenthal, chief of staff of the crown prince's Third Army. These two men knew each other well and stayed in close touch with each other and with Moltke from 24 June right through to 2 September.[102]

As the mobile or war General Staff moved, an abandoned school was usually selected to house its work, with quarters arranged near by. Every 24 hours a duty officer was appointed as deputy chief. He was always available. In combat the General Staff became a 24-hour operation.

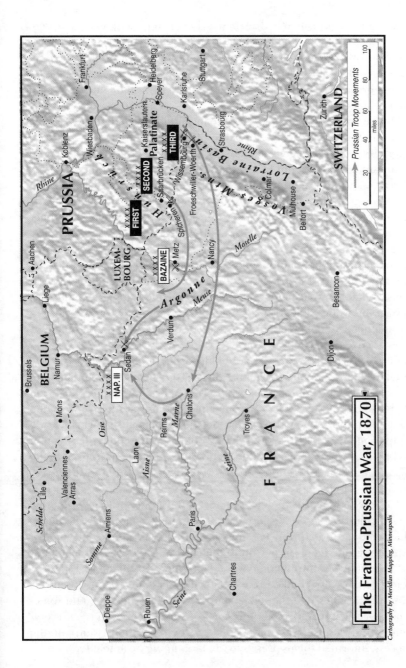

Figure 6.1　North-eastern France, the German and Belgian border areas (Philip Schwartzberg © Meridian Mapping)

A supply of metal-etched map sketches of the campaign area were available. Every morning an officer marked on these sketches the location and size of friendly and enemy forces, then block printed them up on a small portable press. Along with these, Moltke had on his desk a railroad map of central Europe, a compass, a magnifying glass and maps of many different scales.

Moltke knew the maximum force that could be moved in a given time frame and terrain to deploy for battle.[103] He figured that a corps armed for war would move about ten miles in one day.[104] And he reckoned on maximum and minimum forced marches. For example at the best time of year – spring or autumn – with good weather and an early morning start after a good night's rest, cavalry or horse artillery might go nearly 20 miles before noon. After a halt for rest and food, it might go another 20 miles by 7 p.m. If the unit was in very good condition, after five hours' rest, it might, under emergency conditions, be asked to resume march at midnight, gaining another 20 miles by 6 a.m. Thus 50 or 60 miles in 24 hours. During the same time period and with similar conditions, infantry might march 30 miles.[105] As conditions changed, these maximums would slide to an average or to a minimum: thus in bad winter weather, without a good night's rest, reserve troops not hardened by recent active duty might perform very differently from this.

Every morning Podbielski assembled the department chiefs, the bureau chiefs, the first adjutant, Stosch the general intendant and Maydam, the chief of telegraphic bureau, for a wide-ranging discussion of the situation. Moltke led the meeting, asking questions, requesting additional information, and laying out the details of his plans, clearly and succinctly. After this, Moltke and Podbielski presented the situation and plans to the king, and, after getting his approval, went back to the GGS, where the operations orders were drawn up. Key orders were drafted by Moltke himself.

To deliver them, the mobile General Staff used several methods. One was a group of *Jäger*, supported by a regiment of infantry. Secondly, older General Staff officers might deliver very important orders, explaining the details in person to the chief of staff and commander at the other end. A third method was telegraphic.[106] And a fourth was the field post. Finally, Moltke wrote personal letters and routinely sent his closest colleagues into the field. They reported to the army and sometimes corps commanders and his chief of staff, checked to see if everything from Moltke was understood, fielded questions, and, in the process, informed themselves as to what was going on at that location.[107]

When possible, army and corps chiefs of staff also initiated this system, appearing at the mobile General Staff to discuss and confer directly with Moltke. Between 22 July and 2 September, Blumenthal, chief of staff to the Third Army, communicated with Moltke or his chief aides virtually once in every 24 hours. Towards the end these communications increased to roughly one every six hours.[108]

Moltke usually stayed very close to the king during a battle. Only once did he stray away, during the battle of Gravelotte-St Privat when he went with the attack of II Corps against the French left wing, until he was warned by officers of his entourage that it was not his place to stand in danger of enemy fire.[109] Moltke stayed in close touch with his staff. The simple midday meal was shared around noon with the whole staff, unless Moltke had been requested to eat at the king's table. His eating and drinking habits were legendarily modest and sparse and Moltke did not need much sleep. In spite of being 70 years old, his energy never flagged. After a period of intense work and tension, staying up and working at all hours of the night before a major decision, he was completely refreshed with a few hours of sleep. In the evening a few officers played whist in his quarters. They played for only five pfennigs a point, but with passion and concentration. Continuous mistakes or misadventures bothered Moltke, even if he said nothing.[110] In the GGS, the spirit of Moltke dominated everything.[111]

By 26 July, the tenth mobilization day, the East Prussian, Pomeranian and Silesian corps began to move into position behind the Second and the Third armies. One active infantry division and two *Landwehr* divisions moved by rail to coastal defence positions. By 3 August, the nineteenth mobilization day, the main forces were assembled and march ready. The clockwork of industrial war planning processes had produced 456 000 men and 135 000 horses war ready.[112]

The French Mobilization

Meanwhile, the French mobilization allowed the German armies the luxury of time. Time is one factor that cannot be called back. If lost, it cannot be found later.

According to the printed German war plan, French armies were expected to cross the Rhine River and attack. To begin the war on German territory. Even the French expected this. That it did not happen came as a profound shock to everyone. But for the Germans, it was a welcome surprise, for the French a sudden negative jolt which got worse and worse, becoming a numbing exercise in chaos and leading to their first lost war in more than half a century.[113]

In France, mobilization was expected to produce 300 000 men and almost 1000 guns ready for action in about three weeks. Three armies were to arrive at Metz, Strasbourg and Chalons ready to invade German territory.

For five days operations with this in mind went forward. Then, on 19 July, there was a sudden, total change. Emperor Napoleon III ordered a complete reorganization. He was to be in command, not General Leboeuf. There would be only one army, not three. Napoleon III, counting on Austrian intervention against the German southern flank, would lead a sweep across the Rhine against their ancient foe.

The sudden, premature French war declaration of 14 July had stunned the Austrians. Amid profuse declarations of loyalty and a formal statement of neutrality, Austria nevertheless began secretly to mobilize cavalry and artillery reserves.[114] Italy wavered: some Italians remembered what they owed to Prussia for 1866, others thought that military support for France now would help remove French garrisons in Rome. Not to worry: the French had already sent transports to bring home the Rome garrison. While Austria and Italy consulted, Russia meanwhile, with 200 000 men stationed on the Austrian border, threatened to match Austrian mobilization with one of her own.[115] On 3 August, Napoleon received a proposal suggesting that Austria and Italy might both declare armed neutrality, but press ahead with war preparations, either to enter the war or to mediate it. He rejected this, saying only immediate military intervention was acceptable.

Although Austrian intervention remained an open possibility, even after 2 September – and a possibility that Moltke kept contingency forces ready to deal with – in reality Austria was unready and unwilling to fight in 1870. Her leadership was divided and she was still recovering from 1866.[116] But the crucial factor was the battlefield: German victories and French defeats. If at any time this had been slowed, changed or reversed, Austria might have become very dangerous, very quickly.

Meanwhile French mobilization was in chaos. They had no war-planning process and no functioning General Staff. They had not done the planning and preparation to fight with an army of 300 000. Instead of being a week or two ahead of the Germans, they were a month or two behind. And there was no uniformity. Some parts were ahead, others behind. For example, reservists had to go first to depots for uniforms and equipment and then to their regiments. Soldiers from the depart-ment of the Nord around Lille, assigned to the 2nd Zouaves, had to go to Oran, Algeria, to pick up equipment and supplies, then back north-east to Alsace where their regiment was a part of VI Corps.[117]

Once the troops arrived at their regiments, there was often no food or orders: no one knew what they were supposed to do or where they were supposed to go. Nothing had been arranged. Officers, equipment, food and quarters: all were missing.[118] Single regiments were displaced here and there across France. Huge traffic jams ensued at railroad embarka-tion and disembarkation points.[119] Railroad lines were filled with loaded supply trains sent forward without any thought as to the unloading facil-ities needed at the other end. Even if they could be unloaded, there were no orders to tell them what to do. Active duty units lacked horses and forms of transport, equipment, cooking pots, even money to pay

Figure 6.2   Moltke and the mobile General Staff during the French War. During the 1870 War Moltke conducted combat with about 80 officers. Seventy of them were located in a nearby abandoned schoolhouse or public building, while about a dozen accompanied Moltke himself, in this case to a vantage point in a clear-ing on the wooded hills above Frenois, south of the Meuse River, overlooking the fortress city of Sedan, located two or three miles in the distance beyond Moltke (Courtesy Ullstein Bilderdienst, Berlin)

the troops. Officers had been issued only maps of Germany: they had to borrow maps of France from local schools and real estate offices. The most severe shortage was food: the great fortress of Metz gradually filling up with troops who had no sugar, coffee, rice or salt. Troops were on their own. After they had eaten the locals out of house and home, they turned to pillage. Discipline lapsed. Soldiers did what they wanted. They wandered off, and came back as they pleased. Such an army was in no condition to fight a war.[120] In spite of this a vague outline of the French Army in war positions began to appear. Four corps were in front of Metz and one corps behind it. Another corps was at Thionville, II Corps was at the frontier opposite Saarbrücken, at Strasbourg was I Corps, V Corps was near Sarreguemines, the guard at Nancy, VII Corps gradually moving towards Belfort. On 24 July French forces began to concentrate on the Metz–Saarbrücken road, aiming for Mainz where they suspected the German forces were also going.

Meanwhile authoritative British newspapers expected an early French invasion of Germany and saw no way that the Prussians would be ready in time to do anything about it.[121] Archduke Albrecht, war commander designate of a proposed Austrian army of intervention, told a crown council in Vienna that French forces would cross the Rhine by 30 July and be poised along the border of Saxony for an attack into the heartland of Prussia by the end of August.[122]

Moltke was astonished as more and more German troops arrived at the Rhine, but there were no French attacks. Meanwhile the French had fewer than 200 000 troops. Since they had no intelligence organization to collect information, they were also in the dark as to what military situation they confronted.[123] When Napoleon arrived on 28 July, he had no plan either. Unable to sit on a horse, incoherent in thought, he was lost without his wife's counsel. When one of his generals suggested an attack against Saarbrücken just to fill the time until the Germans arrived from wherever, Napoleon agreed.

Orders went out and six French corps slowly and accidentally converged on Saarbrücken. They marched ten miles a day, in complete confusion, crossed each others' lines, got mixed up and delayed each other. By 2 August they had arrived and were ordered to attack en masse, with no reconnaissance or advance guard, as if on a field review. Officers were told to take some food along because it was not known when they might get back to camp. German forces in Saarbrücken, three companies and two troops of light field guns, stayed for a few hours, fired off a few shots and then withdrew. A few French troops ventured ahead, but the town was not occupied, the bridges not crossed, the telegraph station not destroyed. Parisian newspapers reported that three Prussian divisions had been destroyed and Saarbrücken burned to the ground.

1870: Combat

Lorraine was the decisive battleground in the Franco-Prussian War. After a series of engagements, Prussia and her German allies dislocated the French Army, setting up its investiture in the fortress of Metz, the encirclement of Sedan and the siege of Paris. Even though the war went on beyond 2 September, the day the French Army in Sedan surrendered, the north-eastern campaign was the decisive fighting in the Franco-Prussian War.

Battles of Spicheren and Wissembourg, 4 August

One small canvas in this 180 000 square miles of war tapestry was a region in the foothills of the Vosges, overlooked by mountains to the north and by the hills of the Bavarian Palatinate across the Lauter River to the north-east.[124] More than 300 000 German troops were converging on it across the 100-mile arc from Karlsruhe to Koblenz. The Second Army, six corps strong, was moving south-west around Kaiserslautern through the mountains. The First Army, III Corps was moving directly south towards the lower Saar River. The Third Army, separated by 50 miles of mountains, was at Speyer, due east and threatening Strasbourg. Moltke had intended the Third Army to begin the war and on the evening of 3 July he saw a chance of its flanking the French just as the Second Army was attacking it frontally. He ordered the Third Army to attack the next day. The Third Army was not ready, so he ordered the First Army to do it: strike east and south from the Moselle River, laying down specific date phase lines: clear all the First Army out of the St Wendel–Ottweiler road and allow the Second Army to pass through, move up to the Saar River on 7 July, be ready to cross it on the 9th. Instead, the First Army's commander Steinmetz set off on his own. On the evening of 5 July he launched his corps due south-east, across the path of the Second Army and into a blind frontal attack against an entrenched and well-positioned French hilltop position called Spicheren.[125]

   This battle was made out by the media to be a great German triumph. The French took their defeat as a thunderclap sent from heaven, while the Germans thought so highly of it that streets and squares all across Germany were named in its honour. In reality it was a disaster. The 14th

Division, without orders, attacked a superior force, dug in and entrenched on a hillside. It was the only place in the French line with reinforcements close by. Lacking surprise and cover, from 11 a.m. to 5 p.m. German forces moved steadily uphill against superior weapons. Casualties of roughly 10 per cent were taken by the Germans, and they would have been worse had not German artillery moved in to support. At dusk the French finally withdrew when their position was about to be outflanked by newly arrived German troops.[126]

Meanwhile waiting in the outskirts of Saarbrücken, other French forces did nothing. Troops marched to and fro – in soaking rain or blazing sun – without maps, without orders. Napoleon finally ordered them into a defensive position, having read in the newspapers that German forces were approaching. On the evening of 3 August a single French division, 20 miles out in front of its supporting forces, occupied the town of Wissembourg, 400 yards from the frontier across which four German corps would advance the following day.

The reason they chose Wissembourg was that the division was out of food. One battalion occupied the town, the others camped in the hills behind it while officials from the intendance checked out the availability of provisions. They found food and drink and made a night of it. At dusk their commander sent out a few casual reconnaissance patrols. They missed seeing that three miles away, just across the Lauter River, was the German advance guard. The commander discounted reports from his headquarters and from local residents. He inspected the plain of the Palatinate and found nothing. The threat of the Bavarians was rumour and hearsay, he told his aides.

In the thirteenth century Wissembourg had been one of the ten free cities of Alsace. The land around it forms a natural amphitheatre, facing east. The old town is built directly astride the River Lauter which joins the Rhine, a dozen miles further downstream.

Posting two infantry battalions and a single battery in this small fortress town, overlooking the two bridges providing access from the east, the French commander deployed his nine remaining battalions, three batteries and a Mitrailleuse unit whose gun crews did not know how to fire the new invention, a mile to the south-west in the small fortress called the Geissberg.

German V Corps troops were awakened at 2 a.m. in the rain. They began their approach march two hours later. The first Bavarian shells began to fall on the town at 8 a.m.[127] Douay, the French general, thought he was facing a reconnaissance. He deployed his troops, halted the Bavarian infantry by careful Chassepot fire and then waited. Two battalions of German infantry surrounded the Altstadt, and moved towards the railroad station.[128] They ran point blank into a company of French line infantry. Both opened fire. In the Prussian fusilier battalion of 1000, only four officers and two corporals were not killed or wounded. Two more battalions of the French 47th came up. The railroad station was seized, town houses on the outskirts occupied. Meanwhile two German corps moved against these forces, one to attack frontally, one flanking the town to the south. In preparation 80 pieces of breech-loading artillery zeroed in on the French positions. Shortly before noon, the French commander was killed when a shell exploded the ammunition wagon of his Mitrailleuse battery.

An hour later the lead infantry brigades of German V Corps stormed the defences of Wissembourg, and its two battalions and battery surrendered. Meanwhile the 41st brigade of the German XI Corps had worked its way through the thick woodlands east of the Geissberg and began to assault the slope. Moving forward in closed columns 800 officers and men were shot down in a few minutes by the Chassepot.[129] Four batteries of artillery were brought up and by 2 p.m. the Chassepot were silenced. The 1st Company of the 5th *Jäger* poured so much fire into a French artillery battery that all its horses were killed.[130] The French withdrew towards Woerth, the Prussians did not follow, but bivouacked on the battlefield in heavy rain. They had lost over 1500. The French in fortress Geissberg, having defended it for three hours, surrendered, after taking more than 25 per cent casualties.[131]

Wissembourg was a paradigm battle for the war as a whole. Dominant themes were: (1) overwhelming German numbers, 50000 against 6000 French; (2) the broad envelopment which these numbers made possible; (3) the terrifying and deadly impact of French Chassepot fire on attacking troops and (4) the final reliance on volumes of German rifled artillery fire; and (5) high casualties. Of 6000 engaged, the French lost 33 per cent. From three corps, the Germans lost almost 2000.[132]

Battle of Froeschwiller–Woerth, 29 August

Fifteen miles and a day's march to the south-west, the campaign was resumed as the Prussian Third Army stumbled into the vanguard of the French VI Corps. The terrain was rolling hills and valleys. West of the Saurbach was the Froeschwiller ridge, the foothills of the Vosges Mountains rising like a huge folded comforter, three to four miles long and a mile wide. Green meadows were intersected by a shallow stream crossable on foot but a few bridges allowed the passage of guns and transport. Gently rising slopes, without cover, led up to a crest crowned by a small timbered village. The layout was in the form of a giant 'E' with a central spine along the ridge and three prongs – to the north a ridge of hills covered by forest, in the centre a ridge stretching 600 yards down to the towns of Woerth and Elsasshausen, to the south the forest of Niederwald, a square mile of pines and hills sloping down to the village of Morsbrunn.[133]

Defending it were French forces of 42 000 infantry, 6000 cavalry and 100 guns. A division on the left flank prong, the forest and grassy hill sloping down to the village, another division in the centre prong, down to the villages of Woerth and Elsasshausen, finally 7000 men facing south and the ridge sloping down to the village of Morsbrunn. A fourth division was fed into the left wing, parts of a fifth – the survivors of Wissembourg, were held on the slopes behind Froeschwiller as reserve. Behind them was a cavalry division.

The French arrived haphazardly. Units straggled in here and there. Artillery never arrived, food supplies trickled in. The local inhabitants' hospitality was soon exhausted. Intendants had 6000 rations to feed more than 40 000 troops. When food supplies finally arrived, the French were cooking it as the Prussian offensive began. Bridges were not destroyed, reconnaissance patrols not sent out, sentries not posted, trenches not dug. Nevertheless, these troops radiated confidence. They had defeated the Chinese and the Vietnamese, they would defeat the Prussians. Men wandered in to drink in the taverns of Woerth or water their horses in the Sauerbach as they pleased.[134]

Advancing against these few triumphant colonial veterans were five German corps, nearly 300 guns and 85 000 men. Neither commander expected, wanted or sought a fight that day, not least one with 25 000 casualties. It was a meeting encounter battle, full of the terror of surprise. However, such an encounter as Froeschwiller played exactly into Moltke's strategic and operational strategy: he now knew he had enough forces to attack the French whenever and wherever he found them.

On the evening of 5 August, as the Third Army elements advanced from the battlefield at Wissembourg to the south, German forces approached in two great waves; the first contained the 2nd Bavarian and the II and V Prussian Corps, and the Corps Werder. As V Corps readied its night bivouac near the village of Preuschdorf, a half mile in front of Woerth, its pickets saw the watch fires of the MacMahon army across

Sauer creek on the heights of the woods.[135] During a night of pouring rain, outposts on both sides exchanged shots.

At 5 a.m. French fatigue parties collecting water in the Sauer creek found bullets whizzing around them. French soldiers arriving at the Woerth tavern to seek refreshment after a wet and cool night out were fired upon by Prussian artillery. The French scampered back to their camps, outside of town. A Prussian regiment forded the creek and tried to clear the area. Taking heavy Chassepot and Mitrailleuse fire, it fell back.[136]

Meanwhile the Bavarian 4th Division, two miles to the north, hearing the firing, seeing the French bivouac and assuming an attack, launched one itself just as the outposts of V Corps were falling back from Woerth. They moved across uneven ground, thickly wooded, until towards the top they emerged from the wood's edge to find open ground swept by the Chassepot fire of Ducrot's division. By 10.30 the 4th Bavarian was pinned down in a single confused and unsupported skirmish line.

Meanwhile on the right flank of the French position Lartigue's division, pushed forward close to the creek crossing point, opened artillery fire. Four German batteries from XI Corps replied, reducing the French guns to silence within a few minutes. At 10 a.m., the chief of staff of V Corps, alarmed that this engagement presaged a full-scale attack – opened up with his entire 14 batteries. Within an hour 24 more guns from XI Corps were added. Finally, General von Kirchbach ordered a full attack, throwing in three corps, half the strength of the Third Army. Soon the crown prince, realizing the situation was becoming critical, ordered an attack all along the front.[137] Coming up in support was a single French division which arrived late.

MacMahon's troops withered under superior artillery barrages, unanswered by their own forces. Wherever Chassepot were brought to bear, the German troops were pushed back, but artillery and increasingly larger and larger numbers gradually forced the French into a tight ring. On their left flank XI Corps drove a wedge between two French corps, captured the village of Morsbrunn south of the Niederwald and seized MacMahon's communication lines. By 1 p.m. Lartigue's division, its last reserves used up, called upon Michel's Cuirassier brigade and the 6th Lancers of Duhesme's division to cover his retreat. This body of horsemen, 1000 strong, launched themselves across a terrain of tree stumps, ditches and tangled vines.[138] At a range of 300 feet this group ran into the concentrated fire of the 32nd and 80th German regiments. Only a handful of survivors escaped. It was 2.30 p.m.

The Prussian XI Corps stormed the burning village of Elsasshausen. MacMahon's position was now compromised. Only Drucrot, on the left, kept open the vital escape route to the south-west. French troops in Froeschwiller were caught in a German crossfire of five divisions and their assembled artillery. Two Algerian regiments briefly drove the Germans back, losing 1000 men in 30 minutes or 33 men per minute.

At 4 p.m. MacMahon ordered a general retreat. To cover it he ordered in Bonnemain's reserve cavalry force. The 2000 sabres launched themselves across broken ditches, vineyards and hop gardens at the densely packed advancing infantry. Met by point blank rifle fire and artillery case shot, they were overwhelmed in ten minutes. The second brigade met the same fate; 75 per cent of men and horses went down, over 5000 men in a few minutes, over 260 men per minute.[139] Killed, wounded and taken prisoner at Froeschwiller–Woerth were more than 25 000 French.

German forces also suffered substantial casualties. However, the Prussian system now sustained such large numbers of troops and supplies that even after punishing battles – when in earlier wars armies required a breathing space of two or three months to recover – these German forces took less than 48 hours to regroup, resupply and push on to the next objective.[140]

Battle and siege of Sedan, 1–2 September

The end of the decisive phase of the French War came at Sedan in north-eastern France on Tuesday, 2 September. It came unsurprisingly to those who understood France's lack of preparations for war before it started, an insufficiency which was the hallmark of defeat in industrial mass war. In fact Sedan was a normal conclusion to a contest between two states, one of which used a deep future-oriented war planning process and the other did not.

When Emperor Napoleon III arrived by third-class railroad carriage at Chalons on the evening of 16 August, a new army – without equipment, leadership or direction – was being created. It was a force of over 130 000 men and 400 guns, cobbled together from many sources, including the three right-wing corps of the old Army of the Rhine, arriving by train from the west and south, a new XII Corps, partly made up of a brand new division of men whose training took place during the war, 18 battalions of outrageously wild Garde Mobile sent from Paris, weapons and munitions from here and there.[141]

Supplies and equipment for these men did not arrive. Many had left their packs and equipment elsewhere. There were no artillery or medical services. But the main problem was that no one had planned what to do with these forces. The emperor had no plans. MacMahon asked Marshal François Bazaine, commander of the Army of the Rhine. Bazaine waited on fate.

On 18 August the telegraph line between the fortress city of Metz and the commander's headquarters at Chalons was cut. On the 21st German cavalry closed to within 20 miles. The next day the army of Chalons retreated west to Rheims.[142] Halfway there it was decided they should go north-east to Montmedy on the Aisne River and on 23 August they set out.

Moltke, meanwhile, held his forces in tight control, ordering the crown prince's Second Army forward to Nancy, but splitting it in two. The Army of the Meuse under Crown Prince Albert of Saxony, with the Guard, IV and XII Corps, were to pursue MacMahon to the Meuse River. The remaining four corps of the Second Army would stay at Metz.[143]

Moltke's intelligence of French moves was poor. It came in bits and pieces. On the 24th a dispatch from London, based on Paris newspapers, reported that MacMahon would try to link up with Bazaine. Moltke's staff worked out the complex march tables to allow for that possibility, for example, to intercept MacMahon near Damvilles by 29 August. On that day they got hold of a bundle of newspapers from Paris. *Le Temps* reported that MacMahon was already marching to rescue Bazaine. Yet the picture was not clear. Cavalry reconnaissance confirmed nothing.

Moltke decided to risk assuming that it was valid. But his orders remained open-ended. Unless cavalry reconnaissance to the north-west belied it, the Army of the Meuse was to concentrate between Verdun and Varennes, with the two Bavarian corps swinging north. Moltke's *Auftrag* orders reiterated that, in this situation, he could not exactly specify what to do: Crown Prince Albert had to decide himself. To ensure that something happened, Moltke sent Verdy du Vernois through the night to the Meuse headquarters to talk with the crown prince's chief of staff.

Moltke and his staff rode north-west, trailing MacMahon by only a dozen miles. As he moved, Moltke spewed out telegraph messages, personal letters, couriers and aides-de-camp to confirm, ensure and inform himself.

Crown Prince Albert's Saxon cavalry patrols ran into MacMahon northeast of Grand Pré and Vouziers. Before leaving Rheims MacMahon had ordered his corps to load up with supplies at Rheims railway station, which was brimming with equipment, food and war materials. However the intendants had not the time, staff or ability to distribute it properly. The troops came away empty-handed. This boded ill for these 130 000 men. They soon broke ranks and began to pillage the countryside. To resupply, MacMahon on the 24th veered sharply north-west to reconnect with the railroad line at Rethel.[144] It took two days to load up before again heading east towards Metz.

The main body of the German forces were now moving through the muddy forests of the Argonne. Steady rain made everything worse, especially the roads.

On the 27th MacMahon received reports that the advance guards of the Saxon cavalry had crossed the Meuse River. He knew that German forces occupied Chalons and Rheims to his rear and German cavalry was appearing from the cover of the Argonne Forest to harass his right flank.[145] MacMahon concluded that his only hope lay to the north. He gave up the Metz operation, ordered his army to change course again to the north-west, and sent messages to Bazaine and to Paris. Paris immediately ordered him to go to Bazaine's aid. He countermanded his prior orders and inquired about the possibilities of crossing the Meuse below Stenay.

French cavalry patrols found the bridges at Stenay firmly held by German troops. MacMahon ordered his forces to turn north and head for the crossings at Remilly and Mouzon.[146] The two northern corps could do this, XII Corps reaching Mouzon and I Corps Rancourt six miles further west. VII Corps, harassed by German cavalry, could barely get halfway to La Besace.

Meanwhile V Corps, near Buzancy, never received these orders: the officer carrying them fell into German hands. As its advance patrols topped a rise at Nouart, they received point blank infantry fire and caught a glimpse of the whole of the Saxon XII Corps deployed and ready for action to their immediate front. All afternoon they shot at each other across the valley of the Wiseppe River. Then the French withdrew through the dark, wet forest. When they reached Beaumont they threw themselves on the ground to sleep. The rearguard only arrived at 5 p.m.

An hour or so after the last French soldier had fallen asleep, five German corps began advancing on the outskirts of the French encampment. There were no sentries posted, horses were unsaddled, artillery parks cluttered with guns and supplies. German soldiers said afterwards it seemed unfair to open fire on such a target.[147] With the first signs of movement and activity, they opened up. The French scrambled, officers tumbled out of their billets, wagons and equipment jammed the streets, masses of troops and civilians fled north to Mouzon and east to the Meuse. The cautious and methodical Germans were halted by Chassepot as the French withdrew to a line a mile behind the village. Soon overwhelmed, the French, under constant barrage, withdrew further to the river. They tried cavalry charges to break up the oncoming infantry. These were shot down. Five miles north, fighting all the way, they found the Mouzon bridges crowded with refugees. Officers and men flung themselves into the Meuse. By 7 p.m. the river was in German hands. By evening the French had lost nearly 7500 men. MacMahon ordered his army to fall back on the fortress of Sedan.[148]

On the 30th Bismarck warned the Belgian government that if the French Army crossed the frontier and was not disarmed, Prussian forces reserved the right to pursue it. Moltke passed this on to the troops. On the afternoon of 31 August, German forces moved into Frenois and Donchery, beginning to close off the French retreat avenue to the northwest. More than 200 000 German forces moved into position surrounding Sedan, finding bridges undamaged and watch patrols not out. Additional pontoon bridges were thrown across the Meuse.

MacMahon still assumed he would be in Sedan a day or two, to rest and refit, then break out by massing his troops against German forces too tired and weakened to stop him.

Next morning, 2 September, the battle began at 4 a.m. The Meuse at Donchery was crossed by advance units from the German V and XI Corps. By 7.30 they had reached the Sedan–Mezieres road and turned east towards the sound of the guns. At the same hour, the Ist Bavarians crossed and attacked Bazeilles in the dark, fearing the French would slip away. Not to worry: the French were asleep. But they and the villagers put up a staunch resistance. Finally Saxon artillery began to shell the town. MacMahon, riding out towards Bazeilles caught a fragment in his leg. He turned command over to Ducrot who wanted to abandon the position at once: as a veteran of Froeschwiller he knew the Prussians would soon envelop the entire area. Bazeilles was evacuated. Then General Emanuel Wimpffen appeared, the man who had been given command by the Parisian government. He wanted to fight to the last man.

On this final day, 2 September – as German troops moved into encircling positions, as the artillery bombardment around the position began to heat up and German units began to close – the French cavalry charged. There were four of these.

There was one at 9 a.m. As the batteries of the German V and XI Corps took positions on the sloping hillside crest south of the Floing-Illy ravine, and their infantry advanced over the slope, a detachment of French cavalry galloped across the valley against it. It crashed and went to ground against infantry volleys and artillery fire. Horses and riders, lost and out of control, plunged away, wandering over the frontier. There were thousands of stragglers.[149]

A second occurred at 1 p.m. Ducrot with his infantry overwhelmed and his artillery shattered, asked General Margueritte to use his cavalry as a battering ram to force a passage for the French infantry. As Margueritte began to write out the orders, a bullet passed through his face, and, as he was carried back by his aides, he pointed with one arm towards the enemy. At that his whole mass of horsemen launched themselves as one up the slope, past the disorganized lines of their own infantry and down again into the skirmish lines and formations of breech-loaders. At no point was the German line broken. The charge disintegrated, split in two, and the remainders crashed into the quarries and valleys below.

Ducrot asked the remaining commander if he would try again. Again a charge, again they plunged down the hill to their destruction.

At 2.30 p.m. Ducrot asked a last time. The final charge of General de Gallifet broke totally. Volleys halted it at 140 feet and again at 80 feet.[150] It was reported that Gallifet himself came to within a few feet of the German lines. The infantry ceased fire, the officers saluted, the French commander was allowed to ride slowly away, honoured and unharmed.[151]

The artillery finishes the battle for Sedan

The king, Moltke, Bismarck and assorted attachés and visitors – Philip Sheridan of the Union Army, General Kutosow from Russia, Colonel Walker from Britain, and assorted princes – assembled to watch the end game from the heights of a clearing on the wooded hill above Frenois, south of the Meuse.[152] In the fields below, II Bavarian Corps had deployed its artillery, and, on the right, IV Corps had set up its guns.

In the next few hours, more than 600 guns fired 33 000 rounds. And, in contrast to French artillery shells, set to explode at 3950 and 9200 feet, German shells used percussion fuses, exploding on impact wherever they landed.[153]

This was not random fire but carefully directed. For example, the Guard artillery set up to bombard the Bois de la Garenne. Each of ten batteries took a different section of woods, each gun firing at a different elevation.[154] When a French unit appeared at the wood's edge, it was driven back by the full force of all guns. Eyewitnesses called it a catastrophic rain of artillery shells.[155] At 2.30 the guns ceased and the Guard advanced into the woods. They found masses of demoralized men, incapable of resistance. Some battalions had stacked their arms, waving handkerchiefs. Those who still wanted to fight their way out were dissuaded by others who wanted to quit. By 5 p.m. everything was quiet and thousands were prisoners.[156]

Negotiations

As dusk came on, a white flag was raised from the topmost tower of the Sedan fortress. But who would request an armistice? It had to be Wimpffen. But before that there was one last futile charge against the II Bavarians, on the road to Balan. The Bavarians were driven out of the village, reserves on both sides were alerted to check any attempt to exploit this. Nothing happened. Now Moltke dispatched Bonsart von Schellendorff to find out the meaning of the flag. He was sent back in the company of the emperor's adjutant, General Count Reille, with a letter from Napoleon to the German king.

Moltke was nominated by the king to head the negotiations. The king went back to his quarters at Vendresse. Moltke stayed with his General Staff near Donchery. They had a glass or two of wine, and then Moltke went to bed. As midnight approached he felt his arm touched and awoke. Excellence, the French are here. What do they want? To surrender! Moltke jumped out of bed, splashed his face with cold water and put on his wig. The last act of the play can begin, he said.[157]

Present were General Wimpffen, newly appointed commander-in-chief and General Henri Castelnau as personal representative of Emperor Napoleon III. Moltke led the Prussian delegation, along with Bismarck. Nearly all of the Prussian General Staff was present.

As soon as everyone was seated, there was a long pause. Although it seemed as if the Prussians should lead the discussion, Moltke remained silent. Finally General Wimpffen began by explaining that they had come to hear the surrender conditions of the King of Prussia. They were very simple, replied Moltke. The entire French Army were to be prisoners, along with their weapons and equipment. Officers were to be allowed to keep their weapons as testimony to their bravery, but they were to be prisoners along with the troops.

Wimpffen responded. These conditions are very harsh, General, and my instructions force me to ask for something better in return for the honour and courage of the French Army. We will turn over the fort and our artillery. Our army with weapons, supplies and flags will be let free, on condition they will not again make war on Prussia. The emperor and the officers will assume personal and written responsibility. The army will retire to a specifically designated part of France or to Algiers and will remain there to await conclusion of peace negotiations.

Moltke broke in to say the conditions could not be altered.

Wimpffen changed tactics. Two days ago, he said, I was in the interior of Africa. Up to this time my military record has been faultless. Here I am, given command in the middle of a battle. How can I put my signature to such an unhappy surrender? I must take the whole responsibility for a battle without having done anything to prepare for it. You, General Moltke, an officer like me, can understand the great bitterness of my situation. You can alter the conditions if you will.

As Wimpffen saw that Moltke was unmoved, he became even more earnest. If you cannot change them, then maybe we should fight it out. If I appeal to the honour of my army I can break out to the west or we can defend inside the fortress of Sedan.

It was plain to see that Wimpffen himself was not convinced by his own words.[158]

Moltke replied that he had great respect for Wimpffen. He appreciated his situation and was sorry he could not do what was requested. But the suggestions – either a breakout or a defence of Sedan – were essentially impossible. Certainly French troops were excellent, the best of the infantry was noteworthy, the cavalry audacious and fearless. The artillery wonderful, causing us too much destruction.

But most of your infantry is demoralized, we captured 20000 unwounded soldiers yesterday! You have roughly 80000 troops left. You must realize that we have over 240000 troops and 500 guns. Under such circumstances it will be impossible to break through our lines. As for defending Sedan, you have 48 hours' worth of food and no ammunition.

Wimpffen then shifted to a political discussion. It was in Prussia's interest to arrange an honourable political settlement: you do not want the entire nation of France on your backs.[159] Finally Wimpffin said the French Army would continue the battle.

In that case, Moltke interjected, the armistice ends tomorrow morning at 4 a.m. Punctually at 4 we will open fire.

Everyone had got up from the table. The horses had been brought. The meeting seemed to be over.

At that point Bismarck stepped forward. General Wimpffen, I do not doubt that you have brave and glorious troops, that can do wonderful things and take great casualties. But for what? By tomorrow night you will have accomplished no more than you have now and you will have to forget the great loss of blood in both of our armies. Let us not break up the conference on an argumentative tone.

Everyone sat down again. Moltke reiterated that a breakout would fail even if French troops were in the best possible condition. My army is greatly superior in size, and my artillery can, in a few hours, turn everything in Sedan into ashes. The position is surrounded and all sides are covered.

Oh, you are not as strong as you think, and you do not know the terrain and specific topography around Sedan, replied Wimpffen.

You do not know the position as well as we do, replied Moltke. At the beginning of the campaign all your officers were given maps of Germany, but they were not in position to study the terrain and topography of their own country. I repeat, our position is not only strong, but terribly and impregnably so.

Wimpffen could not answer. After a pause, he continued. I return to the offer you made at the beginning of this conference. Let me send an officer around to look over the situation, when he returns, I will make a decision.

You will send no one. It is pointless. You can believe me. And you have only four hours. It is now midnight, at 4 a.m. the armistice ends and I give you not a minute past that.

Then, Wimpffen said, you must realize I cannot make this decision myself, I have to consult my colleagues. It is impossible to do this by 4 a.m. I need more time.

At this Bismarck drew Moltke aside. They talked. Finally Moltke replied, you have until 9 a.m. The negotiations had lasted an hour.[160]

The next morning very early the emperor appeared in Donchery. He wanted to speak with the king. Bismarck took him to a small hut and they talked. Nothing was possible until the surrender was signed. Wimpffen came back and signed at 11 a.m. The next morning, accompanied by a hussar squadron, the emperor was escorted across Belgian territory and interred as a prisoner in the palace at Wilhelmshoehe, near Kassel.[161]

On the evening after 2 September, celebrated in Germany as 'Sedan Day', Moltke finally sat down with his officers at the whist table. Now we can play again, he said.[162]

After the French surrender at Sedan, the German armies marched on Paris and, by 19 September, had completely surrounded the city. Three

French armies formed up for the relief of Paris. Faidherbe in the north, Chanzy at Orleans and Bourbaki in the south-west. The defeat of Chanzy at Orleans and the victory of General Werder over Bourbaki, whose forces were driven over the Swiss border, caused the Parisians to capitulate. On 1 March, the French National Assembly at Bordeaux ratified the peace conditions and brought the war to a close. Thus the same factors that led to German success at Sedan on 2 September, also made this outcome virtually certain. It was just a question of time.

CONCLUSION

Moltke

Dealing with a legend is always hazardous. Moltke is arguably one of the five or ten most famous Germans of all time. In December 1899, at the turn of the millennium, the *Berliner Illustrierte Zeitung* conducted a reader survey. What was the most important invention of the century? The railroad. What was the most significant event? The unification of Germany. Who was the greatest statesman? Bismarck. Who was the century's greatest thinker? Not Darwin, Kant, Schopenhauer or Nietzsche, but Moltke! He also came in a close second to Napoleon as the most important military leader.[1]

Theodor Fontane wrote that he embodied the Prussian ideal: he looked sound and true, with a Greek soul, the spirit of Frederick the Great and a unique character: judicious, selfless, disciplined, proficient and full of common sense.[2] Writing in 1984, Franz Herre says that of the 'three stars' – 'Dreigestirns' – only Moltke was the 'real German', the complete human being. Bismarck was too complex and too well-known, there was too much to criticize. Roon left too soon: he retired in 1874, became ill and died in 1879. Moltke, in contrast, although he lived for another 20 years after the victory over France in 1871, never became well known. He worked alone in his office or at Kreisau, never said much and offered little to criticize. But, above all, he seemed to be just 'one of the Germans'. When he walked in the Tiergarten with the long general's coat and simple field cap, he looked more like a philosopher. When he travelled in civilian clothes, always second class, carrying his own bag, he looked just like everyone else.[3]

Virtually on a par with Luther and Bismarck, Moltke comes with almost no negative baggage. Yet making sense of him at the dawn of the twenty-first century is a formidable task, given the nature of the sources, on the one hand, and the experience of Germany in the first half of the twentieth century, on the other.

185

No negative baggage means a virtually hagiographic image. And he himself, almost invisibly and perhaps unintentionally, added to this image. For example, take Moltke's natural abstemiousness. One of the reasons he got along so well with the Prussian royalty of the period 1840–88, is that they could also do with less: they had grown up during the French occupation and Napoleonic Wars. For Moltke, work was more important than food. And when he got interested in something, everything else went by the board. He was famous for going on General Staff rides with only a sandwich in his pocket and coming home dead tired and very hungry. Or travelling all day by train without eating. In both cases he got interested in something else. Explaining this, Moltke gave the famous reply that 'he had gone hungry for the first twenty one years of his life'![4]

That may not be the case at all, although his natural tendencies may have been entirely in that direction. As a famous person, late in life, Moltke naturally wanted to fit himself into his reputation. To emphasize the impoverishment of his youth, the difficulty of being sent away from home at age seven, etc. It is a good story. People like to read about orphans who become field marshals.

In the autumn of his eightieth year, early October 1880, Moltke led his last General Staff ride. It was in Schleswig-Holstein. For several days the officers stayed in Kiel, studying its defence from a land side attack. Then they travelled to the fort at Sonderburg and the Dybbol trenches. The navy provided the seven-hour transport from Kiel harbour. At Sonderburg the officers got off and, with Moltke leading the way, walked the distance to Dybbol. There they heard a lecture about the taking of the position in 1864, to which Moltke added his own comments and reminiscences, showing his detailed knowledge of the experience. This was followed by the return walk, a simple meal, and the boat trip back to Kiel. Most of the officers used these hours to rest and sleep. Not so the field marshal: he got the ship's officers to explain to him in detail the inner workings of their vessel. The members of the ride then invited the naval officers to dinner, at which Moltke appeared fresh and punctually as if he had not spent the day in a lengthy exercise. Moltke lead the toasting. And the talking and drinking went on until midnight. The field marshal was not the first to turn in.[5]

Eleven years later, in the spring of 1891, scarcely more than a month before he died, he gave his last formal speech in the Reichstag. In late April, a few minutes before he died, Moltke executed his final grand slam at the whist table.[6] Such vital staying power – and creative energy, perpetual imagination and continuing curiosity – characterized the man who developed and validated modern war processes.

To early twenty-first-century observers Moltke is unique not only because he is a modern, self-made, technically educated, professional officer, but because he put together and perfected existing processes and technologies to create the format for all large-scale twentieth-century wars.

The Cycles of War

The German Wars marked the big change in the cycles of war between Napoleon and World War I. It was a military revolution of the first order. Part of this was technology and part was process. But they were united by thinking about war.[7]

Rifled repeating handguns and artillery, the telegraph and the rail-road: these four all coexisted in the Germanies in the early 1860s. Mean-while a war process had been developing in the Prussian Army: it was there, waiting for these pieces of technology. Moltke put the process and the technology together, first in his mind, then he gave a demonstration of it in real life. The pieces of technology, folded into the first modern war-planning process, allowed a controlled increase in size, space and time – and in the destructive capacities of the armies thus employed – raising war to the next level.

The other mid-century wars – the Crimean, the American Civil and the Chinese Taiping – were big, long, terrible wars. But they were not thought about much, either before, during or after. The Crimean par-ticipants – England, France and Russia – had other concerns than war so far away, with such high casualties, for such paltry gains. America, the looming industrial giant, typically did not enfold war into its mainly business culture. Once over, it was out of mind. The Taipings, whose huge numbers and 'democratic' grass roots organization might have foreshadowed twentieth-century armies, disintegrated internally and then were externally overwhelmed after more than ten years of power. The regional armies which were raised to defeat them began the devo-lution of power away from the imperial system but they did not do it in modern ways, but along traditional, neo-Confucian lines.

Only the Prussian Army had a mechanism for thinking about war before it broke out, employing modern management techniques while it was being fought, and thoroughly assessing what had happened after it was over. It enrolled technology with process so that the size, space and time dimensions of military engagements were systematically manipulated.

The Reverse Salient

Like Austria, which did not react as Moltke expected in 1866, France's war performance in 1870 was so different from expectations that the French process disaster all by itself confounded Prussian plans. These worst-case scenarios which did not materialize meant that, up to September 1870, Moltke's systemic expedients more than compensated for German failings. After that unforeseen political problems surfaced, causing a new kind of war to drag on for more than six months past the climactic 2 September battle at Sedan.

Thus in two out of three wars – the Danes responded pretty much as he had predicted – Moltke's scenarios laid out a far different expectational parameter than the enemy was ready, willing or able to deliver. But Moltke's worst-case scenarios and the plans he formulated to deal with them, provided a row of buffers, a '*system* of expedients'. He built enough extras of men, weapons and accoutrements, that – with the essential but accidental addition of enemy mistakes and errors – his plans worked in spite of the fact that Moltke and the GGS were way out in front of parts of his own army and government.[8] Here was the reverse salient.[9] Prussian governmental leaders were happy to take advantage of Moltke, the technological wizard, who somehow constructed these marvellous battlefield victories, while not really understanding how, in fact, he had done so.

Technology, training and command

In 1864 Prussia had organizational and numerical superiority, and the ability to move, supply and direct a larger force than Denmark. They had this from the start and it got stronger as the war went on. Prussia had technological superiority: Dreyse rifles, siege guns, pontoon bridges. Prussia had strategic and operational planning superiority: Moltke orchestrated a steadily building artillery bombardment at Dybbol and pure surprise at Alsen Island. Finally, Prussia had a tactical – read training – parity which gave them at least fire equality and usually fire superiority in infantry-on-infantry fighting.

In 1866 the numbers were much more equal but the organizational superiority was also more pronounced, especially against the western

German armies – the Hanoverians and Hessians – but even when facing Austrian forces. Benedek was barely able to get his army 150 miles north of Vienna, let alone think about doing anything imaginative with it. Moltke not only moved his 220 000 soldiers 150 miles south but manoeuvred them so that half confronted the enemy face front, the other half got around the side and broadsided the Austrians from a point they were not expecting. Only effective organization, command and training can execute such an idea.

Technological ascendancy was clear. Austrians were outshot in rifle-on-rifle encounters and casualty ratios remained roughly 5 to 1 in favour of Prussia. The Dreyse rifle is a 'sustaining technology': it dramatically improved an existing weapon.[10] Tactical dominance resulted from superior weapons wielded by men whose training was relatively uniform across the whole army. Prussian strategic and operational predominance, and Moltke's risk-taking, extracted war-ending battles in six weeks.

In 1870 the technological tables were turned. France had superior weapons, the Chassepot and Mitrailleuse – but soldiers and units had not been trained to use them. Fortunately for the German armies, there were few direct, large-scale, continuous encounters against these weapons. For when they occurred the Germans were shot down, often from ranges beyond their capacity to reply. Large-scale, continuous war fighting with these huge numbers, over extended periods of time, is a result of deep future-oriented processes and plans. It cannot be improvised. And it was in these mainframe aspects, the ability to move, sustain and coordinate 700 000–800 000 troops over many hundred square miles, that the Germans dominated in 1870.

It was not just their existence, but in how these pieces were fitted into a larger whole that Prussian superiority rested. How can these other advantages be understood?

Organization and Management

The most basic factor is provided by the four fundamental inventions of Prussian war planning: organizational, representational, educational and analytical. Each of these four together anchored a system which enabled command and control of the nearly million-man army, the largest industrial workforce in the world at that time.

It is worth emphasizing that this army was a flat organization in which the tooth-to-tail ratio remained very lean. Few officers and NCOs commanded many men.[11] And these few were endowed with great authority, empowered by the *Auftrag* command system. This had important ramifications for management efficiency as well as organizational decision making. Prussian management allowed a high degree of decentralization yet preserved standardization and uniformity. Much of its work was done through temporary commands, project teams and ad hoc alliances such as brigades, combinations of specialized units that came together to tackle a specific project. All of this flattened the organization. If the army was typically burdened by paperwork, it was never crowded with middle management. And this creative and efficient organization was not merely leaner and flatter. In war games it was often a 'thriving marketplace of aspiring talent'.[12]

Low transportation costs allowed maximum specialization of labour. Moving by rail was much faster and more cost effective for men, horses and equipment: they did not have to be fed as much during travel, they did not get tired, they arrived fresh and ready to work. Siege guns, boats and movable pontoon bridges in Denmark, a war-winning flank attack with over 110 000 troops in Austria, and simply overwhelming numbers – in place, with weapons, equipment, ammunition and orders – almost a million of them, plus over 600 guns confronting a force less than half that size lacking food and ammunition – against France. Each of these was partially a result of changed transportation structures.

As interdependence between units grew, so did the level of coupling between corps, divisions, brigades and regiments. At Dybbol it was artillery, infantry and transportation. At Alsen Island ships, guns and infantry. At Königgrätz three large armies. Around Sedan and spread across the French landscape 13 corps. More accuracy was required at each node and more information, arriving sooner and more closely timed. This kind of war fighting is less tolerant of imprecision. This principle favoured Prussia.

All of the above meant a larger knowledge burden – railroad time schedules, command and control orders, food and supply arrangements – which put pressure all the way down the line. In 1864 to provide 122 heavy guns to fire 4000 shells a day for several weeks required delivery of huge quantities of ammunition 300–400 rail miles, then 50 or 100 road miles to the war front, continuously over a period of several months. The guns themselves took a full six weeks to arrive. These numbers quadrupled from 1864 to 1870. At Mars le Tour, on 16 August 1870, nearly 20 000 shells were fired. Two days later at Gravellotte, 33 000 rounds. And at Sedan, two weeks later, 35 000 shells in a battle which lasted scarcely 36 hours.[13] Maximum specialization of labour in a few large units raised the knowledge threshold: to work with such huge numbers, everyone had to be roughly on the same page.

There were 'rogue outcomes', that is, unexpected or accidental confrontations that turned out badly such as Trautenau and Spicheren. High-casualty attacks, poor command and control, willful disregard of orders and simple mistakes in the heat of battle, all took place. But the system and process of deep future-oriented planning provided expedients, back-ups, fall-backs, supplementary aid and assistance. Individual failures were supported in the meshwork of system and process.

In an environment of new equipment and novel processes, Moltke communicated a minimum amount of certainty by means of the chief of staff system. Although corps commanders were free to make mistakes, Moltke tried to keep the level of surprise under control. Austrian commanders reacted to higher levels of uncertainty by increasing the controls, Prussian commanders did not have to do that.

Moltke and the GGS came out of each war with enhanced power and authority. They guessed the future before other elements of the Prussian government. The military organization grew towards that location where information for resolving uncertainty was chiefly located, the GGS. As the size and structure of the army grew and changed, Moltke's span of responsibility – in men and time – increased. When he became chief of staff to Prince Friedrich Charles in April 1864, he took effective field command of the small Prussian–Austrian armies. In 1866 and 1870, as war commander-in-chief of much larger forces, he effectively replaced the king for the first time in 200 years of Prussian war history.

Above all, Moltke and the GGS attacked a central problem of war: that productivity is highest when most of the activity necessary to win is highly routinized, but specialized work is most valuable when there is uncertainty about how to achieve this goal.[14] At the level of company, regiment and brigade, soldierly combat was highly routinized, but it was coupled with the unique flexibility of the Prussian *Auftrag* command philosophy. Orders were given in terms of very general goals, assuming the commander on the spot would use his imagination and knowledge to come up with the most effective means to achieve these goals. So the Prussian army was in this sense a mixed structure. Very hierarchical and routinized by training, but very decentralized and innovative in executing command decisions. No one was ordered to do what they did not see as feasible and valid. Moltke, at the top, aimed, as he said over and over again, to rapidly inflict maximum destruction on an enemy force so that it would sue for peace as soon as possible. In other words to get out of a war having accomplished its goals with the least casualties. To do this, as Eberhard Kessel said, Moltke proved the perfect master of the calculable and the unpredictable.[15]

Casualties

Casualties are defined here as killed, wounded and missing in action, including prisoners. War casualty figures before the twentieth century, even before the second half of that century, are notoriously erroneous, miscalculated, under- or overestimated.[16] This is true for many reasons. Part of the problem is record keeping but a larger problem is that modern battles create huge numbers of badly destroyed humans, strewn across vast land areas. Armies were very late in trying to keep track of this deadly chaos. It is, in all events, ghastly work to sort out the casualties after a battle.

In the German Wars, the military was often unable to do much about this. Friends or family often went to the scene to try and extract those they held dear. Legendary are the stories of kinfolk and colleagues wandering across these battlefields, searching for their loved ones. A day or two after these battles, the grounds were terrible places: bodies and parts, dead and dying, with terrible images and worse smells: the unburied aftermath. Even though the Prussian Army during the French War included contingents of field hospitals and medical units, it was not enough. Counting up the number 'for whom the bell tolls' is always incomplete after a war. It is a grisly business and no one wants to do it.

A second point is that almost none of the sources for these wars take pains with casualty numbers. Some do not mention the topic. Fontane, who is unusually good for individual battles, makes no summary statements at the conclusions of his volumes. Only recent accounts, such as Craig (1964), Howard (1961) or Wawro (1996), deal with it. Virtually no nineteenth-century historian dwells on it in detail. Perhaps they knew they could not find exact figures. Perhaps they found the topic too black.

The traditional way to measure these is called 'total casualties', and it looks something like this:

	Prussian	Danish
Danish War[17]	1600	8000
	Prussian	Austrian
Austrian War[18]	9000	44 000
	Prussian	French
French War[19]	116 696	370 000

Note the fairly consistent ratios: 1:4 against Denmark. 1:5 against Austria, 1:4 against France.

Another way to measure casualties is as a percentage of total 'present strength'. For example, Boehn argues that in 1864 the number of dead on either Austrian or Prussian side did not go above 0.5 per cent of 'present strength'. In 1866 casualties were 1.09 per cent of present strength for Prussia, 2.7 per cent for Austria. In 1870, with much larger forces, the German Army casualties were not above these figures.[20] The problem here is in determining present strength.

Combat Effectiveness

Related to casualties is combat effectiveness. One scholar says an ideal fighting army is one that consists of born fighters, held in high esteem by their society, well trained, well disciplined and well led. And it is part of an organization that fosters and sustains these qualities.[21] Deleting birth and adding technology, one is tempted to apply this to the Prussian–German armies, 1864–70. But it will not work because the esteem came only well after these wars had been fought.

More to the point, another writer argues that combat efficient armies consistently produce more casualties – and combat victories – using fewer forces than their opponents.[22] Implied in this approach is the assumption that armies are organizations: analysed as processes and systems. They are looked at from top to bottom. It is not just that Moltke's plans were carried out, it is that the whole process for dealing with huge numbers of soldiers, from the 100 000 in the Danish War to the almost million in the French War, was deep future oriented. The Prussian system prepared for this in the deep past. But it also means technology: weapons, transportation and communication. And, above all, training at the small unit level so that individual soldiers know how to use their weapons and how to fit themselves into the larger wholes of which their squad, company or troop was but a part. Moltke was intimately aware of the high quality soldiers he could rely on in the Prussian Army. We have repeatedly emphasized training and education from top to bottom. Arguably the Prussian Army in the German Wars was consistently the most well trained, all the way down to regiments and companies. Its NCOs were the best, and so was its officer corps.

Cumulative Combat Experience

Between 1864 and 1870 war fighting experience built up in the Prussian Army. Each war added a new layer, spreading it out among more soldiers, against opponents lacking this recent experience. What percentage of these soldiers fought in all three? At what ranks? These are questions to be answered.[23] But the explanation for improved performance on increasingly complex, larger and more lethal battlefields may have less to do with age and experience and more with the architecture of the army in which they fought. And also with the planning processes developed and validated by Helmuth von Moltke, the first modern war planner, which multiplied this experience.

Armies as Organizations

The Prussian Army studied here was a dynamic modern organization. And not only because its main war planner was a military genius of the first order. Its companies, regiments and brigades were of high quality, and the integration of effort among these separate parts was conducted at a high level. Small repertoires of activity spread throughout the army added up to a far greater whole. Good modern armies are collections of small units that produce complicated results through interaction. The soldiers' work studied here was less fixed by heredity – the established stanchion of the old Prussian nobility so much celebrated in myth and story – and more subject to environmental and social forces. How exactly do these parts fit together? We have sketched out a general outline at the top, but the truth as to why they won is just as likely to be found near the middle and bottom. Theories of how military units fit together are likely to be grounded in studies of how soldiers relate to one another at the small unit level.[24]

Armies need a minimum amount of certainty to operate and survive. Additional levels of complexity – new weapons, new organizational modes, new larger opponents – reduce organizational predictability and raise the knowledge threshold. To maintain an acceptable level of certainty throughout the system requires an understanding of these increased knowledge levels.[25] Prussian war processes produced a more complex tactical, operational and strategic mixture. Closer coordination was required between all its elements. As the threshold levels of interdependence went up, minimum operational standards followed. In modern war a lack of knowledge has costs: for example the French were armed with weapons they did not know how to use in 1870. Each new weapon, communication and transportation system raises the ante: requiring new levels of knowledge all across the board from soldier to general. When generals such as Steinmetz or Bonin fail to reach this new level, outcomes turn bad.

Generally Prussian war processes were well designed for the knowledge conditions existing in the army at that time: a high level of NCO training, a high level of company and field grade officer training, with the General Staff system for overall command and control. When soldiers were taught how to use the Dreyse rifle and rifled artillery, as Hindersin said, it was important that their instructions were simple enough so that they would be able to carry them out under the stressful conditions of the combat battlefield.

A large increase in the extent and validity of testing was necessary to accommodate these new levels of weapons, transportation and communication and the other unknowns of the new war system. Fortunately there was a foundational element in Prussian military practice called war gaming which continuously tested all these novel introductions. Although the knowledge burden of the new Prussian system was high, so were the level and quality of training used to upgrade soldiers to its requirements.

To Return to the Beginning

'The Prussian Army was as much a marvel for the world of the 1870s as Henry Ford's assembly line was for the world of the 1920s.'[26] Making cars and organizing for war may have similar processes, but they are entirely different kinds of work. Only one of them has to do with the lifeblood of the children. That is the reason historians have been unable to put together a valid image of the Prussian Army before 1914. German military experiences during the first half of the twentieth century – World Wars I and II – have coloured every attempt to deal objectively with its nineteenth-century predecessor. It is time to begin to revise this image.

NOTES

INTRODUCTION   PRUSSIA: WAR, THEORY AND MOLTKE

1. From Stephen J. Gould, *Leonardo's Mountain of Clams and the Diet of Worms* (New York, 1998), p. 393. Gould argues that post-modernist critique should give us a healthy scepticism towards the 'complex and socially embedded reasons behind the original formulations of our established categories'. Surely this applies to the Prussian military before 1914.
2. Gerhard Weinberg, *Germany, Hitler and World War II: Essays in Modern Germany and World History* (Cambridge, 1995), p. 287.
3. Although the image of nineteenth-century Germany had begun to shift a bit before August 1914, the sea change took place thereafter and since 1945 has been fairly uniformly grey, at least in the English cultural world. Fifty years past World War II has not erased the negative image of the 'Hun', German national character and Germany prior to August 1914. Peter E. Firchow, *The Death of the German Cousin: Variations on a Literary Stereotype: 1890–1920* (Lewisburg, 1986), *passim*.
4. These are the three great historiographical controversies which have erupted since the end of World War II. Each one paints nineteenth-century Germany in dark, twentieth-century colours. The first and third confront the Prussian–German Army directly, describing it in militaristic terms. All three describe various attempts to attach the Third Reich, and especially the Holocaust, to German history before 1933, and especially before 1914. The Fischer controversy was touched off by the publication of Fritz Fischer's book, *Griff nach der Weltmacht* (Düsseldorf, 1961), translated as *Germany's Aims in the First World War* (New York, 1967), in which he argued that Nazi foreign policy was a continuation of German foreign policy in 1914–18. See John Moses, *The Politics of Illusion: the Fischer Controversy in German Historiography* (London, 1975); the Sonderweg controversy is best seen in the work of Geoff Eley. It deals with the question of whether German industrialization was unique or whether the process was comparable to what happened in England or France. See for example his recent edited work, *Society, Culture, and the State in Germany, 1870–1930* (Ann Arbor, 1996), especially 'Introduction 1: Is There a History of the Kaiserreich?'; the Goldhagen issue arose out of Daniel Goldhagen's *Hitler's Willing Executioners* (New York, 1996), Goldhagen argues that eliminationist anti-Semitism existed in nineteenth-century Germany long before Nazi Germany. It is best followed in a number of articles. Gordon Craig, 'How

Hell Worked', *NY Review of Books*, 18 April 1996, pp. 4–8; Volker Berghahn, 'The Road to Extermination', *NY Times Book Review*, 14 April 1996; Istvan Deak, 'Holocaust Views: the Goldhagen Controversy in Retrospect', *Central European History (CEH)*, Vol. 30, No. 2 (1997), pp. 295–307; Hans Ulrich Wehler, 'The Goldhagen Controversy: Agonizing Problems, Scholarly Failure and the Political Dimension', *German History*, Vol. 15, No.1 (1997), pp. 80–91; Josef Jaffe, 'Goldhagen in Germany', *NY Review of Books*, 28 November 1996; Ruth Bettina Birn, 'Historiographical Review: Revising the Holocaust', *The Historical Journal*, Vol. 40, No. 1(1997), pp. 195–215.

5. Jean Quataert, 'Introduction 2: Writing the History of Women and Gender in Imperial Germany', p. 49, and Elizabeth Domansky, 'Militarization and Reproduction in World War I Germany', pp. 427–64 in Eley, *Society, Culture and the State 1870–1930*; Fritz Stern, *Einstein's German World* (Princeton, 1999), p. 277.

6. Cf. Correlli Barnett, *Essays on Leadership and War* (1992), Introduction by John Terraine; Geoff Eley, 'Theory and Kaiserreich: Problems with Culture: German History after the Linguistic Turn', *CEH*, Vol. 31, No. 3 (1998), pp. 197–227. Barbara Tuchman wrote that the trap built into all history was the 'disproportionate survival of the negative'. Because what catches people's eye at the time, what is mainly written down, is the bad, the crimes, crises and disasters. Bad news sells newspapers, p. x, Jack Dukes and Joachim Remak (eds), *Another Germany: a Reconsideration of the Imperial Era* (Boulder, 1988).

7. Kenneth Barkin, 'W. E. B. Du Bois and the Kaiserreich', *CEH*, Vol. 31, No. 3 (1998), pp. 158, 162.

8. Firchow, *The Death of the German Cousin*, pp. 30–1.

9. Arden Bucholz, *Moltke, Schlieffen and Prussian War Planning* (Oxford, 1991). Introduction. Hereinafter *Prussian War Planning*.

10. Performance to price ratios of central processing units (CPUs) for information technology currently doubles every 18 months.

11. 'Defense Technology: the Information Advantage', *The Economist*, 10 June 1995, p. 6. Merrill A. McPeak, 'The Key to Modern Airpower', *AIR FORCE Magazine*, September 1993, pp. 43–6; Larry D. Welch, 'Dominating the Battlefield (Battlespace)', *Journal of Electronic Defense*, January 1997 Supplement, pp. 12–14. (Kindness of Sandra Higel, Reference Librarian, USAF Academy, Colorado Springs, Colo.)

12. Ibid., p. 8; Robert H. Scales, 'Cycles of War', *Armed Forces Journal*, July 1997, pp. 38–42; US Department of the Army, *Force XXI Operations*, TRADOC Pamphlet 525–5 (TRADOC, 1994); Dennis Reimer, *Knowledge and Speed: the Annual Report of the Army after Next Project* (Washington, 1997).

13. Arden Bucholz, 'Delbrück: the Artist of War and Politics' in *Zum 150. Geburtstag von Hans Delbrück* (1999); idem, *Delbrück's Modern Military History* (Lincoln and London, 1997), hereinafter *Delbrück's Modern History; idem, Hans Delbrück and the German Military Establishment* (Iowa City, 1985); 'Modern' as a term has been heavily criticized in the past two decades. However, no one has come up with a better way to describe what has happened to many parts of the world in the past 200 years than by using the continuum 'traditional–modern'. It is used here with full awareness of its limitations.

14. Bucholz, *Prussian War Planning*, p. 92.
15. Cf. Michael Crichton, *Jurassic Park* (New York, 1990), pp. 75–7 for interesting correlations.
16. Bucholz, *Prussian War Planning*, p. 2.
17. Ibid., pp. 3–4; Moltke says this in almost the same words at the start of his 'Instructions for Large Group Commanders' of June 1869. Daniel Hughes, *Moltke on the Art of War* (Novato, Calif., 1993), p. 172.
18. This is the principle of *Wu-wei* or non-action. Herlee Creel, *What is Taoism?* (Chicago, 1970), pp. 51–71; Wang Pi, *Commentary on Lao Tzu* (Honolulu, 1979), p. 1018; Lin Yutang, *The Wisdom of Laotze* (New York, 1948), pp. 265, 293.
19. Atul Gawande, 'When Doctors Make Mistakes', *The New Yorker*, 1 Feb. 1999, p. 51.
20. France and England suffered similar casualty rates in the Great War. Cf. Jean-Jacques Becker, *The Great War and the French People* (Oxford, 1985), pp. 5–6. French dead were 1 327 000, English 715 000 and German 2 037 000. To make any sense of these one must consider them in relationship to total population size, and also to examine when they died.
21. Gordon Craig, *The Battle of Koeniggraetz* (Philadelphia, 1964); Michael Howard, *The Franco-Prussian War* (New York, 1961). To complement Craig we have the excellent recent study by Geoffrey Wawro, *The Austro-Prussian War: Austria's War with Prussia and Italy in 1866* (New York, 1996).
22. John Kenneth Galbraith, *The New Industrial State* (2nd edn, London, 1972), Ch. 2; Bucholz, *Prussian War Planning*, introduction.
23. Bucholz, *Prussian War Planning*, introduction.
24. Ibid.
25. Ibid.
26. Arthur L. Stinchcombe, *Information and Organizations* (Berkeley, 1990), pp. 2–6.
27. Ibid., p. 21.
28. Eberhard Kessel, *Moltke* (Stuttgart, 1957), p. 507.
29. Mark Dodgson, 'Organizational Learning: a Review of Some Literatures', *Organizational Studies*, Vol. 14, No. 3 (1993), pp. 377–80; Dodgson, 'Technology Learning, Technology Strategy and Competitive Pressures', *British Journal of Management*, Vol. 2 (1991), pp. 133–9; a fine case study of these ideas is Dodgson, *The Management of Technological Learning: Lessons from a Biotechnology Company* (Berlin, 1991). A minor classic describing organizations is Mary Douglas, *How Institutions Think* (London, 1986). A more formal statement, full of ideas, is Charles Perrow, *Complex Organizations: a Critical Essay* (New York, 1986).
30. Dodgson, 'Organizational Learning', pp. 380–2.
31. Gordon Craig, *Theodor Fontane: Literature and History in the Bismarck Reich* (New York, 1999); Peter Gay, 'Foreword' to *Theodor Fontane, Short Novels and Other Writings*, edited by Peter Demetz (New York, 1982), p. vii.
32. Peter Demetz, 'Introduction' to *Fontane, Short Novels and Other Writings*, p. xv.
33. This work draws heavily on Eberhard Kessel's fine biography of Moltke. Part of the uniqueness of his work, and also those of Bigge and Jaehns – Wilhelm Bigge, *Feldmarschall Graf Moltke: Ein militaerisches Lebensbild* (2 vols, 1901);

and Max Jaehns, *Feldmarschall Moltke* (2 vols, Berlin, 1900) – is that they researched and took careful notes in the General Staff War Archives before 1945. That archive received a direct air strike in spring 1945 and a good deal of it was destroyed. Much of the rest was carted off by Soviet troops to remain unused in various warehouses in Moscow. Ten years ago 45 tons of this material was returned to Berlin. Holger Afflerbach, *Falkenhayn: Politisches Denken und Handeln im Kaiserreich* (Munich, 1994), used this material and so did Annika Mombauer, 'A Reluctant Military Leader? Helmuth von Moltke and the July Crisis of 1914', *War in History*, Vol. 6, No. 4 (1999), pp. 417–46. It is curious that there has been no serious scholarly biography of Moltke in almost half a century and there is still nothing in English.

34. Arden Bucholz, 'Militarism' in *Encyclopedia of Violence, Peace and Conflict*, 3 vols, 1999, Vol. II, pp. 423–32.

35. Peter F. Drucker, *Managing in a Time of Great Change* (New York, 1995), p. 91.

1   NAPOLEON'S LEGACY AND THE PRUSSIAN INVENTION

1. Jürgen Habermas, 'Modernity – an Incomplete Project' in Hal Foster (ed.), *The Anti-Aesthetic: Essays on Postmodern Culture* (Seattle, 1992), p. 5.

2. Paul Virilio, *Speed and Politics* (New York, 1997); *idem, Popular Defense and Ecological Struggles* (New York, 1983); Giles Deleuze and Felix Guattari, *Nomadilogy: the War Machine* (New York, 1989); Paul Virilio and Sylvere Lotringer, *Pure War* (New York, 1983).

3. H. Stuart Hughes, *Consciousness and Society* (New York, 1958), p. 123.

4. Ibid., pp. 121–2. G. J. Whitrow, *Time in History* (1988), p. 173.

5. Rinehard Koselleck, *Futures Past: On the Semantics of Historical Time* (Cambridge, Mass., 1983), pp. xxiii–xxiv. A very close paraphrase from Jürgen Habermas, 'Modernity – an Incomplete Project', p. 5.

6. R. R. Palmer and Joel Colton, *A History of the Modern World* (8th edn, New York, 1998), pp. 391–419; J. Black, *European Warfare, 1660–1815* (London, 1994), pp. 168–75.

7. Arden Bucholz, *Hans Delbrück and the German Military Establishment* (Iowa City, 1985), pp. 9–15, 34–6.

8. Archer Jones, *The Art of War* (New York, 1987), p. 314.

9. Ibid.

10. Ibid., pp. 314–17.

11. Ibid., p. 325.

12. A. H. Robinson et al., *Elements of Cartography* (5th edn, New York, 1984), p. 368; Bucholz, *Prussian War Planning*, Ch. 2.

13. Robinson, *Elements of Cartography*, pp. 29–30.

14. Josef Konvitz, *Cartography in France, 1660–1848* (Chicago, 1987), p. 39.

15. Ibid., pp. 19–21.

16. Ibid., p. 61.

17. W. H. Bruford, *Germany in the Eighteenth Century: the Social Background of the Literary Revival* (Cambridge, 1965), p. 41; W. O. Henderson, *The Industrial Revolution in Europe* (Chicago, 1961), pp. 9–15.

18. Bucholz, *Prussian War Planning*, pp. 18–19; Black, *European Warfare*, pp. 193–9.
19. Jones, *Art of War*, pp. 371–7; Black, *European Warfare*, pp. 168–75.
20. Bucholz, *Prussian War Planning*, Ch. 1; for a contemporary restatement of Massenbach, cf. Kees van der Heijden, *Scenarios: the Art of Strategic Conversation* (New York, 1996).
21. Gabriel Motzkin, 'On Koselleck's Concept of Time in History' in Hartmut Lehmann and Melvin Richter (eds), *The Meaning of Historical Terms and Concepts* (Washington, DC, 1996), pp. 41–3.
22. Bucholz, *Prussian War Planning*, Ch. 1.
23. Ibid., pp. 25ff.
24. Ibid., pp. 22–4.
25. E. S. Mittler, Berlin, was the General Staff publisher from 1816 to 1919.
26. The *Militär-Wochenblatt* included a lot more than history, but military history was one of its staples. Some would call this the house organ of the army because it included promotions, retirements, new appointments and official announcements of all kinds.
27. Bucholz, *Prussian War Planning*, pp. 23–4.
28. Ibid., pp. 20–2.
29. Ibid., p. 31.
30. Thomas B. Allen, *War Games* (London, Heinemann, 1987), p. 160.
31. Hajo Holborn, *A History of Modern Germany, 1648–1840* (New York, Alfred Knopf, 1971), pp. 473ff.
32. Walter von Lossow, 'Mission-Type Tactics versus Order-Type Tactics', *Military Review*, Vol. 57 (June 1977), p. 87; Christian O. E. Millotat, *Understanding the Prussian–German General Staff* (Carlisle, Penn., Strategic Studies Institute, US Army War College, 1992), pp. 23–4; Wolfgang Schall, 'Fuehrungsgrundsaetze in Armee und Industrie', *Wehrkunde*, Vol. 14, No. 5 (1964), pp. 10–18.
33. This is, of course, arguable. First in the world implies some sort of informal standard in which the educational systems of all other countries are also rated and compared. Of course this rarely or never happens in reality. In the nineteenth century Great Power world, there were few players. China, for example, whose education system a century before this might have been considered very strong, was in a period of deepening decline. And of course this was education for a very small percentage of its population. British education itself was considered very good, at least for the small elite. In the nineteenth century, this role model resided in Europe; perhaps Germany, France and England shared dominance. And I would argue that Germany may have held a slight edge. But the point here is that Prussian military education – for certain kinds of persons – may have been a cut above civilian education.
34. Bernard Poten, *Militaer-Erzeihungs- und Bildungswesens in den Landen deutsche Zunge* (4 vols, Berlin, A. Hofmann, 1896), Vol. IV, p. 499.
35. Hubert von Boehn, *Generalstàbsgeschaefte* (Potsdam, 1875), pp. 75ff.
36. Freiherr Ferdinand von Ladebur, *Die Geschichte des deutschen Unteroffiziers* (Berlin: Junker und Duennhaupt Verlag, 1939), p. 228; Henderson, *Industrial Revolution in Europe*, p. 20.
37. Ladebur, *Deutschen Unteroffiziers*, p. 225.

38. Ibid., pp. 249ff.
39. Bucholz, *Prussian War Planning*, pp. 60ff.
40. Jones, *Art of War*, p. 393.
41. Ibid.
42. Wilfried Feldenkirchen, *Werner von Siemens: Inventor and International Entrepreneur* (Columbus, Ohio State University, 1994), pp. 32–3.
43. Henderson, *Industrial Revolution in Europe*, p. 20.
44. Wawro, *Austro-Prussian War*, p. 11.
45. Edward Hagerman, *The American Civil War and the Origins of Modern Warfare* (Bloomington, Ind., Indiana University Press, 1988), pp. 33–5.
46. Ibid., p. 37.
47. Craig, *Koeniggraetz*, p. 18.
48. Ibid., p. 21; Wawro, *Austro-Prussian War*, p. 21.
49. Craig, *Koeniggraetz*, p. 21.
50. Friedrich Engels in 'The History of the Rifle', *Volunteer Journal for Lancashire and Cheshire*, 3 November 1860 and 5 June, 1861 reprinted in Bernard Semmel, *Marxism and the Science of War* (New York, 1981), pp. 126–37; *Engels as Military Critic*, ed. W. H. Chaloner and W. O. Henderson (Westport, 1976).
51. Peter Drucker, *Managing in a Time of Great Change* (New York, 1995), p. 91.

2 HELMUTH VON MOLTKE, 1800–57

1. The famous conclusion of Queen Louise of Prussia.
2. Kessel, Moltke, pp. 11–13. Curiously enough, near the end of his life, when asked which books had influenced him the most, both Homer and the Bible made the short list. Does this suggest to us that Moltke's mind worked over and over a few big ideas and works, plumbing them to depths that others missed?
3. Doris Asmundsson, *Georg Brandes: Aristocratic Radical* (New York, 1981), p. 7; Elias Bredsdorff, *Hans Christian Andersen* (New York, 1975), *passim.*
4. R. R. Palmer and J. Colton, *A History of the Modern World* (8th edn, New York, 1995), p. 422.
5. Monica Stirling, *The Wild Swan: the Life and Times of Hans Christian Andersen* (New York, 1965), p. 265 and *passim*; Bucholz, *Prussian War Planning*, pp. 218ff. We may note that it was from this family that Helmuth von Moltke the younger – Moltke's nephew and long-time personal adjutant who was chief of the GGS from 1906 to 1914 – got his wife Countess 'Lizzy', who was a member of a wealthy and interesting group of Berlin women just prior to the outbreak of World War I.
6. One of Hagermann-Lindencrone's sons would face Moltke in 1864 as commander of a Danish cavalry division. A. Gallenga, *The Invasion of Denmark in 1864* (2 vols, London, 1864), Vol. II, p. 203.
7. Kessel, *Moltke*, p. 15.
8. Cf. the letter of one of the sons of the house when Moltke lived there, 'Erinnerungen des Generalleutnants v. Hegermann-Lindencrone' in GGS, *Moltkes Gesammelte Schriften*, Vol. V, pp. 241–51. The general, six years

younger than Moltke, commanded a Danish cavalry division and then all the forces in Jutland in the Danish War of 1864.

9. Friedrich August Dressler, *Moltke in Seiner Hauslichkeit* (2nd edn, Berlin, 1904), p. 78.
10. Kessel, *Moltke*, p. 19.
11. Stirling, *The Wild Swan*, p. 207.
12. Bucholz, *Prussian War Planning*, p. 3.
13. Showalter, *Frederick the Great*, p. 351, Peter Paret, *Yorck and the Era of Prussian Reform* (Princeton, 1966), pp. 28ff, 210–14; John A. English, *On Infantry* (New York, 1967), pp. 1–4.
14. Kessel, *Moltke*, p. 21.
15. Ibid., p. 20.
16. Bucholz, *Prussian War Planning*, p. 29.
17. Ibid., p. 31; Kessel, *Moltke*, pp. 25–30.
18. Kessel, *Moltke*, p. 32.
19. Ibid., pp. 34, 40; Bucholz, *Prussian War Planning*, pp. 22–32, 45, 51.
20. Dressler, *Moltke in Seiner Hauslichkeit*, written by his personal musician.
21. Kessel, *Moltke*, p. 49.
22. *Websters New International Dictionary*, 1934, pp. 986, 600.
23. Mark Dodgson, 'Technology Learning, Technology Strategy and Competitive Pressure', *British Journal of Management Technology Learning*, Vol. 2 (1991), p. 141.
24. Mark Dodgson, 'Organizational Learning: a Review of Some Literatures', *Organizational Studies*, Vol. 14, No. 3 (1993), pp. 375–94.
25. Ibid., p. 389.
26. Ibid., p. 383.
27. Kessel, *Moltke*, pp. 53–65.
28. Kameke letter, GGS, *Moltkes Gesammelte Schriften*, Vol. VI, pp. 254–5.
29. Bucholz, *Prussian War Planning*, p. 25; Eugene Ferguson, *Engineering and the Mind's Eye* (Cambridge, Mass., 1992), *passim*.
30. Cf. reminiscences of a 17-year-old daughter of the Kospoth house during the time Moltke was with them. She emphasized the simplicity of the household: the privations of the Napoleonic War years were not forgotten, 'Erinnerungen der Frau Louise v Schimpff' in GGS, *Moltkes Gesammelte Schriften*, Vol. V, pp. 251–3.
31. Kessel, *Moltke*, p. 65.
32. One of them is German Ordnance Survey Map No. 4870 for Gross Zoellnitz. Bucholz, *Prussian War Planning*, p. 33.
33. Kessel, *Moltke*, p. 101.
34. Bucholz, *Prussian War Planning*, pp. 28–31.
35. The *Militär-Wochenblatt* was the weekly house organ of the Prussian Army, edited and published by the General Staff. Cf. Max Jaehns, 'Das militair-Wochenblatt von 1816 bis 1876' in Max Jaehns, *Militaergeschichtliche Aufsaetze*, edited by Ursula von Gersdorff (Osnabrück, Biblio Verlag, 1970).
36. Bucholz, *Prussian War Planning*, p. 30.
37. Ibid., pp. 14–15.
38. Letter to his mother of February 1831, cited in Rudolf Peschke, *Moltkes Stellung zur Politik bis zum Jahre 1857* (Kirchhain, 1912), p. 7.

39. Kessel, *Moltke*, p. 90.
40. Ibid., pp. 92–5.
41. Kessel, *Moltke*, pp. 96–100.
42. Showalter, *The Wars of Frederick the Great*, pp. 305–6.
43. Ibid., p. 279; Kessel, *Moltke*, p. 104.
44. Kessel, *Moltke*, p. 110.
45. Ibid., pp. 113–14.
46. Bernard Lewis, *The Emergence of Modern Turkey* (London, 1961), pp. 75–103; Erich Zürcher, *Turkey: a Modern History* (London, 1994), pp. 32–53. Stanford and Ezel Shaw, *A History of the Ottoman Empire and Modern Turkey* (3 vols, Cambridge, 1977), Vol. II, pp. 135–9.
47. Kessel, *Moltke*, p. 118.
48. Ibid., pp. 124–5.
49. Ibid., p. 126.
50. Ibid., pp. 127–31.
51. Ibid., pp. 127–33.
52. Ibid., p. 133.
53. Ibid., pp. 133–7.
54. Ibid., pp. 140–1. Kessel also wrote about Moltke's experiences at Nezib, using General Staff documents, Moltke's reports to General Staff chief Krauseneck and to Prussian Ambassador Koenigsmark in Constantinople, and letters written by Moltke's colleagues, Fischer, Mühlbach, Vinke and Loew, dealing with these same events, and also reproducing Moltke's field topographical sketches of the terrain and troop placement. *Moltkes erster Feldzug* (Berlin, 1939).
55. Kessel, *Moltke*, pp. 142–5.
56. Ibid., pp. 142–6.
57. Ibid., pp. 141–7.
58. Ibid., p. 147.
59. Moltke's letters of 1 May and 12 July 1839, say it all as quoted in Kessel, *Helmuth von Moltke Briefe* (2nd edn, Stuttgart, 1960), pp. 129–54; as quoted in Max Horst, *Moltke, Leben und Werk in Selbstzeugnissen* (Leipzig, 1930), pp. 66–86. The most recent edition of his letters from Turkey is Helmuth Arndt (ed.), *Helmuth von Moltke. Unter dem Halbmond. Erlebnisse in der alten Turkei, 1835–1839* (Berlin, 1988), for Nezib, pp. 156–75.
60. Kessel, *Moltke*, p. 150.
61. Rudolf Peschke, 'Moltke als Mitarbeiter der Augsburger Allgemeinen Zeitung' in *Moltkes Stellung zur Politik bis zum Jahre 1857* (Kirchhain, 1912), pp. 39–45, a review of a dozen articles Moltke published on diverse topics between 1841 and 1844, in the Augsburg newspaper.
62. For Moltke's contributions to German understanding of ancient world topography see Christian Belger, 'Generalfeldmarschall Graf Moltkes Verdienste um die Kenntnis des Alterthums', *Preussische Jahrbücher*, Vol. 51, No. 1 (1883), pp. 70–114.
63. Kessel, *Moltke*, p. 155.
64. James M. Brophy, *Capitalism, Politics and Railroads in Prussia, 1830–1870* (Columbus, 1998), pp. 30–3.
65. Kessel, *Moltke*, p. 167.

66. Rahne, *Mobilmachung*, p. 23.
67. I came to the same conclusions but was comforted to find that Max Horst in *Moltke*, p. xxvii, agreed.
68. Hannah Pakula, *An Uncommon Woman: the Empress Frederick* (New York, 1995), p. 60.
69. Kessel, *Moltke*, p. 175.
70. Horst, *Moltke*, Introduction, p. xxvii.
71. Friederika von Brockdorff, *Marie von Moltke: Ein Lebens- und charakterbild* (Leipzig, 1893), p. 48. Auguste, Moltke's closest sibling, described her step-daughter in 'Marie Moltke', GGS, *Moltkes Gesammelte Schriften*, Vol. V, pp. 29–35. Moltke's mother also knew Marie and wrote to her son about her. 'Marie Moltke' in GGS, *Moltkes Gesammelte Schriften*, Vol. I, pp. 145–58.
72. Brockdorff, *Marie von Moltke*, p. 98.
73. Kessel, *Moltke*, p. 157; Jaehns, *Feldmarschall Moltke*, Vol. I, p. 132.
74. Kessel, *Moltke*, pp. 179–80.
75. Ibid., p. 182.
76. Belger, 'Generalfeldmarshall Graf Moltkes Verdienste', details Moltke's contributions both as cartographer and as terrain describer.
77. Kessel, *Moltke*, p. 185.
78. Moltke's travel writings in fact became famous. In 1879 George von Bunsen, famed natural scientist, published a special edition called *Moltkes Wanderbuch*. Kessel, *Moltke*, p. 769; Marie von Bunsen, *George von Bunsen* (Berlin, 1900), p. 281; Holborn, *Modern Germany*, Vol. II, pp. 528–9.
79. Kessel, *Moltke*, p. 191.
80. Bigge, Moltke, Vol. I, pp. 292–5. Articles were published in the *Militär-Wochenblatt* in April 1848, July and November 1852 and February 1854. The General Staff published *Geschichte des Krieges gegen Daenemark, 1848–1849* as Vol. VIII, *Moltkes Militaerische Werke* (Vol. III, 1893).
81. Cf. the letter of one of his fellow staff officers, H. A. v. Glisczinski, who had been in Moltke's War School class, and was later chief of staff to the Guard Corps during the mobilization of 1850. Glisczinski says that Moltke never changed: his identity was consistent. Even in Berlin during the 1860s, when his wife would stay with the Moltkes, and they played whist from 6 to 8 in the evenings, nothing changed. GGS, *Moltkes Gesammelte Schriften*, Vol. V, *Briefe*, pp. 258–61.
82. Hubert von Boehn, *Generalstabsgeschaefte* (Potsdam, 1875), pp. 108–9.
83. Kessel, *Moltke*, pp. 195–206.
84. Ibid., p. 200.
85. Ibid., p. 195.
86. Jaehns, *Moltke*, Vol. I, p. 189.
87. Bigge, *Feldmarschall Moltke*, Vol. I, pp. 313–14.
88. Craig, *Politics of the Prussian Army*, p. 130.
89. Kurt Jany, *Geschichte der Preussischen Armee von 15. Jahrhundert bis 1914* (2nd edn, 4 vols, Osnabrück, 1967), Vol. IV, pp. 187–9.
90. Hermann Rahne, *Mobilmachung: Militaerische Mobilmachungsplanung und-technik in Preussen und im Deutschen Reich von Mitte des 19. Jahrhunderts bis zum zweiten Weltkrieg* (Berlin, 1983), p. 16.
91. Ibid., p. 15.

92. Bigge, *Feldmarschall Moltke*, Vol. I, p. 312.
93. Ibid., Vol. I, p. 316.
94. GGS, *Moltkes Gesammelte Schriften*, Vol. I, p. 156.
95. Ibid., Vol. V, p. 261.
96. He wrote to his brother that for 24 weeks the entire IV Corps had been mobilized in the field and out of its garrisons. If only Frederick the Great had had such a corps! Millions of thalers for a pointless demonstration. Horst, *Moltke*, p. 184.
97. Cf. Moltke's comments, in *Moltkes Gesammelte Schriften*, Vol. V, pp. 261–4.
98. Kessel, *Moltke*, pp. 313–15.
99. Ibid., p. 211.
100. Ibid., p. 214.
101. Ibid.
102. Bucholz, *Delbrück's Modern Military History*, p. 71.
103. Horst, *Moltke*, pp. 189–93; Kessel, in *Moltkes Briefe*, chose the same letter.
104. Kessel, *Moltkes Briefe*, pp. 271–313, long letters to his wife describing in detail the places and people he met while on official duty as first adjutant to the Crown Prince of Prussia.
105. Ibid., pp. 214–16.
106. Ibid., p. 221.
107. Ibid.
108. Ibid., p. 223.
109. Dressler, *Moltke in Seiner Hauslichkeit*, p. 114.
110. Kessel, *Moltke*, p. 222.

3 MOLTKE AND PRUSSIAN SYSTEM, 1857–63

1. Kessel, *Moltke*, pp. 227ff; Reyher's monthly salary had been 6000 thalers as chief of the General Staff and general of cavalry, plus living quarters on the top floor of the General Staff building, with a staff to run it. His wife was asked to move out, with her children and 500 a month. The administration made a deal: she would move out, but with a pension of 1100. Beginning officers in the Prussian Army of that day earned roughly 25 thalers a month. Kessel, *Moltkes Briefe*, pp. 316–18.
2. Bucholz, *Prussian War Planning*, pp. 128ff.
3. Kessel, *Moltke*, p. 228.
4. Brockdorff, *Marie von Moltke*, p. 48.
5. Helmuth had specifically asked her to write to him in English. They used English at home. His English improved momentously from the days in the 1830s when he translated Edward Gibbon's *Decline and Fall of the Roman Empire* from English into German, but her German probably did not approach court standards. A number of Prussian royal family and high nobles had English wives, including Crown Prince Frederick, Albrecht von Roon and Albrecht von Blumenthal. But the language at court was German, mixed perhaps with French.
6. An example of someone with both lineage and money is Mary Lee Waldersee. Although a wealthy New Yorker, she was related to the

Hohenzollerns by marriage. The combination of being on the court order of presentation, lots of money and a lively personality, combined with the fact that her second husband, Waldersee, was a Hohenzollern relative by blood, meant Mary Lee had lots of access that Marie Burt did not.

7. Brockdorff, *Marie von Moltke*, p. 110.
8. Ibid., p. 123.
9. Kessel, *Moltke*, p. 230.
10. Ibid., p. 231.
11. Moltke was initially appointed 'acting' chief. It was almost a year later, 18 September 1858, that he became chief. In 1857 he was a general major and only became general lieutenant in 1859, the year after he became chief. Each of these designations and ranks had remunerative as well as command and staff implications. Jaehns, *Moltke*, Vol. II, p. 276.
12. Ibid.
13. Craig, *Politics*, p. 193.
14. Kessel, *Moltke*, pp. 232–3.
15. Ibid., pp. 233–4.
16. Julius von Verdy du Vernois, *With the Royal Headquarters, 1870–71* (London, 1897); Paul Bronsart von Schellendorff, *The Duties of the General Staff* (4th edn, London, 1905).
17. Count Albrecht von Blumenthal (ed.), *Journals of Field-Marshal Count von Blumenthal for 1866 and 1870–71* (London, 1903), pp. 57–9.
18. Kessel, *Moltke*, pp. 232–64.
19. Owen Connelly, *Blundering to Glory: Napoleon's Military Campaigns* (Wilmington, 1987), pp. 7–9 and *passim*; cf. Black, *European Warfare*, pp. 182–99; Alan Schom, *Napoleon Bonaparte* (New York, 1997), *passim*.
20. Kees van der Heijden, *Scenarios: the Art of Strategic Conversation* (New York, 1996).
21. Ron S. Dembo and Andrew Freeman, *Seeing Tomorrow* (Toronto, 1998) pp. 9–40.
22. See below, Ch. 6, pp. 123–5.
23. Hajo Holborn quotes approvingly Moltke's famous statement that no war plan can really go much beyond the first meeting with the enemy: after that everything was up for grabs; in Peter Paret, *Makers of Modern Strategy from Machiavelli to the Nuclear Age* (Princeton, 1986), p. 289; J. F. C. Fuller wrote that Moltke took his armies to the starting point and then let them go, abdicating command. Fuller, *A Military History of the Western World* (3 vols New York, 1954), Vol. 3, p. 134. Gunther Rothenburg, 'Moltke, Schlieffen and the Doctrine of Strategic Envelopment' in Paret, *Makers of Modern Strategy*, Ch. 11, is closer to the interpretation presented here.
24. This volte-face probably explains some of the friction between Moltke and Bismarck which is supposed to have developed from time to time during these wars. If Bismarck got used to the Moltke in his type B role during peacetime, he had some adjusting to do in combat where Moltke emerged in his type A personality to fight a war.
25. Walter von Lossow, 'Mission-Type Tactics versus Order-Type Tactics', *Military Review*, Vol. 57 (June 1977), pp. 87–91; Christian Millotat, *Understanding the Prussian–German General Staff System* (Carlisle, Pa, 1992),

pp. 20–4; Wolfgang Schall, 'Führungsgrundsaetze in Armee und Industrie', *Wehrkunde*, Vol. 14, No. 5 (1964), pp. 10–18; Franz Uhle-Wettler, 'Auftragstaktik: Mission Order and the German Experience,' in Richard D. Hooker, Jr, *Maneuver Warfare: an Anthology* (Novato, Calif., 1983), pp. 235–47.

26. Clayton R. Newell, *The Framework of Operational Warfare* (1991), pp. 168–73; Carl-Gero von Ilsemann, 'Das operative Denken des Aelterer Moltke' in Horst Boog et al., *Operatives Denken und Handeln in deutschen Streitkraeften im. 19. und 20. Jahrhundert* (Bonn, 1988), pp. 17ff.

27. Arthur T. Coumbe, 'Operational Command in the Franco-Prussian War' in *Parameters*, Vol. 21, No. 2 (summer 1991), pp. 92–3; Michael D. Krause, 'Moltke and the Origins of the Operational Level of War' in R. E. Foerster (ed.), *Generalfeldmarschall von Moltke: Bedeutung und Wirkung* (Munich, 1991).

28. Newell, 'Operational Warfare', p. 169.

29. Millotat, *Understanding the Prussian–German General Staff*, pp. 23–4. Cf. Schall, 'Führungsgrundsätze in Armee und Industrie', pp. 10–18.

30. Prinzen Kraft zu Hohenlohe-Ingelfingen, *Aus meinen Leben: Aufzeichnungen* (3 vols, Berlin, 1906), Vol. III, p. 17.

31. Max Horst, *Moltke: Leben und Werk in Selbstzeugnissen* (Leipzig, 1930), p. xiii.

32. Bucholz, *Delbrück's Modern Military History*, p. 66.

33. Kessel, *Helmuth von Moltke, Briefe, 1825–1891* (2nd edn, Stuttgart, 1960), introduction; pp. 5–6; Eberhard Kessel (ed.), *Moltke Gespraeche* (Hamburg, 1940), pp. 9–11.

34. Kessel, *Moltke Gespraeche*, pp. 20–3.

35. Kessel, *Moltke*, p. 235.

36. Ibid., p. 252.

37. Theodore Ropp, *War in the Modern World* (New York, 1967), pp. 164ff.

38. Jeremy Black, *War in the World: Military Power and the Fate of Continents* (New Haven, 1998), pp. 165–76.

39. Larry Addington, *The Patterns of War since the Eighteenth Century* (Bloomington, Ind., 1984), p. 61.

40. Wawro, *Austro-Prussian War*, p. 11.

41. Addington, *Patterns of War*, p. 62.

42. Kessel, *Moltke*, p. 244.

43. Max Jaehns, 'Das Militaer-Wochenblatt von 1816 bis 1876' in *Max Jaehns, Militaergeschichtliche Aufsaetze*, ed. Ursula von Gersdorff (Osnabrück, 1970), pp. 301ff.

44. Ibid., p. 311.

45. Ibid., p. 312.

46. Kessel, *Moltke*, p. 244.

47. Jaehns, 'Das Militaer-Wochenblatt', p. 313.

48. Daniel Hughes (ed.), *Moltke on the Art of War: Selected Writings* (Novato, Calif., 1993), pp. 171ff.

49. General Guillaume Bonnal, 'Le Plan de Moltke pour 1870', in *Journal des Sciences Militaires*, July and August 1903, p. 7. From 28 November 1857 to 6 May 1870 Bonnal wrote, his preparatory ideas for a war against France were clear and thematic. Moltke's military correspondence, he went on, allows us to appreciate how much Moltke's immense labours contributed to the actual outcome of his wars, p. 6.

50. Kessel, *Moltke*, p. 282.
51. (Bavaria, Württemberg, Baden and Rhine Hesse.) Kessel, *Moltke*, p. 247.
52. The X Federal Corps was Hanover, Braunschwieg, North and Eastern Small; the IX Federal Corps was Saxony, Kur Hesse and Nassau.
53. Kessel, *Moltke*, p. 245.
54. Bucholz, *Prussian War Planning*, p. 39.
55. Kessel, *Moltke*, p. 247.
56. Ibid., p. 243.
57. Bucholz, *Prussian War Planning*, p. 40.
58. Kessel, *Moltke*, p. 252.
59. Ibid., p. 264.
60. Ibid., pp. 265–89.
61. Ibid., p. 269.
62. Ibid., p. 271.
63. Ibid., p. 275.
64. Jaehns, *Moltke*, Vol. II, p. 297.
65. Ibid.
66. Horst, *Moltke, Leben und Werk*, p. 246, letter to his brother Adolf dated July 1859.
67. Kessel, *Moltke*, p. 277.
68. 'First General Staff officer', also known as the 'chief of staff' to corps and divisional commanders.
69. Wawro, *Austro-Prussian War*, p. 34.
70. Kessel, *Moltke*, p. 281.
71. R. A. Doughty et al., *American Military History and the Evolution of Western Warfare* (Lexington, Mass., 1996), p. 126; cf. Michael D. Krause, 'Moltke and Grant: a Comparison of Their Operational Thinking and Perspective', in Foerster (ed.), *Generalfeldmarschall von Moltke: Bedeutung und Wirken*.
72. Kessel, *Moltke*, p. 286.
73. Bucholz, *Prussian War Planning*, p. 40.
74. Ibid., p. 41.
75. Kessel, *Moltke*, p. 295.
76. Ibid., pp. 295–302.
77. Pakula, *An Uncommon Woman*, p. 135; Craig, *Politics*, pp. 142–4; Kessel, *Moltke*, p. 349; *Denkwürdigkeiten aus dem Leben des General-Feldmarschalls Kriegsministers Grafen von Roon* (3rd edn, 3 vols, 1892); Reinhard Hübner, *Albrecht von Roon* (Hamburg, 1933).
78. Jaehns, *Moltke*, Vol. II, pp. 309–11.
79. Ibid., pp. 311–12.
80. Ibid., p. 313.
81. Ibid., pp. 315–16.
82. Kessel, *Moltke*, p. 292.
83. Ibid., p. 293.
84. Ibid., p. 308; Bucholz, *Prussian War Planning*, p. 42.
85. Kessel, *Moltke*, p. 309.
86. Ibid., p. 315.
87. Horst, *Moltke, Leben und Werk*, pp. 254–5.
88. Jay Luvaas, *The Military Legacy of the Civil War* (Chicago, 1959), p. 52.
89. Erich Eyck, *Bismarck and the German Empire* (New York, 1964), p. 166.

90. Luvass, *Military Legacy*, p. 124.
91. Ibid., p. 60.
92. Russell B. Nye, *George Bancroft: Brahmin Rebel* (New York, 1944), p. 278; Lilian Handlin, *George Bancroft: the Intellectual as Democrat* (New York, 1984), pp. 292–5; *The Life and Letters of George Bancroft*, edited by M. A. D. Howe (2 vols, 1971), Vol. II, pp. 174ff.
93. Examples are 'Der Feldzug 1862 in Nord-America', *Preussische Jahrbuecher*, Vol. 10, No. 4 (1863), pp. 362–86; 'Der Feldzug 1863 in Nord-America', *Preussische Jahrbuecher*, Vol. 12, No. 3 (1863), pp. 480–506; 'Der Krieg in Nordamerika', *Die Grenzboten*, Vol. 23, No. 4 (1964), pp. 325–34; Heinrich Korthoeber sums up a great deal of what Germans knew about the American Civil War in his essay, 'Ein merkwürdiger Krieg: der amerikanische Bürgerkrieg in zeitgenoessicher deutscher Perspektive', paper given at the German Historical Institute Conference, Washington, DC in April 1994. Otto Graf zu Stollberg-Wernigerode, *Deutschland und die Vereinigten Staaten von America in Zeitalter Bismarks* (Berlin, 1933); Ralph Lutz, *Die Beziehungen zwischen Deutschland und den Vereinigten Staaten waehrend des Sezessionskriegs* (Heidelberg, 1911).
94. Edward Hagerman, *The American Civil War and the Origins of Modern Warfare* (Bloomington, Ind., 1988), pp. xii–xiii and *passim*.
95. Roger Pickenpaugh, *Rescue By Rail: Troop Transfer and the Civil War in the West* (Lincoln and London, 1998), *passim*.
96. Kessel, *Moltke*, p. 321. Did Moltke image the German topography as Grant the American? In both cases the rivers run north and south, the railroads mainly east and west.
97. Dennis Showalter, *Railroads and Rifles: Soldiers, Technology and the Unification of Germany* (Hamden, Conn., 1975), pp. 44–8; Jaehns, *Moltke*, Vol. II, pp. 305ff.
98. Lother Gall, *Bismarck: The White Revolutionary* (2 vols, London, 1986), Vol. I, p. 155.
99. Ibid.
100. Ibid., p. 158.
101. Ibid., p. 159.
102. Ibid., p. 169.
103. Edward Crankshaw, *Bismarck* (London, 1983), p. 114.
104. Gall, *Bismarck*, Vol. I, pp. 171–7.
105. David Blackbourn, *The Long Nineteenth Century: a History of Germany, 1780–1918* (New York, 1998), p. 242.
106. Kessel, *Moltke*, p. 322.
107. Ibid., pp. 325–6; Jaehns, *Feldmarschall Moltke*, Vol. II, pp. 325–7.
108. Kessel, *Moltke*, p. 334.
109. Blackbourn, *The Long Nineteenth Century*, p. 242.

4   THE DANISH WAR, 1864

1. Kessel, *Moltke*, p. 359.
2. Both Gordon Craig's *Politics*, Ch. 5, and Gerhard Ritter's *Sword and Sceptor* (1954), Vol. I, Ch. 8, make much of the tension between political and

military goals and methods; none of Bismarck's biographers comments on Bismarck's assessment and evaluation of the instrument he chose to accomplish his political goals. For example, Emil Ludwig, *Bismarck: the Story of a Fighter* (1927); Erich Eyck, *Bismarck and the German Empire* (New York, 1964); Werner Richter, *Bismarck* (1965); Otto Pflanze, *Bismarck and the Development of Germany* (3 vols, 1963–90); Crankshaw, *Bismarck*; Gall, *Bismarck*.

3. Hans-Joachim Schoeps, *Bismarck über Zeitgenossen, Zeitgenossen über Bismarck* (Frankfurt, 1972), p. 128.

4. Nye, *George Bancroft: Brahmin Rebel*, p. 253.

5. Max Holzing says that Moltke's writings on the Danish War are substantial. Holzing, a Badisch first lieutenant probably assigned to the GGS at the time, presumably used these writings in his lecture presentation to the Military Society in Berlin on 1 December 1897. Holzing, 'General v. Moltkes Einwirkung auf den Strategischen Gang des Krieges gegen Daenemark 1864' in *Militär-Wochenblatt*, Beiheft 3, No. 4 (1897); Gordon Craig sums up Fontane's Danish War book in *Theodor Fontane*, pp. 79–85.

6. Kessel, *Moltke*, p. 362.

7. Ibid., pp. 364–6.

8. Carr, *Origins*, p. 71.

9. Sheehan, *German History*, pp. 888–92.

10. Ibid., p. 368; in the *Manchester Guardian* of 16 February 1864, Friedrich Engels wrote that, in contrast to the general assumption that the Germans outnumbered the Danes three to one, in reality it was slightly less than two to one. About the same, Engels said, that Wellington and Blücher had over Napoleon in 1815. *Engels as Military Critic*, eds W. H. Chaloner and W. O. Henderson (Westport, Conn., 1959), pp. 118–20.

11. Kessel, *Moltke*, p. 371.

12. Ibid., p. 383.

13. Ibid., p. 376.

14. Theodor Fontane, *Der Schleswig-Holsteinische Krieg im Jahr 1864* (Berlin, 1866), 2 vols, Vol. I, p. 31.

15. Prinzen Kraft zu Hohenlohe-Ingelfingen, *Aus meinen Leben: Aufzeichnungen* (3 vols, Berlin, 1906), Vol. III, p. 17.

16. Ibid., pp. 13–14. 'Zu Befehl' – yes Sir!

17. Fontane, *Schleswig-Holsteinische Krieg*, Vol. I, p. 48.

18. Ibid., Vol. I, pp. 1–7.

19. Few historians have dealt with weather as a factor in war. The reasons for this are varied. Discounting the extreme examples of French and German armies nearly perishing in Russian winters, in 1812–13 and 1941–44, respectively, perhaps nineteenth-century armies mainly tried to fight during the traditional campaign season, from April to October, when they could find food for their horses in the fields. Harold A.Winters, *Battling the Elements: Weather and Terrain in the Conduct of War* (Baltimore, 1998).

20. Daniel Hughes, *Moltke on the Art of War* (Novato, Calif., 1993), p. 207.

21. Fontane, *Schleswig-Holsteinische Krieg*, Vol. I, p. 57.

22. Hans Delbrück, 'Dybbol und Alsen' in *Preussischer Jahrbücher*, Vol. 60 (October 1887), pp. 18–63.

23. Kessel, *Moltke*, p. 388.

24. Delbrück, 'Dybbol und Alsen', p. 384. These numbers are too high.
25. Ibid., p. 376.
26. Holzing, 'General v. Moltkes Einwirkung', pp. 138–41.
27. Delbrück, 'Dybbol und Alsen', pp. 384–5.
28. Fontane, *Schleswig-Holsteinische Krieg*, p. 52.
29. Austrian accounts calls this the battle of 'Oeversee'. Frederick von Fischer, *Der Krieg in Schleswig und Jütland im Jahre 1864* (Vienna, 1870). pp. 123–6. Danish writers describe it as 'Overso-Sankelmark'. Johs Nielsen, *1864 Da Europa gik af lave* (Copenhagen, 1975) and N. Neergaard, *Under Junigrund-loven. En Fremstilling af Det Danske Folks Politscke histories fra 1848 til 1866* (Copenhagen, 1916).
30. A. Gallenga, *The Invasion of Denmark* (2 vols, 1864), Vol. II, pp. 136–9.
31. Fontane, *Schleswig-Holsteinische Krieg*, Vol. I, p. 55.
32. F. J. G. Count Waldersee, *Krieg gegen Daenemark im Jahre 1864* (Berlin, 1865), Beilage No. 7. B, der Schanzen bei Missunde.
33. Gallenga, *The Invasion of Denmark*, Vol. II, p. 140.
34. *Weapons: an International Encyclopedia* (1990), pp. 13, 21.
35. Craig, *Fontane*, p. 87.
36. Edward Dicey, *The Schleswig-Holstein War* (2 vols, London, 1864), Vol. I, pp. 113–15.
37. Herman Granier, *Der Feldzug von 1864* (Berlin, 1897). p. 36.
38. Waldersee, *Krieg gegen Daenemark*, p. 38.
39. Ibid., pp. 40–1; Fontane, *Schleswig-Holsteinische Krieg*, Vol. I, p. 46.
40. Waldersee, *Krieg gegen Daenemark*, pp. 43–5.
41. Granier, *Feldzug von 1864*, p. 37; Waldersee, *Krieg gegen Daenemark*, p. 48.
42. Ibid., p. 51.
43. This correspondence was referred to by Holzing, 'General v. Moltkes Einwirkung', p. 143.
44. Fontane, *Schleswig-Holsteinische Krieg*, Vol. I, p. 46.
45. Ibid., Vol. I, p. 78.
46. *Weapons: an International Encyclopedia*, pp. 113, 190.
47. Fontane, *Schleswig-Holsteinische Krieg*, Vol. I, p. 92; Fischer, *Der Krieg in Schleswig*, pp. 94ff.; Waldersee, *Krieg gegen Daenemark*, pp. 88ff.
48. Fontane, *Schleswig-Holsteinische Krieg*, Vol. I, p. 92.
49. Kraft zu Hohenlohe, *Aufzeichnungen*, Vol. III, p. 125.
50. Christopher Duffy, *The Fortress in the Age of Vauban and Frederick the Great, 1660–1789* (1985), pp. 1–3.
51. Holzing, 'General v. Moltkes Einwirkung', p. 133.
52. Delbrück, 'Dybbol und Alsen' p. 376.
53. Ibid., p. 380.
54. Dicey, *Schleswig-Holstein War*, Vol. II, pp. 31–52.
55. Ibid.
56. Alfred Vagts, *Landing Operations* (Harrisburg, Pa, 1946), preface.
57. Kessel, *Moltke*, pp. 379–430; Delbrück, 'Dybbol und Alsen', p. 377; Lawrence Sondhaus, *Preparing for Weltpolitik* (Annapolis, Md, 1997), pp. 71–9.
58. Ibid., p. 379.
59. Delbrück, 'Dybbol und Alsen', p. 380.

60. *Denkwürdigkeiten des Generals und Admirals Albrecht v. Stosch, Briefe und Tagebuchblaetter,* ed. Ulrich v. Stosch (2nd edn, Stuttgart, 1904), p. 55.
61. For Hindersin see 'A Little Military History' in Bucholz, *Delbrück's Modern Military History,* pp. 60ff.
62. Twenty-two 24-pound rifled siege guns, sixteen 25-pound siege mortars, thirty-four 12-pounders, twenty-two 6-pounders, sixteen light 12-pounders, and a dozen 7-pounders.
63. Wilhelm Rüstow, *Der deutsch–daenish Krieg 1864* (Zurich, 1864), p. 464.
64. Dicey, *Schleswig–Holstein War,* Vol. II, p. 159.
65. Rüstow, *Deutsch–daenische Krieg,* p. 456.
66. Nielsen, *1864,* pp. 242–3; Neergaard, *Under Junigrundloven,* pp. 1101–19.
67. Rüstow, *Deutsch–daenische Krieg,* p. 454; Bucholz, *Delbrück's Modern Military History,* pp. 61ff.
68. Rahne, *Mobilmachung,* p. 42.
69. Dicey, *Schleswig-Holstein War,* Vol. II, p. 137.
70. Ibid., Vol. II, p. 119.
71. Ibid., Vol. II, p. 31.
72. Ibid., Vol. I, pp. 284–8.
73. Ibid., Vol. II, p. 25.
74. Ibid., Vol. II, p. 65.
75. Ibid., Vol. II, p. 66; *Websters New International Dictionary,* 1934, p. 793.
76. Delbrück, 'Dybbol und Alsen', p. 381.
77. Dicey, *Schleswig-Holstein War,* Vol. II, pp. 138–42.
78. Ibid., Vol. II, pp. 147–56.
79. Ibid., Vol. II, p. 159.
80. Ibid., Vol. II, p. 166.
81. Ibid., Vol. II, pp. 74–175.
82. Ibid., Vol. II, p. 176.
83. Ibid., Vol. II, p. 78.
84. Ibid., Vol. II, p. 105.
85. Ibid., Vol. II, p. 106.
86. Delbrück, 'Dybbol und Alsen', p. 58.
87. Ibid., p. 59; Wrangel was kept on for a few weeks as a '*Schaustück*' for the Austrians, but he no longer was in operational command. Stosch, *Denkwürdigkeiten,* p. 56; Kessel, *Moltke,* pp. 403–4.
88. Delbrück, 'Dybbol und Alsen', p. 384.
89. Ibid., Vol. II, p. 309.
90. Fontane, *Schleswig-Holsteinische Krieg,* Vol. II, p. 310.
91. Cf. Moltke's account for Marie, in Horst, *Moltke,* pp. 265–75, in which he writes that Marie may let other, interested persons, read the letter if they wish. So he is not giving away any secrets in this account. He also says that this is not at all an official account, but merely the impressions of an observer.
92. Werner von Siemens had graduated from it in the 1830s and spoke glowingly about its mathematicians, chemists and physicists: he said the school gave him a clear edge over his peers. Wilfried Feldenkircken, *Werner von Siemens: Inventor and International Entrepreneur* (Columbus, 1994), pp. 32–3.
93. Fontane, *Schleswig-Holsteinische Krieg,* Vol. II, pp. 312–14.

94. Ten-page letter to his wife, dated 3 July 1864. Horst, *Moltke*, pp. 265–75.
95. Fontane, *Schleswig-Holsteinische Krieg*, Vol. II, p. 325.
96. Ibid., Vol. II, p. 331.
97. Nielsen, *1864*, p. 329; Waldersee, *Krieg gegen Daenemark*, pp. 506–8.
98. Prussian officers called their men 'children', using the same grammatical structure used in adult–child discourse. Alfred Vagts, a mortar platoon leader in World War I, told me this long ago from his own experiences in the World War I German Army.
99. Fontane, *Schleswig-Holsteinische Krieg*, Vol. II, p. 347.
100. Waldersee, *Krieg gegen Daenemark*, pp. 545–7; Fischer, *Krieg in Schleswig*, pp. 356–7.
101. For a view of Lundby from Schlutterbach's regiment, there is Albert von Boguslawski, *Geschichte des 3. Niederschlesischen Infanterie-Regiments Nr. 50* (Berlin, 1887), pp. 55–65.
102. Fontane, *Schleswig-Holsteinische Krieg*, Vol. II, p. 349.
103. Ibid., Vol. II, p. 350. Kessel, *Moltke*, p. 425.
104. Carr, *Origins*, p. 85.
105. Horst, *Moltke*, pp. 278–9.
106. Ibid., p. 279.
107. Letter to Marie, dated 25 August 1864, GGS, *Moltkes Gesammelte Schriften*, Vol. VI, p. 421.
108. Kessel, *Moltke*, pp. 417–18.

5   THE AUSTRIAN WAR, 1866

1. Geoffrey Wawro, *The Austro-Prussian War* (New York, 1996), p. 277; Gordon Craig, *The Battle of Koeniggraetz* (Philadelphia, 1964), p. 166.
2. The critic was Friedrich Engels. James Sheehan, *German History, 1770–1866* (New York, 1989), p. 902.
3. Larry Addington, *The Patterns of War since the Eighteenth Century* (Bloomington, Ind., 1984), p. 65.
4. Craig, *Koeniggraetz*, p. 25.
5. Fontane, *Deutsche Krieg*, Vol. I, pp. 248–9.
6. Istvan Deak, *Beyond Nationalism: a Social and Political History of the Habsburg Officer Corps, 1848–1918* (1990), p. 52; Wawro, *Austro-Prussian War*, pp. 56–65.
7. Craig, *Koeniggraetz*, p. 15.
8. This was a reverse salient or cultural lag.
9. Bucholz, *Delbrück's Modern Military History*, pp. 73–4.
10. Wawro, *Austro-Prussian War*, pp. 24–32.
11. Kessel, *Moltke*, pp. 426–7.
12. Prinz Friedrich Karl von Preussen, *Denkwürdigkeiten aus seinem Leben*, ed. Wolfgang Foerster (3 vols, Stuttgart, 1910), Vol. 1, pp. 362–3.
13. Edward Taaffe, Howard Gauthier and Morton O. Kelly, *Geography of Transportation* (2nd edn, 1996), pp. 70–140.
14. Ibid., pp. 73ff., 134ff.

15. Michael F. Barnsley, *Fractals Everywhere* (2nd edn, 1988), p. 1.
16. T. S. Eliot, 'Tradition and the Individual Talent' quoted in Calvin Tomkins, 'The Escape Artist: a New Rothko Retrospective at the Whitney', *The New Yorker*, 28, Sept. 1998, pp. 102–3; Kessel, *Moltke*, p. 428.
17. Bucholz, *Prussian War Planning*, p. 41.
18. Ibid., p. 44.
19. Ibid., p. 48; Michael Salewski, 'Moltke, Schlieffen und die Eisenbahn' in Roland G. Foerster (ed.) *Generalfeldmarschall von Moltke: Bedeutung und Wirkung* (Munich, 1991), p. 91.
20. Bucholz, *Prussian War Planning*, pp. 44–5.
21. Max Jaehns, *Feldmarschall Moltke* (3 vols, Berlin, 1900), Vol. II, p. 375; Carr, *Origins*, pp. 119–20.
22. Sheehan, *German History*, pp. 899–907.
23. Carr, *Origins*, pp. 135–6.
24. Jaehns, *Moltke*, Vol. II, p. 376.
25. Ibid., Vol. II, p. 378.
26. Nomenclature borrowed from Timothy O'Brien, 'Taking the Danger out of Risk: Chase says Models Helped it Avoid Financial Minefields', *NY Times*, 20 January 1999, pp. C1, C9.
27. Jaehns, *Moltke*, Vol. II, pp. 379–80.
28. Ibid., Vol. II, p. 382.
29. Kessel, *Moltke*, p. 332.
30. Waldersee, *Denkwürdigkeiten des General-Feldmarschalls Alfred Grafen von Waldersee*, ed. Heinrich O. Meisner (3 vols, 1922), Vol. I, pp. 22–3.
31. Ibid., Vol. I, pp. 22–4.
32. Kessel, *Moltke*, pp. 433–7.
33. Ibid., p. 438.
34. Ibid.
35. Ibid., p. 444.
36. Hermann Rahne, *Mobilmachung*, p. 50; not much has been written about horses in nineteenth-century war, except for cavalry actions. Horse usage goes far beyond that. F. M. L. Thompson, *Horses in European Economic History* (1983); R. L. DiNardo and Austin Bay, 'Horse-Drawn Transport in the German Army', *Journal of Contemporary History*, Vol. 23 (1988), pp. 129–42.
37. Bucholz, *Prussian War Planning*, p. 162.
38. Kessel, *Moltke*, p. 445.
39. Ibid., pp. 445–6.
40. Jaehns, *Moltke*, Vol. II, p. 385.
41. Kraft zu Hohenlohe, *Aus meinem Leben*, Vol. III, p. 211.
42. Jaehns, *Moltke*, Vol. II, p. 385.
43. Carr, *Origins*, p. 129.
44. Ibid., p. 128. Although Prussia could not fight at all without horses it could and did fight without food, in 1866 only 3 of $8\frac{1}{2}$ corps had full supplies with them. Wolfgang Petter, 'Die Logistic des deutschen Heeres im deutsch–franzoesischen Krieg von 1870/71', in *Die Bedeutung der Logistik für die militarische Führung von Antike bis in die neueste Zeit*, p. 113. Schellendorff estimated that an army corps, advancing by two roads to a depth of ten

miles, would do fine in large towns but would need five miles of country farms to live for one or two days without military supply. And that an army of 100 000–120 000, in a country of average population and agricultural fertility, with its units within a day's march of each other, could subsist without magazines or supply arrangements during an advance that was interrupted by halts of a single day's duration. Schellendorff, *Duties of the General Staff*, p. 411. It was early summer, before the harvest in most places: sufficient food was available.

45. Kessel, *Moltke*, p. 445.
46. Wawro, *Austro-Prussian War*, p. 54, Craig, *Koeniggraetz*, pp. 34–5.
47. Kraft zu Hohenlohe, *Aus meinem Leben*, pp. 211–25.
48. Carr, *Origins*, p. 129.
49. Showalter, *The Wars of Frederick the Great*, pp. 342–52.
50. Jaehns, *Moltke*, Vol. II, p. 386.
51. Ibid., Vol. II, p. 389.
52. Kessel, *Moltke*, pp. 446–7.
53. Michael Salewski emphasizes the central role railroads played in Moltke's operational and strategic thinking, 'Moltke, Schlieffen und die Eisenbahn' in Foerster (ed.), *Generalfeldmarschall von Moltke, Bedeutung und Wirkung*, pp. 89–102.
54. Kessel, *Moltke*, p. 449.
55. Jaehns, *Moltke*, Vol. II, p. 391.
56. Ibid.
57. Carr, *Origins*, p. 130.
58. Kessel, *Moltke*, p. 332.
59. Carr, *Origins*, p. 130.
60. Jaehns, *Moltke*, Vol. II, p. 393.
61. Ibid., Vol. II, p. 392.
62. Ibid., Vol. II, p. 395.
63. Ibid., Vol. II, p. 428.
64. Wilhelm Bigge, *Feldmarschall Graf Moltke* (2 vols, 1901), Vol. II, p. 197.
65. Martin van Creveld, *Command in War* (1985), pp. 122–3.
66. Bronsart von Schellendorff, *The Duties of the General Staff* (rev. edn, 1905), p. 288.
67. An example is the war diary of W. von Klenck, squadron commander in the Royal Saxon Guard Cavalry Regiment for the battle of St Privat, 15–19 August 1870, translated and published as *St. Privat, German Sources,* translated by Harry Bell (1914).
68. Ibid., p. 294.
69. Ibid., pp. 295–7.
70. Carl-Gero von Ilsemann, 'Das operative Denken des Aelteren Moltke' in Horst Boog et al., *Operatives Denken und Handeln in deutschen Streitkraeften im 19 und 20. Jahrhundert* (Bonn, 1988); Roland G. Foerster, 'The Operational Thinking of the Elder Moltke and its Consequences' in *Operational Thinking in Clausewitz, Moltke, Schlieffen and Manstein* (1988), pp. 21–40; Shimon Naveh, *In Pursuit of Military Excellence: the Evolution of Operational Theory* (1997), pp. 36–7, 57–8 and *passim*.

71. Michael D. Krause, 'Moltke and the Origins of the Operational Level of War' in Foerster (ed.), *Generalfeldmarschall von Moltke, Bedeutung und Wirkung*, pp. 65–79.
72. Christopher Bellamy, *The Evolution of Land Warfare* (1990), p. 60, quoted from Moltke, *Taktische-strategische Aufsaetz aus den Jahren 1857 bis 1871* (1891), Vol. V, p. 291.
73. Kraft zu Hohenlohe, *Aus meinem Leben*, p. 226.
74. Salewski, 'Moltke, Schlieffen and die Eisenbahn', p. 92.
75. Carr, *Origins*, p. 132.
76. Ibid., p. 134.
77. For Falckenstein cf. *Denkwürdigkeiten des General-feldmarschalls Alfred Grafen von Waldersee*, ed. H. O. Meisner (2 vols, 1922), Vol. I, pp. 30–3.
78. Wawro, *Austro-Prussian War*, p. 77.
79. Using telegraphic communications to speed up the process. Dennis Showalter, 'Soldiers into Postmasters? The Electric Telegraph as an Instrument of Command in the Prussian Army', *Military Affairs*, Vol. 46, No. 2 (April 1973), p. 50.
80. For this whole affair of Langensalza cf. Hans Delbrück, 'Langensalza und Vogel von Falckenstein', *Preussische Jahrbücher*, Vol. 59 (May 1887), reprinted in Delbrück, *Erinnerungen, Aufsaetze und Reden* (1907), pp. 12–47.
81. Wawro, *Austro-Prussian War*, p. 80.
82. Ibid., p. 77.
83. Ibid., p. 78.
84. Craig, *Koeniggraetz*, p. 40; Wawro, *Austro-Prussian War*, p. 77.
85. Ibid., p. 118.
86. Two other well-known equations for estimating mathematically the results of combat are the Lanchester and the Dupuy equations. Lanchester equations link casualty and attrition rates to target acquisition, fire rates and weapons effectiveness on both sides of the battle.The Lanchester model evolved at about the same time as Naumann. Dupuy is a late twentieth-century American model, which factors in tanks, artillery and other equipment as well as relative casualty rates. Michael O'Hanlon, *Defense Planning for the Late 1990s: Beyond the Desert Storm Framework* (1995), appendix A.
87. Bucholz, *Prussian War Planning*, p. 88.
88. Theodor Fontane, *Der Deutsche Krieg von 1866* (2 vols, 2 edn, Berlin, 1871), Vol. I, p. 293.
89. Wawro, *Austro-Prussian War*, p. 137.
90. Ibid., p. 144.
91. Ibid., pp. 137–40.
92. Fontane, *Deutsche Krieg*, Vol. I, p. 301.
93. Ibid., Vol. I, p. 303.
94. Wawro, *Austro-Prussian War*, p. 143; Fontane's casualties were 7372 Austrian and 1120 Prussian; *Deutsche Krieg*, Vol. I, p. 317.
95. Wawro, *Austro-Prussian War*, pp. 144–5.
96. Craig, *Koeniggraetz*, p. 62.
97. H. M. Hozier, *The Seven Weeks War* (2 vols, London, 1867), Vol. I, pp. 265–7.
98. Fontane, *Deutsche Krieg*, Vol. I, p. 360.
99. Craig, *Koeniggraetz*, p. 63; Fontane, *Deutsche Krieg*, Vol. I, pp. 356–89.

100. Wawro, *Austro-Prussian War,* p. 147. Blumenthal thought Bonin should have been removed on the spot. Craig, *Koeniggraetz,* p. 64.
101. Fontane, *Deutsche Krieg,* Vol. I, pp. 383–9.
102. Wawro, *Austro-Prussian War,* pp. 151–2.
103. Craig, *Koeniggraetz,* p. 114.
104. Ibid., p. 64; Wawro, *Austro-Prussian War,* p. 152.
105. Fontane, *Deutsche Krieg,* pp. 322–39.
106. Schowalter, *Wars of Frederick the Great,* p. 363.
107. Fontane, *Deutsche Krieg,* Vol. I, pp. 322–5; Wawro, *Austro-Prussian War,* pp. 165–7; Craig, *Koeniggraetz,* pp. 64–6.
108. Wawro, *Austro-Prussian War,* pp. 169–70.
109. Fontane, *Deutsche Krieg,* Vol. I, p. 326.
110. Wawro, *Austro-Prussian War,* pp. 173–4.
111. John English, 'The Operational Art: Development in the Theories of War' in *The Operational Art: Developments in the Theories of War,* ed. B. J. C. McKercher and Michael A. Hennessy (Westport, Conn., 1996), p. 8.
112. Daniel J. Hughes, *Moltke on the Art of War* (Novato, Calif., 1993), p. 231.
113. Franz Uhle-Wettler, 'Auftragstaktik: Mission Orders and the German Experience' in Richard D. Hooker, Jr, *Maneuver Warfare: an Anthology* (Novato, Calif., 1993).
114. Hughes, *Moltke on the Art of War,* pp. 12, 177.
115. Craig, *Koeniggraetz,* p. 40.
116. Hughes, *Moltke on the Art of War,* p. 184.
117. Van Creveld describes 14 of these. *Command in War,* pp. 118–40.
118. Cf. Albrecht von Stosch's comments from his position on the staff of the crown prince's Second Army, in *Denkwürdigkeiten des Generals und Admirals Albrecht von Stosch,* ed. Ulrich von Stosch (2nd edn, Stuttgart, 1904), pp. 70–85.
119. Tom Clancy and Fred Franks, Jr, *Into the Storm: a Study in Command* (1997), p. 292.
120. Craig, *Koeniggraetz,* p. 72.
121. Ibid.
122. Ibid., p. 85.
123. Ibid.
124. GGS, *Moltkes Gesammelte Schriften,* Vol. VI, p. 446.
125. Craig, *Koeniggraetz,* p. 92.
126. Ibid., p. 97.
127. Ibid., p. 112.
128. Ibid., p. 109.
129. Ibid., p. 123.
130. Ibid., p. 124.
131. Paret, *Makers of Modern Strategy,* p. 294.
132. Ibid.
133. Craig, *Koeniggraetz,* p. 198.
134. Ibid., pp. 159–60.
135. Ibid., p. 162.
136. Horst, *Moltke,* p. 288.
137. Ibid., p. 289.

138. Moltke's letters to Marie, describing the battle, are remarkably close to the best twentieth-century accounts such as Gordon Craig. On the other hand, in one letter, he gives her leave to let others read it, saying it is only an account of his impressions.
139. Wawro, *Austro-Prussian War*, p. 27; Craig, *Koeniggraetz*, p. 166.
140. Richard M. Swain, *'Lucky War': Third Army in the Desert Storm* (1994), p. xxvii.
141. Van Creveld's examples tend to support the 'near-run' thesis, but his conclusions are closer to those advanced here. He says that Moltke's risks were based on a realization that individual Prussian forces were strong enough to withstand larger Austrian forces for a certain period of time and that Moltke built into his system large margins of safety to ensure that these periods of time were not exceeded and things allowed to get out of hand. *Command in War*, p. 121.
142. Gordon Craig, *The Politics of the Prussian Army* (New York, 1955), p. 198.
143. Ibid., p. 203.
144. Horst, *Moltke*, p. 293; John C. G. Roehl, *The Kaiser and and his Court: Wilhelm II and the Government of Germany* (1996), pp. 87–90.
145. This was followed by nearly 50 pages of etchings of more than 100 of the important memorials, with the words, military units and names inscribed written beside each illustration. Fontane, *Deutsche Krieg 1866*, Vol. II, appendix, pp. 1–2.

6 THE FRENCH WAR, 1870–71

1. Michael Howard, *The Franco-Prussian War* (New York, 1961), pp. 1, 12–13. The opposite view is also possible. That the French, because they fought mainly colonial wars against small, less well-equipped and technologically backward native peoples, were, in reality, not up to the quality levels of the European military. Nor were French commanders experienced and practised in handling armies: their experience had been with regiments and divisions and they had little practical experience with large-scale manoeuvres.
2. It is impossible to render this into English as it sounded in German, where it was a play on three verbs – 'erdacht, gebracht, gemacht' – which sounded alike. 'Der den Feldzugsplan erdacht, Der ihn zu Ende gebracht, Moltke hat es gut gemacht.' Bigge, *Moltke*, Vol. II, p. 251; GGS, *Moltkes Gesammelte Schriften*, Vol. VI, p. 464.
3. Howe, *Letters of Bancroft*, Vol. II, p. 218.
4. Friedrich A. Dressler, *Moltke in his Home* (London, 1907), a translation of the same author's *Moltke in seiner Hauslichkeit* (Berlin, 1904). Dressler was a pianist and composer who was befriended by the family for his musical abilities. He often dined and played the piano in Moltke's home from late1868 up to and including the night Moltke died, p. 66.
5. Jaehns, *Moltke*, Vol. II, p. 463.
6. Ibid., Vol. II, p. 465; Kessel, *Moltke*, p. 494.
7. Kessel, *Moltke*, p. 494.

8. GGS, *Moltkes Gesammelte Schriften*, Vol. V, p. 42.

9. Kessel, *Moltke*, p. 495.

10. Jaehns, *Moltke*, Vol. II, p. 476. Kessel, *Moltke*, p. 476. His younger and favourite sister Auguste had lost her husband in 1856. His brother Fritz had lost his wife in 1864. In December 1868 in Berlin for the funeral of Marie von Moltke, she had been taken aside by Queen Auguste, who told her it was her and her brother's duty to Germany to move into Moltke's apartment in Berlin to provide support for the General Staff chief. From then on they took over day-to-day management of his household. GGS, *Moltkes Gesammelte Schriften*, Vol. V, p. 30.

11. GGS, *Moltkes Gesammelte Schriften*, Vol. VI, p. 456. At the ratification ceremony for the preliminary peace treaty, 29 July 1866, the king inducted both Moltke and Roon into the order of the Black Eagle.

12. *Das Tagebuch der Baronin Spitzenberg* (5th edn, Göttingen, 1989), *passim*.

13. Lilian Handlin, *George Bancroft, the Intellectual as Democrat* (New York, 1984), p. 295; Russell B. Nye, *George Bancroft, Brahmin Rebel* (New York, 1944), pp. 267–78.

14. Handlin, *Bancroft*, p. 292; cf. James M. Brophy, *Capitalism, Politics, and Railroads in Prussia, 1830–1870* (Columbus, 1998), *passim*. Bancroft, *Letters*, Vol. II, p. 196.

15. This is confirmed by General Philip Sheridan, American Civil War commander who was an observer at the battle of Sedan and spoke with Moltke several times. P. H. Sheridan, *Personal Memoirs* (2 vols, New York, 1888), Vol. II, pp. 362–410; Joseph Hergescheimer, *Sheridan: a Military Narrative* (Boston, 1931), pp. 3–8.

16. M. A. DeWolfe Howe, *The Life and Letters of George Bancroft* (2 vols, 1971) (originally published in 1908), Vol. II, pp. 219–20.

17. Handlin, *Bancroft*, Ch. 10; Nye, *Bancroft*, Ch. 7.

18. Invisible to historians because research using regimental rolls has not yet been put together at this level. Kraft zu Hohenlohe remarks that many of the same officers commanded in 1866 and 1870. Prince Kraft zu Hohenlohe-Ingelfingen, *Letters on Artillery* (London, 1888), pp. 4–5.

19. Kessel, *Moltke*, p. 546.

20. Harry Bell, *St. Privat, German Sources* (1914), Appendix A, pp. 473–7.

21. Moltke uses virtually these same words in his 'Instructions for Large Unit Commanders', Hughes, *Moltke on the Art of War*, p. 172.

22. Kessel, *Moltkes erster Feldzug*, p. 1; Hughes, *Moltke on the Art of War*, p. 172.

23. Bucholz, *Prussian War Planning*, pp. 47–8.

24. Kessel, *Moltke*, p. 502.

25. Bucholz, *Prussian War Planning*, p. 49.

26. Ibid., pp. 51–2; Rahne, *Mobilmachung*, p. 58.

27. Rahne, *Mobilmachung*, p. 58.

28. 'The German Railroad Concentration of 1870', *The Military Historian and Economist*, Vol. 3, No. 2 (1910), pp. 1–32; Gustav Lehmann, *Die Mobilmachung von 1870–71* (Berlin, 1905); Bucholz, *Prussian War Planning*, p. 51.

29. 'The German Railroad Concentration of 1870', p. 32.

30. Public utilities in the USA still use this method to supply coal via railroad, for example, to their electrical generating plants.

31. Bucholz, 'Armies, Railroads and Information: the Birth of Industrial Mass War' in Jane Summerton (ed.), *Changing Large Technical Systems* (1994).

32. Lehmann, *Mobilmachung 1870*, p. 34.

33. Rahne, *Mobilmachung*, p. 58.

34. Bucholz, *Prussian War Planning*, p. 49; Kessel, *Moltke*, pp. 503ff.

35. Kessel, *Moltke*, pp. 508–10.

36. Ibid., p. 518.

37. Ibid., pp. 505–12.

38. Craig, *Koeniggraetz*, pp. 50, 114; Wawro, *Austro-Prussian War*, p. 145; Fontane, *Deutsche Krieg*, Vol. I, pp. 356–89.

39. Hughes, *Moltke on the Art of War*, pp. 237, 241.

40. Dennis Showalter, 'Prussian Technology and War: Artillery from 1815 to 1914' in Ronald Haycock and Keith Neilson, *Men, Machines and War* (Waterloo, 1987), p. 125.

41. Kraft zu Hohenlohe, *Letters on Artillery*, p. 53.

42. Dennis Showalter, *Railroads and Rifles: Soldiers, Technology and the Unification of Germany* (Hamden, 1975), is useful on artillery questions.

43. Schowalter, 'Prussian Technology and War', pp. 128–30.

44. Bucholz, *Delbrück's Modern Military History*, pp. 60–5.

45. Ibid.

46. Ibid.

47. Ibid.

48. Kraft zu Hohenlohe, *Letters on Artillery*, p. 169.

49. Ibid., p. 182.

50. Kessel, *Moltke*, p. 521.

51. Kraft zu Hohenlohe, *Aus meinem Leben*, pp. 357–93.

52. Kraft zu Hohenlohe, *Letters on Artillery*, p. 223.

53. Van Creveld, *Supplying War*, p. 2.

54. Ibid., p. 112.

55. Ibid., pp. 84, 103ff.

56. Bucholz, *Prussian War Planning*, p. 50.

57. Crichton, *Jurassic Park*, p. 67.

58. Kessel, *Moltke*, p. 503.

59. Ibid., p. 504.

60. Ibid., p. 536.

61. Rahne, *Mobilmachung*, p. 56.

62. Kessel, *Moltke*, p. 477.

63. Connelly, *Blundering to Victory*, p. 195; Kessel, *Moltke*, p. 536.

64. Kessel, *Moltke*, p. 524.

65. Ibid., pp. 528–38.

66. There is a description of this terrain and the opening phase of the 1870 War in Patrick O'Sullivan and Jesse W. Miller, Jr, *The Geography of Warfare* (New York, 1983), pp. 69–73.

67. Ibid., p. 477.

68. Kessel, *Moltke*, p. 481.

69. Jaehns, *Moltke*, Vol. II, pp. 562–70.

70. Kessel, *Moltke*, pp. 527–30.

71. Ibid., p. 332.

72. Compare Max Jaehns' ideas in Jaehns, *Moltke*, Vol. II, p. 470.
73. Ibid., Vol. II, p. 469.
74. Kessel, *Moltke*, p. 499.
75. Bradley J. Meyer, 'The Operational Art: the Elder Moltke's Campaign Plan for the Franco-Prussian War' in *The Operational Art*, edited by B. J. McKercher and Michael Hennessy (Westport, Conn., 1996), mainly for the final format these war plans took.
76. Ibid., p. 540.
77. Ibid., p. 541.
78. Kessel, *Moltke*, p. 521.
79. Ibid., pp. 503–21; Hughes, *Moltke on the Art of War*, pp. 171–224.
80. Kessel, *Moltke*, pp. 523–43.
81. Carr, *Origins*, pp. 183ff; David Blackbourn, *The Long Nineteenth Century: a History of Germany, 1780–1918* (New York, 1998), pp. 255ff; Howard, *Franco-Prussian War*, p. 55.
82. Kessel, *Moltke*, pp. 543–4.
83. Ibid., p. 546.
84. Jaehns, *Moltke*, Vol. II, p. 486.
85. Howe, *Letters of George Bancroft*, Vol. II, p. 238.
86. Handlin, *Bancroft*, p. 295; Nye, *Bancroft*, pp. 267–78.
87. Kessel, *Moltke*, p. 545.
88. Rahne, *Mobilmachung*, pp. 61–2.
89. Schellendorff, *Duties of the General Staff*, p. 247.
90. Howard, *Franco-Prussian War*, p. 60 .
91. Boehn, *Generalstabsgeschaefte*, p. 284.
92. Rahne, *Mobilmachung*, pp. 61–8; Lehmann, *Mobilmachung 1870, passim*.
93. Boehn, *Generalstabsgeschaefte*, p. 321.
94. Ibid., p. 324.
95. Ibid.
96. Ibid., p. 327.
97. Ibid., p. 324.
98. Rahne, *Mobilmachung*, p. 63; Boehn, *Generalstabsgeschaefte*, p. 284.
99. Howard, *Franco-Prussian War*, p. 62.
100. Ibid.
101. Major von Blume, 'Vom Generalstabe des Grossen Hauptquartiers im Kriege 1870/71' in GGS, *Moltkes Gesammelte Schriften*, Vol. V, p. 286.
102. Cf. Julius von Verdy du Vernois, *With the Royal Headquarters in 1870–71* (London, 1897) and *Journals of Field-Marshal Count von Blumenthal for 1866 and 1870–71*, ed. Albrecht von Blumenthal (London, 1903).
103. Schellendorff, *Duties of the General Staff*, p. 331.
104. Most recently Brad Meyer deals with these issues in McKercher and Hennessy, *The Operational Art*, pp. 39–42.
105. Schellendorff, *Duties of the General Staff*, p. 353.
106. Dennis Showalter, 'Soldiers into Postmasters? The Electric Telegraph as an Instrument of Command in the Prussian Army', *Military Affairs*, Vol. 46, No. 2 (April 1973), pp. 48–52.
107. Ibid., p. 283. Both Bronsart von Schellendorff and Verdy du Vernois circulated continuously among the army and corps commanders, visiting the

crown princes of Prussia and Saxony, bringing news of Mars le Tour, gathering news and clarifying orders. As they travelled they repeatedly ran into men they knew. Typical of this, during the final battle for Sedan, Verdy liaised with General von Kirchbach, commander of V Corps, his old teacher at the War Academy, whose chief of staff, Lt. Col. von der Esch, was an old friend from regimental days. Verdy du Vernois, *With the Royal I Headquarters*, pp. 45–51, 72, 129. There are some indications that this liaison was routinely carried out in the late afternoon, so that they could report the latest troop dispositions for the following day's operations.

108. *Journals of Blumenthal*, pp. 75–111.
109. Ibid., p. 284.
110. Ibid., p. 285.
111. Ibid. , p. 286.
112. Schellendorff, *Duties of the General Staff*, p. 313.
113. Thomas J. Adriance, *The Last Gaiter Button: a Study of the Mobilization and Concentration of the French Army in the War of 1870* (Westport, Conn., 1982); Richard Holmes, *The Road to Sedan: the French Army, 1866–70* (London, 1984).
114. Scott Lackey, 'The Habsburg Army and the Franco-Prussian War: the Failure to Intervene and its Consequences', *War in History*, Vol. 2, No. 2 (1995), p. 169.
115. Howard, *Franco-Prussian War*, p. 64; Lackey, 'Habsburg Army', p. 169.
116. Lackey, 'The Habsburg Army', pp. 150–79.
117. William Serman, 'French Mobilization in 1870', paper delivered at the German Historical Institute Conference, *On the Road to Total War: the American Civil War and the German Wars of Unification, 1861–1871*, Washington, DC, April 1994, p. 4.
118. Ibid., p. 10.
119. Howard, *Franco-Prussian War*, p. 68.
120. Ibid., p. 71.
121. Ibid., p. 77.
122. Lackey, 'The Habsburg Army', p. 165.
123. Howard, *Franco-Prussian War*, p. 79.
124. Ibid., p. 100.
125. Bucholz, *Prussian War Planning*, pp. 80–1.
126. G. F. R. Henderson, *The Battle of Spicheren* (London, 1902), describes and analyses this battle in great detail. Especially good for artillery.
127. D. Ascoli, *A Day of Battle: Mars-La-Tour, 16 August 1870* (London, 1987), p. 73.
128. Fontane, *Krieg gegen Frankreich*, Vol. I, p. 148.
129. Ibid., Vol. I, p. 102.
130. Ibid., Vol. I, p. 151.
131. Ibid., Vol. I, p. 152.
132. Howard, *Franco-Prussian War*, pp. 102–3.
133. Ibid., p. 105.
134. Ibid., p. 107.
135. Fontane, *Krieg gegen Frankreich*, Vol. I, p. 158.
136. Howard, *Franco-Prussian War*, p. 109.

137. Ascoli, *A Day of Battle*, p. 81.

138. Ibid., p. 81.

139. Ibid., p. 82.

140. One of Michael Howard's general observations in *The Franco-Prussian War*, p. 127.

141. Ibid., p. 183.

142. Ibid., p. 188.

143. Ibid., p. 191.

144. Ibid., p. 195.

145. Ibid., p. 196.

146. Ibid., p. 198.

147. Ibid., p. 200.

148. Ibid., p. 199.

149. Ibid., p. 211.

150. Fontane, *Krieg gegen Frankreich*, Vol. I, p. 539.

151. Howard, *Franco-Prussian War*, p. 216.

152. Sheridan, *Personal Memoirs*, Vol. II, pp. 362–410; Hergescheimer, *Sheridan*, pp. 3–8.

153. Howard, *Franco-Prussian War*, p. 118.

154. Ibid., p. 217.

155. Fontane, *Krieg gegen Frankreich*, Vol. I, pp. 513–15, 531–5.

156. Ibid., Vol. I, pp. 536–58.

157. Kessel, *Moltke*, p. 568; Kessel (ed.), *Moltke Gespraeche* (Hamburg, 1940), pp. 138ff.

158. Ibid., p. 141; Fontane, *Krieg gegen Frankreich*, Vol. I, pp. 563–74.

159. Ibid., p. 146.

160. Ibid., p. 148; Kessel, *Moltke*, p. 568.

161. J. M. Thompson, *Louis Napoleon and the Second Empire* (New York, 1955), p. 313; Alistair Horne, *The Fall of Paris* (New York, 1967), p. 57.

162. Kessel, *Moltke*, p. 569.

CONCLUSION

1. Franz Herre, *Moltke, Der Mann und sein Jahrhundert* (2nd edn, Stuttgart, 1984), p. 9.

2. Ibid., p. 12.

3. Ibid., p. 10.

4. Dressler, *Moltke in seiner Hauslichkeit*, p. 101.

5. GGS, *Moltkes Gesammelte Schriften*, Vol. V, pp. 290–1.

6. Friedrich A. Dressler, *Moltke in His Home* (London, 1907), pp. 152–8.

7. Robert H. Scales, Jr, 'Cycles of War', *Armed Forces Journal International*, July 1997, pp. 38–42.

8. It is not that the Prussian armies did not make mistakes: they repeatedly made them. But that Prussia's opponents made more of them. For example, Prince Friedrich Charles, commander of the Second Army, was given the mission of overtaking and surrounding Bazaine's army on its retreat

from Metz on 16 August. Moltke had given the prince carte blanche and the latter, assuming that Bazaine had escaped, threw his army to the west, away from the main body of the French. Confronted with a situation which could have been a serious disaster for the German forces in the area, Bazaine did nothing and allowed Alvensleben's III Corps to bluff his way to victory or at least a draw at Vionville. Two German corps had held the entire French Army at bay. Bazaine was oblivious to his overwhelming superiority. David Ascoli, *A Day of Battle: Mars-la-Tour, 16 August 1870* (London, 1987), pp. 160–5; Howard, *Franco-Prussian War*, pp. 144ff; although many of Martin van Creveld's examples seem to support the opposite view, his conclusions agree with these. He admits that Moltke's system provided a large safety margin to ensure that the inevitable mistakes did not develop into catastrophes. *Command in War*, p. 121.

9. Reverse salients are technical or organizational anomalies resulting from uneven evolution within a system: progress on one front is accompanied by stagnation on others. Thomas Hughes, 'The Evolution of Large Technical Systems', in *The Social Construction of Technological Systems*, ed. W. E. Bijker, T. P. Hughes and R. J. Pinch (Cambridge, Mass., 1987); Bernward Joerges, 'Large Technical Systems: Concepts and Issues', in *The Development of Large Technical Systems*, eds Renate Mayntz and Thomas Hughes (Boulder, Colo., 1988).

10. Clayton M. Christensen, *The Innovator's Dilemma* (Cambridge, Mass., 1999); Fred Andrews, 'A Primer on Weathering Technologies Storms', *New York Times*, 3 November 1999, p. C10.

11. Bucholz, *Prussian War Planning*, p. 102.

12. Fred Andrews, 'Merger Mania Got You Down? So, Start Thinking Small', *New York Times*, pp. C1, C14. This statement may strike those familiar with 50 years of scholarship describing this army as over the top. But the evidence must be re-examined. Look at the way Schlieffen conducted his General Staff war games and rides two generations later: they remind one of a university seminar, conducted in the law or business school, where the adversarial system prepares its students for the harsh real work which this pedagogical situation mimics. And Schlieffen learned his craft by watching Moltke. Bucholz, *Prussian War Planning*, Chs 3 and 4.

13. Martin van Creveld, *Supplying War*, p. 102.

14. Stinchcomb, *Organizations*, p. 21.

15. Kessel, *Moltke*, p. 439.

16. When the US Department of Defense's Defense Intelligence Agency tried to estimate Iraqi casualties after the Gulf War of 1991, it admitted its numbers had an error factor of 50 per cent or more. John Mueller, 'The Perfect Enemy: Assessing the Gulf War', *Security Studies*, Vol. 5, No. 1 (autumn 1995), p. 87.

17. Kessel, *Moltke*, pp. 412–19; Nielsen, *1864*, p. 354; Neergaard, *Under Junigrundloven*, p. 1377.

18. Wawro, *Austro-Prussian War*, p. 274.

19. Howard, *Franco-Prussian War*, pp. 116, 127, 144, 181, 203, 222, 453; Alistair Horne says 300 000 for the French, 116 696 for the Germans in 1870. *The Fall of Paris* (New York, 1967), p. 268; Larry Addington in *Patterns of War* says 238 00 for the French, 133 750 for the Germans, p. 90.

20. Boehn, *Generalstabsgeschaefte*, pp. 53–62.
21. Martin van Creveld, *Fighting Power: German and US Army Performance, 1939–1945* (Wesport, Conn., 1982), pp. 3–6; Trevor N. Dupuy, *A Genius for War* (London, 1977), pp. 234–6.
22. Dupuy, *A Genius for War*, pp. 234–6.
23. An interesting place to begin is regimental histories. For example, Albert von Boguslawski served in the 3rd Lower Silesian Infantry Regiment No. 50 in each of the three German wars, starting as a first lieutenant and ending up a captain. The 50th IR fought at Lundby in the Danish War, at Königgrätz in 1866 against Austria and at Woerth in the French War. His *Geschichte des 3. Niederschlesischen Infanterie-Regiments Nr. 50* (Berlin, E. S. Mittler, 1887), lists the officers and many of the men and describes the nature of their combat in detail.
24. Cf. Douglas Foster, 'Bugged' in the *New York Times Magazine*, 31 October 1999, p. 68.
25. For this and what follows I am indebted to Chris C. Demchak, *Military Organizations, Complex Machines* (Ithaca, 1991), pp. 163–70.
26. Drucker, *Managing*, p. 91.

BIBLIOGRAPHY

Books

Addington, Larry, *The Pattern of War since the Eighteenth Century* (Bloomington, Ind.: Indiana University Press, 1984).

Adriance, Thomas J., *The Last Gaiter Button: a Study of the Mobilization and Concentration of the French Army in the War of 1870* (Westport, Conn.: Greenwood Press, 1982).

Afflerbach, Holger, *Falkenhayn: Politische Denken und Handeln im Kaiserreich* (Munich: Oldenbourg, 1994).

Allen, Thomas B., *War Games* (London: Heinemann, 1987).

Andreas, Willy, *Moltkes Briefe*. 2 vols (Leipzig, 1922).

Arndt, Helmuth, *Helmuth von Moltke unter dem Halbmond: Erlebnisse in der alten Turkei, 1835–1839* (Berlin: Verlag Neues Leben, 1988).

Ascoli, David, *A Day of Battle: Mars-La-Tour, 16 August 1870* (London: Harrap, 1987).

Asmundsson, Doris, *Georg Brandes: Aristocratic Radical* (New York: New York University Press, 1981).

Becker, Jean-Jacques, *The Great War and the French People* (Oxford: Berg Publishers, 1985).

Bell, Harry, *St. Privat: German Sources* (Fort Leavenworth: Staff College Press, 1914).

Bigge, Wilhelm, *Feldmarschall Graf Moltke: Ein militärisches Lebensbild,* 2 vols (C.H. Beck'sche Verlag, 1901).

Bijker, W. E., Hughes, T. P. and Pinch, R. J., *The Social Construction of Technological Systems* (Cambridge: MIT Press, 1987).

Black, Jeremy. *European Warfare, 1660–1815* (London: Yale University Press, 1994).

——, *War in the World: Military Power and the Fate of Continents* (New Haven: Yale University Press, 1998).

Blackbourn, David, *The Long Nineteenth Century: a History of Germany, 1780–1918* (New York: Oxford University Press, 1998).

Blumenthal, Albrecht von, *Journals of Field-Marshal Count von Blumenthal for 1866 and 1870–71* (London: Edward Arnold, 1903).

Boehn, Herbert von, *Generalstabsgeschaefte* (Potsdam, 1875).

Boguslawski, Albert von, *Geschichte des 3. Niederschlesischen Infanterie-Regiments Nr. 50* (Berlin: E.S. Mittler, 1887).

Boog, Horst et al., *Operatives Denken und Handeln in deutschen Streitkraeften im. 19. und 20. Jahrhundert* (Bonn: E.S. Mittler, 1988).

Boog, Horst et al., *Die Bedeutung der Logistik für die militaerische Führung von der Antike bis in die neueste Zeit* (Bonn: E.S. Mittler, 1986).

Bredsdorff, Elias, *Hans Christian Andersen* (New York: Charles Scribners, 1975).

Brockdorff, Friederika von, *Marie von Moltke: Ein Lebens-und charakterbild* (Leipzig: Verlag von Georg Weigand, 1893).

Brophy, James M., *Capitalism, Politics and Railroads in Prussia, 1830–1870* (Columbus, Ohio: Ohio State University Press, 1998).

Bruford, W. H., *Germany in the Eighteenth Century: the Social Background of the Literary Revival* (Cambridge: Cambridge University Press, 1965).

Bucholz, Arden, *Hans Delbrück and the German Military Establishment* (Iowa City: University of Iowa Press, 1985).

——, *Moltke, Schlieffen and Prussian War Planning* (Oxford: Berg Publishers, 1991).

——, *Delbrück's Modern Military History* (Lincoln and London: University of Nebraska Press, 1997).

Carr, William, *The Origins of the Wars of German Unification* (London: Longman, 1991).

Chaloner, W. H. and Henderson, W. O., *Engels as Military Critic* (Westport, Conn.: Greenwood Press, 1976).

Christensen, Clayton M., *The Innovator's Dilemma* (Cambridge: Harvard Business School, 1999).

Connelly, Owen, *Blundering to Glory: Napoleon's Military Campaigns* (Wilmington, Del.: Scholarly Resources, 1987).

Craig, Gordon, *The Battle of Koeniggraetz* (Philadelphia: Lippincott, 1964).

——, *Theodor Fontane: Literature and History in the Bismarck Reich* (New York: Oxford University Press, 1999).

——, *The Politics of the Prussian Army* (New York: Oxford University Press, 1955).

——, *Germany, 1866–1945* (New York: Oxford University Press, 1978).

Crankshaw, Edward, *Bismarck* (London: Penguin Books, 1983).

Creel, Herlee, *What is Taoism?* (Chicago: University of Chicago Press, 1970).

Crichton, Michael, *Jurassic Park* (New York: Alfred Knopf, 1990).

Deleuze, Giles and Guattari, Felix, *Nomadilogy: the War Machine* (New York: Columbia University Press, 1989).

Dembo, Ron S. and Freeman, Andrew, *Seeing Tomorrow* (Toronto: McClelland & Stewart, 1998).

Demchak, Chris, *Military Organizations, Complex Machines* (Ithaca: Cornell University Press, 1991).

Demetz, Peter (ed.), *Theodor Fontane: Short Novels and Other Writings* (New York: Continuum, 1982).

Dicey, Edward, *The Schleswig-Holstein War*, 2 vols (London: Tinsely Brothers, 1864).

Dodgson, Mark, *The Management of Technological Learning: Lessons from a Biotechnology Company* (Berlin: Walter de Gruyter, 1991).

Doughty, R. A. et al. *American Military History and the Evolution of Western Warfare* (Lexington, Mass.: D.C. Heath, 1996).

Douglas, Mary, *How Institutions Think* (London: Routledge & Kegan Paul, 1986).

Dressler, Friedrich A., *Moltke in seiner Hauslichkeit*, 2nd edn (Berlin: F. Fontane, 1904).

Dressler, Friedrich A., *Moltke in his Home* (London: John Murray, 1907).

Drucker, Peter, *Managing in a Time of Great Change* (New York: Dutton, 1995).

Duffy, Christopher, *The Fortress in the Age of Vauban and Frederick the Great, 1660–1789* (London: Routledge & Kegan Paul, 1985).

Dukes, Jack and Remak, Joachim (eds), *Another Germany: a Reconsideration of the Imperial Era* (Boulder, Colo.: Westview Press, 1988).

Dupuy, Trevor, *A Genius for War* (London, 1977).

Eley, Geoff (ed.), *Society, Culture and the State in Germany, 1870–1930* (Ann Arbor: University of Michigan Press, 1996).

English, John A., *On Infantry* (New York: Frederick Praeger, 1978).

Eyck, Erich, *Bismarck and the German Empire* (New York: Collier Books, 1964).

Feldenkirchen, Wilfried, *Werner von Siemens: Inventor and International Entrepreneur* (Columbus: Ohio State University, 1994).

Ferguson, Eugene, *Engineering and the Mind's Eye* (Cambridge: MIT Press, 1992).

Firchow, Peter E., *The Death of the German Cousin: Variations on a Literary Stereotype, 1890–1920* (Lewisburg: Bucknell University Press, 1986).

Fischer, Friedrich von, *Der Krieg in Schleswig und Jütland im Jahre 1864* (Vienna: Verlage der oesterreichischen militaerischen Zeitschrift, 1870).

Fischer, Fritz, *Griff nach der Weltmacht* (Düsseldorf: Droste Verlage, 1961).

——, *Germany's Aims in the First World War* (New York: W. W. Norton, 1967).

Foerster, Roland, G. (ed.), *Generalfeldmarschall von Moltke: Bedeutung und Wirkung* (Munich: R. Oldenbourg, 1991).

Fontane, Theodor, *Der Krieg gegen Frankreich, 1870–1871*, 2 vols (Berlin: Verlag der Koeniglichen Ober-hofbuchdruckerei, 1875).

——, *Der Schleswig-Holsteinische Krieg im Jahr 1864*, 2 vols (Berlin: Verlag der Koeniglichen Geheim Ober-hofbuchdruckerei, 1866).

——, *Der deutsche Krieg von 1866*, 2 vols (Berlin: Verlag der Koeniglichen Geheim Ober-hofbuchdruckerei, 1871).

Foster, Hal. (ed.), *The Anti-Aesthetic: Essays on Postmodern Culture* (Seattle: Bay Press, 1992).

Fuller, J. F. C., *A Military History of the Western World*, 3 vols (New York: Macmillan, 1954).

Galbraith, John Kenneth, *The New Industrial State*, 2nd edn (London, 1972).

Gall, Lother, *Bismarck: the White Revolutionary*, 2 vols (London: Allen & Unwin, 1986).

Gallenga, A., *The Invasion of Denmark in 1864*, 2 vols (London: Richard Bentley, 1864).

Goldhagen, Daniel, *Hitler's Willing Executioners* (New York: Alfred Knopf, 1996).

Gould, Stephen J. *Leonardo's Mountains of Clams and the Diet of Worms* (New York: Harmony Books, 1998).

Graf Moltke als Redner, edited by Gustav Karpeles (Stuttgart: Spemann, 1887).

Granier, Herman, *Der Feldzug von 1864* (Berlin: Verlag R. Felix, 1897).

Great General Staff, *Moltkes Gesammelte Schriften und Denkwürdigkeiten*, 8 vols (Berlin: E.S. Mittler, 1892).

——, *Moltkes Militaerische Werke*, 13 vols (Berlin: E.S. Mittler, 1892–1912).

——, *Der Deutsch–Daenisch Krieg 1864*, 2 vols (Berlin: E.S. Mittler, 1887).

——, *Der Feldzug von 1866 in Deutschland* (Berlin: E.S. Mittler, 1867).

Great General Staff, *Der deutsch–franzoesische Krieg, 1870–71* 8 vols (Berlin: E.S. Mittler, 1874–1881).

Hagerman, Edward, *The American Civil War and the Origins of Modern Warfare* (Bloomington, Ind: Indiana University Press, 1988).

Handlin, Lillian, *George Bancroft: the Intellectual as Democrat* (New York: Harper & Row, 1984).

Haycock, Ronald and Neilson, Keith, *Men, Machines and War* (Waterloo, Ontario: Wilfred Laurier University Press, 1977).

Helmert, Heinz and Usczeck, Hans-Juergen, *Preussischdeutsche Kriege von 1864 bis 1871* (Berlin: Deutscher Militaerverlag, 1967).

Henderson, G. F. R., *The Battle of Spicheren* (London: Gale & Polden, 1902).

Henderson, W. O., *The Industrial Revolution in Europe* (Chicago: Quadrangle Books, 1961).

Hergescheimer, Joseph, *Sheridan: a Military Narrative* (Boston: Houghton Mifflin, 1931).

Herre, Franz, *Moltke: Der Mann und sein Jahrhundert*, 2nd edn (Stuttgart: Deutsche Verlags Anstalt, 1984).

Hoenig, Fritz, *24 Stunden: Moltkescher Strategie entwickelt und erläutert an den Schlachten von Gravelotte und St. Privat am 18 August 1870*, 2nd edn (Berlin: Verlag von Friedrich Luckhardt, 1891).

Hohenlohe-Ingelfingen, Kraft von, *Aus meinem Leben: Aufzeichnungen*, 3 vols (Berlin: E.S. Mittler, 1906).

——, *Letters on Artillery* (London: Edward Stanford, 1888).

Holborn, Hajo, *A History of Modern Germany*, 3 vols (New York: Alfred Knopf, 1971).

Holmes, Richard, *The Road to Sedan: the French Army, 1866–1870* (London: Royal Historical Society, 1984).

Hooker, Richard D., *Maneuver Warfare: an Anthology* (Novato, Calif.: Presidio, 1983).

Horne, Alistair, *The Fall of Paris* (New York: Doubleday Anchor, 1967).

Horst, Max, *Moltke, Leben und Werk in Selbstzeugnissen* (Leipzig: Dieterich'schen Verlagsbuchhandlung, 1930).

Howard, Michael, *The Franco-Prussian War* (New York: Collier Books 1961).

Hozier, H. M., *The Seven Weeks War*, 2 vols (London: Macmillan, 1867).

Hübner, Reinhard, *Albrecht von Roon* (Hamburg: Hanseatische Verlagsanstalt, 1933).

Hughes, Daniel, *Moltke on the Art of War* (Novato, Calif.: Presidio, 1993).

Hughes, H. Stuart, *Consciousness and Society* (New York: Harper Torchbook, 1958).

Hürshner, Joseph, *Moltkes Briefe aus Russland*, 2 vols (Berlin, 1877, 2nd edn, 1893).

Jaehns, Max, *Feldmarschall Moltke*, 2 vols (Berlin: Ernst Hofmann, 1900).

——, *Militaergeschichtliche Aufsaetze*, ed. Ursula von Gersdorff (Osnabrück: Biblio Verlag, 1970).

Jany, Kurt, *Geschichte der Preussischen Armee von 15. Jahrhunderts bis 1914*, 2nd edn, 4 vols (Osnabrück: Biblio Verlag, 1967).

Jones, Archer, *The Art of War* (New York: Oxford University Press, 1987).

Kessel, Eberhard, *Moltke* (Stuttgart: K. F. Koehler, 1957).

Kessel, Eberhard, *Moltkes erster Feldzug* (Berlin: E.S. Mittler, 1939).

——, *Helmuth von Moltke Briefe*, 2nd edn (Stuttgart: Deutsche Verlags-Anstalt, 1960).

——, *Moltke Gespraeche* (Hamburg: Hanseatische Verlagsanstalt, 1940).

Klein-Wuttig, Anneliese, *Politik und Kriegführung in den deutschen Einigungs-kriegen 1864, 1866 und 1870/71* (Berlin: Verlag für Staatswissenschaften und Geschichte, 1934).

Konvitz, Josef, *Cartography in France, 1660–1848* (Chicago: University of Chicago Press, 1987).

Koselleck, Rinehard, *Futures Past: On the Semantics of Historical Time* (Cambridge: Harvard University Press, 1983).

Ladebor, Ferdinand von, *Die Geschichte des deutschen Unteroffiziers* (Berlin: Junker und Duennhaupt, 1939).

Lehman, Hartmut and Richter, Melvin (eds), *The Meaning of Historical Terms and Concepts* (Washington, DC: The German Historical Institute, 1996).

Lehmann, Gustav, *Die Mobilmachung von 1870–71* (Berlin: E.S. Mittler, 1905).

Lewis, Bernard, *The Emergence of Modern Turkey* (London: Oxford University Press, 1961).

Life and Letters of George Bancroft, edited by M. A. DeWolfe Howe, 2 vols (London: Kennikat Press, 1971).

Lutz, Ralph, *Die Beziehungen zwischen Deutschland und den Vereinigten Staaten waehrend des Sezessionskriegs* (Heidelberg: Carl Winter, 1911).

Luvaas, Jay, *The Military Legacy of the Civil War* (Chicago: University of Chicago Press, 1959).

McKercher, B. J. and Hennessy, Michael, *The Operational Art* (Westport, Conn.: Praeger, 1996).

Mayntz, Renate and Hughes, T. J., *The Development of Large Technical Systems* (Boulder, Colo.: Westview Press, 1988).

Millotat, Christian O. E., *Understanding the Prussian–German General Staff* (Carlisle, Pa.: US Army War College, 1992).

Moltke, Helmuth von, *Briefe an die Braut und Frau*, 2 vols, edited by Henry von Burt (Leipzig, 1894).

Moses, John, *The Politics of Illusion: the Fischer Controversy in German Historiography* (London: Macmillan, 1975).

Müller, Wilhelm, *Generalfeldmarschall Graf Moltke*, 2nd edn (Stuttgart: Carl Krabbe, 1879).

Naso, Eckart von, *Moltke, Mensch und Feldherr* (Hamburg, 1937).

Neergaard, N., *Unter Junigrundloven. En Fremstilling af Det Danske Folks Politische histories fra 1848 til 1866* (Copenhagen: Nordisk Forlag, 1916).

Newell, Clayton R., *The Framework of Operational Warfare* (London: Routledge, 1991).

Nielsen, Johs, *1864 Da Europa gik af lave* (Copenhagen: Odense Universitets-forlag, 1895).

Nye, Russell B., *George Bancroft: Brahmin Rebel* (New York: Alfred Knopf, 1944).

O'Sullivan, Patrick and Miller, Jesse W., *The Geography of Warfare* (New York: St. Martin's Press, 1983).

Pakula, Hannah, *An Uncommon Woman: the Empress Frederick* (New York: Simon & Schuster, 1995).

Palmer, R. R. and Colton, Joel, *A History of the Modern World*, 8th edn (New York: McGraw-Hill, 1998).

Paret, Peter, *Yorck and the Era of Prussian Reform* (Princeton: Princeton University Press, 1966).

——, *Makers of Modern Strategy from Machiavelli to the Nuclear Age* (Princeton: Princeton University Press, 1986).

Perrow, Charles, *Complex Organizations: a Critical Essay*, 3rd edn (New York: McGraw-Hill, 1986).

Peschke, Rudolf, *Moltkes Stellung zur Politik bis zum Jahre 1857* (Kirchhain: Max Schmeresow, 1912).

Pi, Wang, *Commentary on Lao Tzu* (Honolulu: University of Hawaii Press, 1979).

Pickenpaugh, Roger, *Rescue by Rail: Troop Transfer and the Civil War in the West* (Lincoln and London: University of Nebraska Press, 1998).

Poten, Bernard, *Militaer-Erzeihungs-und Bildungswesens in den Landen deutscher Zunge*, 4 vols (Berlin: A. Hofmann, 1896).

Prinz Friedrich Karl von Preussen, *Denkwürdigkeiten aus seinem Leben*, edited by Wolfgang Foerster, 2 vols (Stuttgart: Deutsche Verlags-Anstalt, 1910).

Rahne, Hermann, *Mobilmachung* (Berlin: Militaerverlag der Deutschen Demokratischen Republik, 1983).

Reimer, Dennis, *Knowledge and Speed: the Annual Report of the Army After Next Project* (Washington, DC: United States Army, 1997).

Robinson, A. H., *Elements of Cartography*, 5th edn (New York: John Wiley, 1984).

Roon, Albrecht von, *Denkwürdigkeiten aus dem Leben des General-Feldmarschalls und Kriegsministers Grafen von Roon*, 3rd edn, 3 vols (Breslau: Verlag von Eduard Trewendt, 1892).

Ropp, Theodore, *War in the Modern World* (New York: Macmillan, 1967).

Rüstow, Wilhelm, *Der deutsch–daenish Krieg 1864* (Zurich: Friedrich Schulthess, 1864).

Schellendorff, Bronsart von, *The Duties of the General Staff*, 4th edn (London: Harrison & Sons, 1905).

Schlichting, Sigismund von, *Moltke und Benedek: Eine Studie über Truppenführung* (Berlin: E.S. Mittler, 1900).

Schoeps, Hans-Joachim, *Bismarck über Zeitgenossen, Zeitgenossen über Bismarck* (Frankfurt: Verlag Ullstein, 1972).

Schom, Alan, *Napoleon Bonaparte* (New York: Harper Collins, 1997).

Semmel, Bernard, *Marxism and the Science of War* (New York: Oxford University Press, 1981).

Shaw, Stanford and Ezel, *A History of the Ottoman Empire and Modern Turkey*, 3 vols (Cambridge: Cambridge University Press, 1977).

Sheehan, James J., *German History, 1770–1866* (New York: Oxford University Press, 1989).

Sheridan, P. H., *Personal Memoirs*, 2 vols (New York: Charles L. Webster, 1888).

Showalter, Dennis, *The Wars of Frederick the Great* (London: Longman, 1996).

——, *Railroads and Rifles: Soldiers, Technology and the Unification of Germany* (Hamden, Conn.: Archon Books, 1975).

Sondhaus, Lawrence, *Preparing for Weltpolitik: German Sea Power before the Tirpitz Era* (Annapolis, Md: Naval Institute Press, 1997).

Spitzenberg, Baronin von, *Das Tagebuch der Baronin Spitzenberg*, edited by Rudolf Vierhaus (Göttingen: Vandenhoeck & Ruprecht, 1989).

Stern, Fritz, *Einstein's German World* (Princeton: Princeton University Press, 1999).

Stinchcombe, Arthur L., *Information and Organizations* (Berkeley: University of California Press, 1990).

Stirling, Monica, *The Wild Swan: the Life and Times of Hans Christian Andersen* (New York: Harcourt, Brace & World, 1965).

Stollberg-Wernigerode, Otto von, *Deutschland und die Vereinigten Staaten von America in Zeitalter Bismarck* (Berlin: Walter de Gruyter, 1933).

Stosch, Albrecht von, *Denkwürdigkeiten des Generals und Admirals Albrecht v Stosch*, edited by Ulrich von Stosch, 2nd edn (Stuttgart: Deutsche Verlags Anstalt, 1904).

Thompson, J. M., *Louis Napoleon and the Second Empire* (New York: W.W. Norton, 1955).

US Department of the Army, *Force XXI Operations* (Fort Monroe, Va: TRADOC, 1994).

Vagts, Alfred, *Landing Operations* (Harrisburg, Pa: Military Service Publishing Co., 1946).

Van Creveld, Martin, *Supplying War* (Cambridge: Cambridge University Press, 1977).

——, *Command in War* (Cambridge: Harvard University Press, 1985).

——, *Fighting Power: German and US Army Performance, 1939–1945* (Westport, Conn.: Greenwood Press, 1982).

Van der Heijden, Kees, *Scenarios: the Art of Strategic Conversation* (New York: John Wiley, 1996).

Verdy du Vernois, Julius von, *With the Royal Headquarters, 1870–71* (London: Macmillan, 1897).

Virilio, Paul, *Speed and Politics* (New York: Columbia University Press, 1977).

——, *Popular Defense and Ecological Studies* (New York: Columbia University Press, 1983).

—— and Lotringer, Sylvere, *Pure War* (New York: Simniotext, 1983).

Wagner, Arthur L., *The Campaign of Koeniggraetz* (Fort Leavenworth: Staff College Press, 1889).

Waldersee, F. J. G. Count von, *Krieg gegen Daenemark im Jahre 1864* (Berlin: Alexander Duncker, 1865).

Wawro, Geoffrey, *The Austro-Prussian War: Austria's War with Prussia and Italy in 1866* (New York: Cambridge University Press, 1996).

Weapons: an International Encyclopedia (New York: St. Martins Press, 1990).

Weinberg, Gerhard, *Germany, Hitler and World War II: Essays in Modern Germany and World History* (Cambridge: Cambridge University Press, 1995).

Whitton, F. E., *Moltke* (New York: Henry Holt, 1921).

Winters, Harold A., *Battling the Elements: Weather and Terrain in the Conduct of War* (Baltimore: Johns Hopkins University Press, 1998).

Yutang, Lin, *The Wisdom of Laotze* (New York: Modern Library, 1948).

Zürcher, Erich, *Turkey: a Modern History* (London: I.B. Touris, 1994).

Articles

Andrews, Fred, 'A Primer on Weathering Technologies Storms', *New York Times*, 3 November 1999, p. C-10.

Andrews, Fred, 'Merger Mania Got You Down? So, Start Thinking Small', *New York Times*, 26 November 1999, pp. C-1, C-14.

Barkin, Kenneth, 'W.E.B. Du Bois and the Kaiserreich', *Central European History*, Vol. 31, No. 3 (1998), pp. 158–69.

Belger, Christian, 'Generalfeldmarschall Graf Moltkes Verdienste um die Kenntnis des Alterthums', *Preussische Jahrbücher*, Vol. 51, No. 1 (1883), pp. 70–114.

Berghahn, Volker, 'The Road to Extermination', *New York Review of Books*, 14 April 1996.

Binder, Robert, 'Defense Technology: the Information Advantage', *The Economist*, 10 June 1995, pp. 5–10.

Birn, Ruth Bettina, 'Historiographical Review: Revising the Holocaust', *The Historical Journal*, Vol. 40, No. 1 (1997), pp. 195–215.

Bonnal, General Guillaume, 'Le Plan de Moltke pour 1870', *Journal des Sciences Militaires*, July and August 1903, pp. 2–14.

Bucholz, Arden, 'Militarism', *Encyclopedia of Violence, Peace and Conflict*, 3 vols (San Diego: Academic Press, 1999), Vol. II, pp. 423–32.

——, 'Armies, Railroads and Information: the Birth of Industrial Mass War' in Jane Summerton (ed.), *Changing Large Technical Systems* (Boulder, Colo.: Westview Press, 1994).

Coumbe, Arthur T., 'Operational Command in the Franco-Prussian War', *Parameters*, Vol. 21, No. 2 (Summer 1991), pp. 86–99.

Craig, Gordon, 'How Hell Worked', *New York Review of Books*, 18 April 1996.

Deak, Istvan, 'Holocaust Views: the Goldhagen Controversy in Retrospect', *Central European History*, Vol. 15, No. 1 (1997), pp. 295–307.

Delbrück, Hans, 'Dybbol und Alsen', *Preussische Jahrbücher*, Vol. 60 (October 1887), pp. 18–63.

——, 'Moltke', three essays from the *Preussische Jahrbücher* (November 1890, May 1891 and October 1900), reprinted in Delbrück's *Erinnerungen, Aufsaetz und Reden* (Berlin: Georg Stilke, 1902), pp. 546–75.

Dodgson, Mark, 'Organizational Learning: a Review of the Literature', *Organizational Studies*, Vol. 14, No. 3 (1993), pp. 377–80.

——, 'Technology Learning, Technology Strategy and Competitive Pressures', *British Journal of Management*, Vol. 2 (1991), pp. 133–9.

Eley, Geoff, 'Theory and the Kaiserreich: Problems with Culture: German History after the Linguistic Turn', *Central European History*, Vol. 31, No. 3 (1998), pp. 197–227.

'German Railroad Concentration of 1870', *The Military Historian and Economist*, Vol. 3, No. 2 (1910), pp. 1–32.

Gewande, Atul, 'When Doctors Make Mistakes', *The New Yorker*, 1 February 1999, pp. 48–55.

Holzing, Max, 'General v. Moltkes Einwirkung auf den Strategischen Gang des Krieges gegen Daenemark 1864', *Militaerwochenblatt*, Beiheft 3, No. 4 (Berlin: E.S. Mittler, 1897).

Jaffe, Josef, 'Goldhagen in Germany', *New York Review of Books*, 28 November 1996.

Korthoeber, Heinrich, 'Ein merkwürdiger Krieg: Der amerikanische Buergerkrieg in zeitgenoessischer deutsche Perspektive' (Washington, DC: German Historical Institute, 1994).

Lackey, Scott, 'The Habsburg Army and the Franco-Prussian War: the Failure to Intervene and its Consequences', *War in History*, Vol. 2, No. 2 (1995), pp. 151–79.

Lawlor, Julia, 'A Passion for Community', *New York Times*, 3 November 1999, p. C-10.

Lossow, Walter von, 'Mission-Type Tactics versus Order-Type Tactics', *Military Review*, Vol. 57 (June 1977), pp. 86–95.

McPeak, Merrill A., 'The Key to Modern Airpower', *AIR FORCE Magazine*, September 1993, pp. 43–6.

Mombauer, Annika, 'A Reluctant Military Leader: Helmuth von Moltke and the July Crisis of 1914', *War in History*, Vol. 6, No. 4 (1999), pp. 417–46.

Mueller, John, 'The Perfect Enemy: Assessing the Gulf War', *Security Studies*, Vol. 5, No. 1 (autumn 1995), pp. 77–117.

Scales, Robert H., 'Cycles of War', *Armed Forces Journal*, July 1997, pp. 38–42.

Schall, Wolfgang, 'Führungsgrundsaetze in Armee und Industrie', *Wehrkunde*, Vol. 14, No. 5 (1964), pp. 10–18.

Serman, William, 'French Mobilization in 1870' (Washington, DC: German Historical Institute, 1994).

Showalter, Dennis, 'Prussian Technology and War: Artillery from 1815 to 1914' in Ronald Haycock and Keith Neilson, *Men, Machines and War* (Waterloo, Ontario: Wilfrid Laurier University Press, 1977).

——, 'Soldiers into Postmasters? The Electric Telegraph as an Instrument of Command in the Prussian Army', *Military Affairs*, Vol. 46, No. 2 (April 1973), pp. 48–52.

Wehler, Hans Ulrich, 'The Goldhagen Controversy: Agonizing Problems, Scholarly Failure and the Political Dimension', *German History*, Vol. 15, No. 1 (1997), pp. 80–91.

Welch, Larry D., 'Dominating the Battlefield (Battlespace)', *Journal of Electronic Defense*, January 1997, Supplement, pp. 12–14.

INDEX

A

Adalbert, Prince of Prussia and Admiral, 91
Albert, Crown Prince of Saxony, 158,177
Albrecht, Archduke of Austria, 123
Albrecht, Prince of Prussia, 157
Alexander II, Tsar, 48
Alexander, Prince of Hesse, 122
Alsen Island, battle of (1864), 86, 91–2, 97–100
Alvensleben, General Gustav von, 105, 133
American Civil War, 23, 71–3, 104, 146, 187
Andersen, Hans Christian, 25–6
Augusta, Queen of Prussia, 141
Austerlitz, battle of (1805), 121
Austrian Army, 67–71, 103–38
Austro-Prussian War (1779), 116
Austro-Prussian War (1866), 6, 24, 103–38

B

Bach, Johann Sebastian, 30
Bancroft, Ambassador George, 78, 142–3, 161
Bavarian Army, 114
Bazaine, Marshal François, 58, 177
Beethoven, Ludwig von, 30
Benedek, Field Marshal Ludwig, 104–5, 130, 133–6, 189
Benedetti, Count Vincent, 160
Bergson, Henri, 12
Berlin Illustrierte Zeitung, 185
Bernadotte, Jean-Baptiste, 155

Bernhardi, Theodore von, 48, 72, 116–17
Betzholz, Lieutenant Conrad, 101–2
Beyer, General Friedrich von, 122
Bismarck, Otto von, 1, 10, 69, 72, 77–80, 84, 90, 111, 114, 127, 134, 137, 143, 160–1, 163, 179, 181–2, 185
Bittenfeld, Herwarth von, 133
Blücher, Gebhard Leberecht von, 155
Blumenthal, General Albrecht von, 53, 83–4, 92, 94, 133, 143, 164, 167
Boguslawski, Albert K. F. W. von, 144
Bonin, Adolf von, 52, 68–9, 128–9, 149
Bonnal, General Guillaume, 63
Bourbaki, General, 139,184
Brandenstein, Freiherr von, 143,147,158,164
Budritski, Rudolf Otto von, 144
Bugeaud, Thomas Robert de, 139
Burt, Henry, son of Auguste von Moltke Burt, 35,141
Byron, Lord, 29

C

Canrobert, General, 139–40
Canstein, Freiherr von, 88
Carr, William, 80, 111
Castelnau, General Henri, 181
Casualties in battle, 192–3
  Danish War: Missunde, 87;
    Sankelmarkt, 89; Dybbol, 96–7;
    Lundy, 101
  Austrian War: Nachod, 127;
    Trautenau, 129; Skalitz, 129,
    131; Königgrätz, 137

Casualties in battle – *continued*
  French War: Wissembourg, 173;
    Froeschwiller–Woerth, 176;
    Sedan, 179–80, 192
Chanzy, General Antoine Eugene, 184
Chosref Pasha, 36–9
Claer, Major de, 164
Clausewitz, Carl von, 5, 15, 48, 54,
    158–9
Copenhagen, 25–6, 28, 32, 35
Craig, Gordon, 6, 192
Creveld, Martin van, 2
Crimean War (1854–56), 23, 61, 187
Custova, battle of (1866), 123

D
Danenberg, Ferdinand von, 144
Danish Army, 25, 42
  3rd Infantry Division, 88
  Copenhagen Guards, 94
Danish Cadet Academy, 25–6
Danish War (1848), 43
Danish War (1864), 77–102
Darwin, Charles, 185
Decker, Captain Thomas, 61
Delbrück, Hans, 3, 84
De Meza, General Christian Julius, 81,
    83, 88
Denmark, 25–9, 41, 77–103
Dicey, Edward, 91, 94–5
Dickens, Charles, 29
Doering, Hermann, 52, 117
Dohna, Oberstkammer, Field Marshal
    Count, 46–7
Douey, General Abel, 172
Dreyse breech-loading rifle, 24, 106
DuBois, W. E. B., 1
Ducrot, General Auguste Alexander,
    176
Dybbol, battle of (1864), 84, 89–97, 151,
    186

E
Eisenhower, Dwight David, 150
Elizabeth, Queen of Prussia, 47
Engels, Friedrich, 24,104
Eugénie, Empress, 48

F
Faaborg, Colonel Carl, 99
Faidherbe, General Louis Leon, 184
Falckenstein, General Vogel von, 46,
    122, 132
Fichte, J. G., 20
Finkenstein, Fink von, 133
Fischer, Friedrich Leopold, 38
Fischer, Fritz, 1
Flies, General Eduard, 122, 149
Fontane, Theodor, 7, 9–10, 85, 138, 185
Ford, Henry, 11, 195
Franco-Prussian War (1870), 139–84
Franks, General Fred, 132
Fransecky, Lt General Eduard Friedrich
    Karl von, 134
Franz Joseph, Austrian Emperor, 48, 85,
    97, 118
Frederick the Great, 25, 29, 35, 48,
    118–19, 130
French mobilization in 1870, 167–71
French Revolution, 13, 15–16, 20, 26
Friedrich Charles, Prince of Prussia,
    41–2, 80, 83, 85, 92, 94, 97, 102,
    132–4, 143, 163, 191
Friedrich, Crown Prince of Prussia, 41,
    47, 65, 129
Friedrich Wilhelm IV, King of Prussia
    (1840–61), 34, 40, 42, 46–7, 74
Friedrich IV, King of Denmark, 79
Froeschwiller–Woerth (battle of, 1870),
    173–6

G
Gablenz, General Ludwig, 85, 89, 97,
    121, 128–9
Gallifet, General de, 180
General Staff (Prussian)
  analytical, 18–20, 26–7: war games,
    19–20, 31, 33–4, 36, 64–5, 70,
    103, 112–13, 157–8, 195; force
    ratios, 209
  district commands, 110–11
  educational, 17–18, 63: War Academy,
    29–30, 111; double-loop
    learning, 43; analysis of
    contemporary wars, 83–4, 197–8

General Staff (Prussian) – *continued*
  intelligence gathering, 153
  mobilizations: of 1850, 44–6; of 1859,
    65–9; of 1862, 73–6; of 1864,
    80–3; of 1866, 112–19, 153; of
    1870, 161–3; 'counteractivity',
    113–19, 159–62; horse
    purchases, 114
  organizational, 8, 11, 17–20, 51–4,
    146, 189–92
  Railroad Commission, 68, 147
  railroad line commands, 147
  Railroad Section, 110, 146: military
    travel plan, 146–8, 162–3
  representational, 17–18, 52, 111
  'royal manoeuvres', 148
  war planning processes: writing battle
    orders, 78–9, 120, 131–2;
    periodization and timing
    patterns, 65–6, 74–5, 157–8, 162;
    chief of staff system ('1-A's), 80,
    90
German Confederation, 70, 75, 79–80,
  91, 111, 117–18
German Customs Union (1834), 15, 75
Gibbon, Edward, *The Decline and Fall of
  the Roman Empire*, 36, 42
Goethe, Johann von, 9, 15
Goldhagen, Daniel, 1
Gramont, Duke de, 160
Grant, U. S., 67, 104, 142
Gribeauval, Jean de, 14
Groeben, General Count, 45, 80, 122
Grolmann, Wilhelm von, 143
Gulf War (1991), 2, 11

H
Hafiz Pasha, Ottoman commander,
  38–9
Hagermann-Lindencrone, General
  Friedrich von, 26, 33
  Louise von, 26
Haydn, Franz Joseph, 30
Henikstein, General Alfred, 105
Henry, Prince of Prussia, 41–2, 51
Herodotus, 38
Herre, Franz, 185

Heydt, August Count van der, 142
Hinderson, General Eduard von, 92, 94,
  151–2
Holstein, Wilhelm, Duke of, 28
Holstein-Glucksburg, Prince of, 36
Howard, Michael, 7, 192
Humboldt, Alexander von, 42
Humboldt, Wilhelm von, 20, 43

I
Ibraham Pasha, Egyptian commander,
  38
Italian War of 1859, 23, 62

J
Jomini, Baron Antoine de, 54

K
Kaiser Alexander Guard Grenadier
  Regiment, 49
Kanawha Valley campaign (1861), 23
Kant, Immanuel, 185
Karl, Prince of Bavaria, 122
Karl August, Duke of Saxe-Weimar, 15
Kessel, Bernhard H.A. von, 144
Kessel, Eberhard, 36, 48, 192
Kiepert, Heinrich, 40
Kierkegaard, Søren, 26
Kirchbach, General von, 175
Knowledge theory, 7–9
Koenigsmarck, Count Wilhelm, 36
Königgrätz, battle of (1866), 53, 56,
  121, 123, 131–8
Kraft zu Hohenlohe, Prince, 92, 143,
  150–1, 158
Krismanic, General Gideon, 105
Kunersdorff, battle of (1759), 33
Kutahia, Peace of (1933), 37

L
Langensalza, battle of (1866), 122,
  149
Lao Tzu, 5
Learning organization, Prussian Army
  as, 30–2
Leboeuf, Marshal Edmond, 130
Leopold, Archduke, 171

Leopold, Prince of Hohenzollern-
    Sigmaringen, 160
Liegnitz, battle of (1760), 33
Lilienstern, Colonel Ruhle von, 61
List, Friedrich, 40
Loee, Freiherr von, 134, 153
Lundy, battle of (1864), 56, 86, 100–3
Luther, Martin, 185

M
MacMahon, Marshal Patrice, 139, 175–9
Magenta, battle of (1859), 66
Mahmud II, Ottoman Sultan, 37, 39
Mann, Thomas, 9
Mannstein, General Albrecht E. Gustave
    von, 134, 143
Manteuffel, Otto Freiherr von, 44
Marshall, George C., 150
Marwitz, General von der, 29
Massenbach, Christian von, 16–17
Maximilian, Emperor of Mexico,
    Archduke of Austria, 160
Mecklenburg-Strelitz, Count Karl von,
    20
Mehmet Ali, 37
Mendelssohn, Felix, 30
Mertens, Col. Karl Friedrich von, 98
Militär-Wochenblatt, 18, 34, 61–2
Missunde, battle of (1864), 84–8
Mittler, Ernst S., 61
Moltke, Adolf von, 60, 161
Moltke, Auguste, favourite sister of
    Helmuth, 35, 141
Moltke, Fritz von, 141
Moltke, Helmuth von (1800–91)
    and American Civil War, 71–3
    becomes a famous person, 140–1
    becomes Freiherr, 141
    birth family, 25
    The Campaign of 1866 in Germany, 146
    and concept of risk, 54–7: use of
        scenarios and hypotheticals,
        205 ff.
    Danish cultural impact, 25–8
    education, 25–42
    and education of the army, 84
    A Guidebook to Rome (1852), 42

History of the Danish War, 142
    'Instructions for Large Unit
        Commanders' (1869), 63, 145,
        158–9
    'The Italian Campaign of 1859', 63
    Letters from Turkey (1841), 40
    marriage and family, 69–70
    The Military Drawing of the Land
        (1828), 32
    mobile General Staff, 157–67
    mobilization of 1850, 44–6
    mobilization of 1859, 89ff.
    operational procedures, 131–2
    and operations, command and
        control, 119–21, 163–7
    Order of the Black Eagle (1866), 138,
        141
    personality and character, 185–7
    pour le Mérite, 39, 41
    purchases Silesian estate 'Kreisau',
        141
    and relations with Bismarck, 77–81
    'Remarks on the Influence of
        Improved Rifles on the Attack',
        63
    The Russo-Turkish War of 1829 (1844),
        40, 42
    'system of expedients', 77–8
    The Two Friends (1822), 29
    underestimation of, 61–2
    use of railroads, 72–3, 110, 113,
        116–17, 146–8, 163
    uses of artillery in operations, 149–53
    war fighting management processes,
        77–82, 163–7: Auftrag orders, 20,
        57–8; principle of consultation
        and joint responsibility, 80
    and War of 1859, 90ff.
    war plans: against Denmark, 78–9;
        against Austria, 69–71, 94–5,
        112–19, 137–8, 147–9; against
        France, 63–4, 69–71, 154–9
Moltke, Helmuth von, the younger
    (1848–1916), 141
Moltke, Marie von (née Burt), wife of
    Helmuth, 41, 46, 50–1, 102, 141
Müffling, Karl Freiherr von, 45, 47

Mühlbach, Heinrich von, 38, 52, 54
Mynster, Jacob Peter, 26

N
Nachod, battle of (1866), 125–7
Napoleon Bonaparte, 12–15, 22, 26, 29,
    54–5, 61, 67, 139, 155, 187
Napoleon III, 48, 61, 137, 140–60, 170,
    176
National Socialism, 1
NATO, 2, 3
Naumann, Lieutenant von, casualty
    tables and stress in combat, 56,
    123–5, 127, 131
Navarino, battle of (1827), 37
Nezib, battle of (1839), 31, 39, 44, 48,
    145
Nicholas I, Tsar of Russia (1796–1855),
    44, 48
Niebuhr, Barthold, 42
Niel, Marshal Adolf, 140, 161
Nietzsche, Friedrich, 185

O
Oehlenschlaeger, Adam, 26
Oerstedt, Anders Sandoe, 26
Oerstedt, Johann Christian, 26
Ollech, Werner, 52, 61
Olmütz, 44
Organizational theory, 7–9
Ottomans, 36–40
Ottoman–Egyptian War (1839), 38–40,
    105

P
Pape, Alexander von, 143
Palmerston, Lord Henry John Temple,
    95
Peterson, Johann, 52
Pestalozzi, John Heinrich, 20
Podbielski, General Ferdinand, 98, 119,
    143, 164, 166
Prussia
    Armies: 1866: Elbe Army, 116, 133–4;
        First Army, 116, 132–4; Second
        Army, 116, 132–3, 177; 1870:
        First Army, 163, 171; Second

Army, 163, 167, 171; Third
    Army, 58, 163, 171, 173; Army of
    the Meuse, 58, 177
Army: Central Military Examination
    Commission, 29; NCO Corps,
    20–2; NCO schools, 20–2;
    writing orders, 28, 158, 174;
    'Auftrag orders', 174; 'directive
    orders', 174; 'order commands',
    174; delivery of orders, 166–7;
    Railroad Law of 1838, 40; reserve
    force system, 22–4, 145–6; Trade
    Ministry, 45; War Ministry, 18,
    52, 61, 69; General Staff, 4,
    10–13, 139; as modern
    organization, 7–9, 194–5
Artillery Shooting School, 201
Corps: 1866: Guards, 128, 136; I,
    128; V, 125; 1870: II, 174; V,
    172–3; XI, 176
Divisions: 10th, 127; 7th, 134
Italian-Prussian Alliance (1866), 111,
    116
Regiments: 24th Brandenburg
    Infantry, 87; 18th Infantry, 120;
    64th Infantry, 99; 50th Lower
    Silesian Infantry, 133; 37th
    Infantry, 126; 5th Jäger, 230
War Ministry, 45, 158

R
Radziwill, Anton Prince, 43, 72
Ramming, Lt. Field Marshal Freiherr
    von, 125–7
Ranke, Leopold von, 42
Rechberg, Count Johann, 80
Reille, General Count, 118
Reitzenstein, Karl von, 49
Reyher, General von, Chief of the
    General Staff, 43, 47–8
Rhinebaben, Albert von, 143
Richter, Eugen, 69
Ritter, Karl, 40
Roon, Albrecht von, 68–9, 78, 114, 138,
    143, 161, 163, 185
Russell, Lord John, 96
Rüstow, W. W., 123

S

Saarbrücken, battle of (1870), 170–1
Sankelmarkt, battle of (1864), 86,
    88–9
Saxe-Weimar, Duke Karl August von, 15
Saxony, 69–71, 75, 117, 121–2
Sedan, battle of (1870), 153, 176–83
Seven Years War, 33
Schaubach, Adolf, 60
Schellendorff, Paul Bronsart von, 53,
    143, 164, 181
Schellendorff, Walter Bronsart von, 81
Schiebert, Justus, 72
Schleswig-Holstein War of 1848–49, 79
Schlieffen, Alfred Count, 3, 127, 153
Schliemann, Heinrich, 40
Schlutterbach, Captain von, 100–2
Schoeler, General von, 42
Schopenhauer, Arthur, 185
Schubert, Franz, 30
Shakespeare, William, 5, 26–7, 29
Sheridan, General Philip, 180
Sherman, William Tecumseh, 67, 73
Shiloh, battle of (1862), 23, 67
Skalitz, battle of (1866), 129–31
Solferino, battle of (1859), 66, 121
Somme, battle of (1916), 6
Spicheren, battle of (1870), 171–3, 191
Spitzemberg, Baroness Hildegard von,
    142
Steffens, Heinrich, 26
Stein, Karl von, 15
Steinmetz, General Karl Friedrich von,
    125–31, 143, 163, 171
Stiehle, Hans von, 52, 143
Stülpnagel, General von, 120

T

Taiping Revolution, 187
Technology, 23–4, 188–9
Teil, Chavalier du, 14
Thile, General August von, 43, 47
Tilsit, Treaty of (1807), 26
Torgau, battle of (1760), 33
Trautenau, battle of (1866), 121, 127–9,
    149, 191

Treaty of Vienna (1864), 102
Tümpling, General Ludwig von, 47
Turkey, 36–40

U

United States, 1
Unkiar Skelessi, Treaty of (1831), 37
US Department of Defense, 3

V

Vagts, Alfred, 91
Verdy du Vernois, Julius von, 52, 143,
    158, 164, 177
Victor Emmanuel, King of Italy, 118
Victoria, Queen of England
    (1837–1901), 48
Victoria, wife of King Friedrich III of
    Germany, 48
Vieth, Gunther, 52, 143
Vincke-Olbendorf, Freiherr von, 38
Voights-Rhetz, Lt. General Konstantin
    Bernhard von, 132–3, 143

W

Waldersee, Count Alfred von, 69
Walker, Colonel Sir Charles, 180
Warsaw Pact, 2
Wartensleben, Count Herman von, 52,
    70, 81, 110, 119, 143, 148, 158
Washington, George, 149
Werder, General Carl Wilhelm von, 184
Wilhelm I (King of Prussia, 1861–88),
    44, 46, 49, 51, 63, 69, 74, 76, 81,
    85, 97, 112, 116, 118–19, 135,
    140–1, 143
Wimpffen, General Emanuel, 181–5
Wissembourg, battle of (1870), 56, 171–3
Wittich, Frederick Wilhelm von, 143
World War I, 1–2, 5–6, 187
World War II, 2, 10
Wrangel, Field Marshal Friedrich von,
    53, 59, 81, 83, 85, 90, 97

Y

Yorktown, battle of (1781), 149